"IT is about technology and people. This book is for and about the people who develop and use IT. Jeff Feldman and Lou Russell provide unique insights into the leadership roles people play in the management and development of information technology systems."

Peter Henderson
Department of Computer Science
and Software Engineering
Butler University
Indianapolis, IN

"What I find so engaging about this book is how Lou Russell and Jeff Feldman masterfully blend systems thinking methodology with practical advice and 'real deal' examples. In essence, this is what they do so well. I wish this book had been available during my favorite years in IT."

Andy Proctor, CIO, Citizens Gas
Indianapolis, IN

"The use of technology continues to grow and drive business success. IT Leadership is an important component in that growth. This book gives valuable insight and helpful hints as to how to promote that growth. It is also an engaging and easy read!"

Nadine Martin, IS Learning Manager
LL Bean
Freeport, ME

"I have personally participated in a variety of leadership experiences. Leadership in IT shares many of the same requirements as other management. The challenge is to apply the principles in an ever changing technological context with highly technical people. This book offers practical tools for IT leaders at all levels to learn, adapt, and improve their ability to lead."

· Jeff Clancy, CIO, State of Indiana,
Family & Social Services Administration
Indianapolis, IN

"Who else has the passion and the resolve to take on this difficult issue? I have not come across many in the field of IT who really get it. To know from the soul what makes up a leader; to have the courage to deal on a personal level; to lead with compassion and honesty, that is what Lou and Jeff bring to the table."

Elizabeth Fancher Hoisi
Northeast Utilities
Director, IT Operations and Support

IT Leadership Alchemy

ISBN 0-13-009403-X

ABOUT THE SERIES

In today's world of ever-improving technology—with computers that get faster, cheaper, smaller, and more powerful with each passing month—there is one commodity that we seem to have less and less of: time. IT professionals and managers are under constant pressure to deliver new systems more quickly than before; and one of the consequences of this pressure is that they're often thrown into situations for which they're not fully prepared. On Monday, they're given a new assignment in the area of testing, or risk management, or building a new application with the latest tools from IBM or Microsoft or Sun; and on Tuesday, they're expected to be productive and proficient. In many cases, they don't have time to attend a detailed training course; and they don't have time to read a thousand-page *War and Peace* tome that explains all the details of the technology.

Enter the Just Enough Series of books from Yourdon Press. Our mission is, quite literally, to provide just enough information for an experienced IT professional or manager to be able to assimilate the key aspects of a technology and begin putting it to productive use right away. Our objective is to provide pragmatic "how-to" information—supported, when possible, by checklists and guidelines and templates and wizards—that can be put to practical use right away. Of course, it's important to know that the refinements, exceptions, and extensions do exist; and the Just Enough books provide references, links to Web sites, and other resources for those who need it.

Over time, we intend to produce "just enough" books for every important aspect of IT systems development: from analysis and design, to coding and testing. Project management, risk management, process improvement, peopleware, and other issues are also covered while addressing several areas of new technology, from CRM to wireless technology, from enterprise application integration to Microsoft's .NET technology.

Perhaps one day life will slow down, and we'll be able to spend as much time as we want, learning everything there is to be learned about IT technologies. But until that day arrives, we only have time for "just enough" information. And the place to find that information is the Just Enough Series of computer books from Prentice Hall PTR/Yourdon Press.

ABOUT THE SERIES EDITOR

Edward Yourdon is an internationally recognized consultant, lecturer, and author/coauthor of more than 25 books, including *Managing High-Intensity Internet Projects, Death March, Time Bomb, The Rise and Resurrection of the American Programmer, Modern Structured Analysis,* and others. Widely known as the lead developer of the structured analysis/design methods in the 1970's and the popular Coad/Yourdon object-oriented methodology in the early 1990's, Edward Yourdon brings both his writing and technical skills as Series Editor while developing key authors and publications for the Just Enough Series/Yourdon Press.

Selected Titles from the
YOURDON PRESS SERIES
Ed Yourdon, *Advisor*

JUST ENOUGH SERIES
DUÉ Mentoring Object Technology Projects
MOSLEY/POSEY Software Test Automation
RUSSELL/FELDMAN IT Leadership Alchemy
THOMSETT Radical Project Management
ULRICH Legacy Systems: Transformation Strategies
YOURDON Managing High-Intensity Internet Projects

YOURDON PRESS COMPUTING SERIES
ANDREWS AND STALICK Business Reengineering: The Survival Guide
BOULDIN Agents of Change: Managing the Introduction of Automated Tools
COAD AND MAYFIELD with Kern Java Design: Building Better Apps and Applets, Second Edition
COAD AND NICOLA Object-Oriented Programming
COAD AND YOURDON Object-Oriented Analysis, Second Edition
COAD AND YOURDON Object-Oriented Design
COAD WITH NORTH AND MAYFIELD Object Models, Strategies, Patterns, and Applications,
    Second Edition
CONNELL AND SHAFER Object-Oriented Rapid Prototyping
CONSTANTINE The Peopleware Papers: Notes on the Human Side of Software
CONSTANTINE AND YOURDON Structure Design
DEGRACE AND STAHL Wicked Problems, Righteous Solutions
DEMARCO Controlling Software Projects
DEMARCO Structured Analysis and System Specification
FOURNIER A Methodology for Client/Server and Web Application Development
GARMUS AND HERRON Measuring the Software Process: A Practical Guide to Functional
    Measurements
HAYES AND ULRICH The Year 2000 Software Crisis: The Continuing Challenge
JONES Assessment and Control of Software Risks
KING Project Management Made Simple
PAGE-JONES Practical Guide to Structured Systems Design, Second Edition
PUTNAM AND MEYERS Measures for Excellence: Reliable Software on Time within Budget
RUBLE Practical Analysis and Design for Client/Server and GUI Systems
SHLAER AND MELLOR Object Lifecycles: Modeling the World in States
SHLAER AND MELLOR Object-Oriented Systems Analysis: Modeling the World in Data
STARR How to Build Shlaer-Mellor Object Models
THOMSETT Third Wave Project Management
ULRICH AND HAYES The Year 2000 Software Crisis: Challenge of the Century
YOURDON Byte Wars: The Impact of September 11 on Information Technology
YOURDON Death March: The Complete Software Developer's Guide to Surviving "Mission
    Impossible" Projects
YOURDON Decline and Fall of the American Programmer
YOURDON Modern Structured Analysis
YOURDON Object-Oriented Systems Design
YOURDON Rise and Resurrection of the American Programmer
YOURDON AND ARGILA Case Studies in Object-Oriented Analysis and Design

IT Leadership Alchemy

Lou Russell

Jeff Feldman

Prentice Hall PTR
Upper Saddle River, NJ 07458
www.phptr.com

Library of Congress Cataloging-in-Publication Data

A CIP catalog record for this book can be obtained from the Library of Congress.

Editorial/Production Supervision: *Nick Radhuber*
Acquisitions Editor: *Paul Petralia*
Editorial Assistant: *Richard Winkler*
Marketing Manager: *Debby vanDijk*
Manufacturing Manager: *Alexis Heydt-Long*
Cover Design: *Anthony Gemmellaro*
Cover Design Director: *Jerry Votta*
Interior Design: *Gail Cocker-Bogusz*

© 2003 by Pearson Education, Inc.
Publishing at Prentice Hall PTR
Upper Saddle River, NJ 07458

Prentice Hall books are widely used by corporations and government agencies for training, marketing, and resale.

The publisher offers discounts on this book when ordered in bulk quantities. For more information, contact Corporate Sales Separtment, phone: 800-382-3419; fax: 201-236-7141; email corpsales@prenticehall.com

Or write: Corporate Sales Department. Prentice Hall PTR. One Lake Street, Upper Saddle River, NJ 07458.

Product and company names mentioned herin are the trademarks or registered trademarks of their respective owners.

Printed in the United States of America

10 9 8 7 6 5 4 3 2 1

ISBN 0-13-009403-X

Pearson Education LTD.
Pearson Education Australia PTY, Limited
Pearson Education Singapore, Pte. Ltd.
Pearson Education North Asia Ltd.
Pearson Education Canada, Ltd.
Pearson Educación de Mexico, S.A. de C.V.
Pearson Education—Japan
Pearson Education, Malaysia, Pte. Ltd.

Contents

Chapter 3

Resiliency

Chapter 4

Interpersonal and Team Skills

Chapter 5
Communication Skills

Chapter 8
Strategic Business Acumen

Chapter 11
The Journey to Change

Chapter 12
A Plan for Action

Foreword

In my 15 years of managing and working closely with IT professionals, I've learned many things about this unique breed. Full of energy and enthusiasm, technologists possess unlimited creativity and innovation. Intellectuals frequently feel most comfortable working alone, deep in the details of a project. Every day they work to meet the needs of multiple masters, despite often being held at arm's length from the business.

All of this presents a unique challenge for the IT leader. How do you harness the talents of IT professionals, balance competing priorities from the business, keep costs down, and facilitate teamwork to meet and exceed business goals?

With a degree in nutrition and a background in quality measurement, the road to CIO was not smoothly paved for me. I forged into the technical side of business management without a technology bone in my body. Although I was brought in for my leadership skills, I quickly abandoned my old, proven methodology, assuming I had to think like a technologist to lead an IT organization. In my eagerness to gain respect and credibility with my new staff, I immersed myself in technology buzzwords and trends.

Of course, this approach didn't produce the results I needed to deliver. Luckily, like most managers under stress, I reverted back to my instincts. I began focusing on the fundamentals—establishing trust, opening the flow of communication, setting the vision, developing and empowering employees—and things turned around. Service improved, deadlines were met, costs went down, morale went up, and goals were achieved. When I began *leading*, we began delivering real value to the business.

If your organization is anything like mine was, it doesn't need another technologist. It needs a leader. It needs someone who can create the vision and share the strategy for achieving it, someone to rally the troops and help them embark on the journey. Your organization needs someone who can bring IT the respect it deserves and the tools it needs to succeed.

Throughout *IT Leadership Alchemy,* Lou Russell and Jeff Feldman use an alchemy metaphor to describe leadership: salt, sulfur, and mercury combine to produce something more precious and valuable, much in the same way that IT skills and competencies, combined with leadership, produce something precious and valuable. The role of the leader is to harness IT professionals' intelligence, energy, creativity, enthusiasm, and innovation to deliver true business value. No small task, but one that is made much simpler with Lou and Jeff's insights on leadership and the techniques for their practical application.

I've studied countless articles and publications on leadership. But what I really like about *IT Leadership Alchemy* is that it doesn't matter if you're a born leader or a self-made leader. If you're a natural leader who simply needs to refresh your innate skills, this book will energize those competencies you already possess. You can use Lou and Jeff's leadership alchemy to re-synthesize the leader in you. If you're looking to develop the leadership skills necessary to help your staff succeed, this book will help you identify your strengths and weaknesses and chart a personal plan for improvement.

Like many of us, I'm a hands-on learner. I need to dig around a subject and approach it from different angles to really anchor into what I've learned. I encourage you to do the same with this book. Just as combining salt, sulfur, and mercury in different ways yields unique results, combining Lou and Jeff's leadership methodology with your own personal development strategy will reveal the unique leader in you.

Jane Niederberger
Chief Information Officer
Anthem, Inc.

Preface

I wanted to write this book for many reasons. I have been employed in IT since 1979. I thought I'd died and gone to heaven when I got a highly paid ($13.5K) job as a programmer at AT&T. I had started college as a math major because I liked it. I eventually switched to Computer Science because it seemed like you could make money at it, it was new, and, ironically, I didn't want to teach. Thanks to my Mom for modeling the value of teaching that I so cherish now.

In one way I felt I belonged with IT people; my father is a highly analytical and technical microwave engineer by schooling. Thanks, Dad, for teaching me to understand and translate technical people's brilliance. In another way, spending the rest of my life with people who rarely went outside and who read compiler books for fun over the summer scared me. I thought about getting out of this career decision many times along the way.

I share this because it illustrates why leadership is so critical to the future of IT. The seemingly magic technology truly does make or break a company's ability to compete in the present market. Unfortunately, business people do not want to be around IT people (nerds). IT people tend to be weaker at people skills, so this reinforcing cycle of miscommunication and avoidance spawns insufficient technology solutions that prevent the business from competing. The cycle of miscommunication, blame, and frustration is omnipresent in most IT organizations today.

IT organizations are over equipped to deal with the technical issues but ill equipped to deal with the people issues. IT is an immature discipline; the technology has changed but the processes and behaviors of IT have not changed in 25 years. It is time for that change. The business needs IT to survive. IT needs to learn to lead through collaboration with the business to enable this survival. To do this, IT must exhibit strong leadership within its own troops. Unfortunately, many of the people who could play this role were promoted because of their technical, not their people, skills.

The fallout is evident everywhere you look—sick companies, depressed people, lost markets, and drifting families. The cost of IT staying here is too high for our world. My daughters, Kelly, Kristin, and Katherine, who have patiently supported my work, deserve a better future. They know that technology is a tool, not a religion. They know, and I hope will not forget as they grow up, that people are what matter.

As Ed Yourdon notes in his book *Byte Wars,* the events of 9/11 have created a new playing field for everyone, especially technologists. Thanks to Ed for inviting us to help with this transition with this book.

I believe that there are IT people who know that there is a big problem with IT leadership. They know that they have to grow a new kind of IT, with a new set of leadership competencies in addition to the obvious technical ones. This book is based on leadership competencies established by an elite group of people. Thank you for your brainpower and passion. Thanks to Susan Mosey and the Advisory Board: Christine Trum, Martha Heinrick, Jeff Clancy, Lisa Hoisl, Debra Limm Grommons, Marty Morrow, Susan Fehl, Chuck Geigner, Michael Ayers, and Naomi Karten.

Are you ready to grow your own leadership competencies and encourage the same in the people that work with you? This book is only a starting point. Change will require a stubbornness and determination that leadership matters. Thank you for this in advance. The truly special, gifted CIOs, like Jane Neiderberger of Anthem who wrote the Foreword, know this. That's why they are different and successful. Thanks, Jane, for proving that there is such a thing as an IT leader.

Jeff Feldman, my co-author, is an amazing thinker, with a deep desire to help people. He has been such a joy to work with, and I want to thank his wife, Kristin, for loaning him to me. My husband, Doug Martin, who is the leader of three companies, has helped me see the complexity of leading highly technical people. He is one of those rare IT people who is both a brilliant technologist and an advocate of people. He is also a realist, so he keeps my thoughts from getting too academic and impractical. Thanks for being my partner and rock. Finally, thanks to Vija, Margie, and Carol at Russell Martin & Associates who are the glue that allows me to do what I love.

People and relationships make technology useful. This is the primary message I hope you get from this book. The work you do is extremely important, so take care of yourself. And hug your kids. Along that line, I promised Jon Tripp and Amanda Huffine that I would put their names in this book. Here you go, little friends!

Lou Russell

For me, this project began long before we ever started talking about this book. In August of 2000, Susan Mosey from Russell Martin called to invite me to take part in the design of a new IT leadership development initiative called *i*Leadership. The vision for this project was grand and far-reaching and I was excited by the opportunity. Several months and a lot of phone calling, emailing, dreaming, designing, and redesigning later, we had the framework for what we felt was an exceptional approach to developing IT leaders. We had built a program with wings but for a variety of reasons, it was not yet time to fly. *i*Leadership still exists—the message behind the program was too important to lay dormant—it has now simply taken a different shape.

With the manuscript fully written now and ready to go to press, I must say how proud I am to have had a hand in creating this work. In the book, we talk about how we as leaders need to hold a guiding vision. My vision has always been a simple one: to make the world a better place. I've been accused of being an idealist, and perhaps I am, but I truly believe that each of us holds the power to influence the world in a more positive direction. This work is one small attempt on my part to do just that. By strengthening the capacity for leadership within organizations doing good and important work, in both large and small ways we make the world a better place—for our customers, our employees, for anyone touched by the products and services we provide, and ultimately for ourselves. My hope here is to be an enabler, to enable the growth and fulfill the potential of the authentic leader residing within each of us. This is what I hope I've brought to this work and what I hope you'll take from it.

My contributions to this effort are built upon a foundation of support from many teachers, partners, and loved ones. I have much to be thankful for and many to be thankful to.

To Kristin, for her love, bottomless flexibility, endless understanding, and gentle encouragement.

To my parents, for nurturing the potential they recognized in me and guiding the first steps along the path of this journey.

To the colleagues I've been fortunate enough to partner with through the years, each of whom has directly or indirectly added value and insight to this work: Karl, Bruce, Chris, Corky, and so many others.

A special thanks to Lou for her dreams and vision, support and encouragement, confidence and trust, sense of humor and flexibility, grace and style. I'd write again with you anytime!

Special thanks also to the Russell Martin team who supported this project in so many ways behind the scenes—Carol, Margie, Vija, and to Susan who began this leadership journey with us.

And thanks to you, the reader, for your willingness to explore our approach and engage our ideas. We hope you find a piece of what you seek among these pages.

Jeff Feldman

The Value of Technical Leadership

Strong Information Technology (IT) leadership will grow IT teams who can meet and exceed business goals—it makes market sense for the business and for IT professionals. Unfortunately, IT leadership is a rare commodity due to confusion about what it really is, as well as economic, time, and cost pressures. Alchemy, the study of changing what is common to what is precious, is a good analogy for what we would like to accomplish with this book. We would like to leverage the strengths of ordinary IT managers and provide them with tools that they can use to transform themselves into leaders.

In today's IT shops, the inability of IT to show value-added to the business, coupled with increasing demand for its services, is creating agony. What's creating agony in the IT environment?

- The complexity of IT work has increased due to rising time and cost constraints, ever-changing technological options, and a highly competitive business climate that demands quick innovation at low cost.

- Most IT project managers manage global, enterprise-sized projects (ERP) with virtual teams, multiple external vendors, and priorities and requirements that change constantly.
- IT project managers who are not on ERP-sized projects juggle 10 to 20 different projects, acting as project manager, developer, and implementer, with the constant challenge of prioritizing this work.
- At the same time these situations demand more, IT organizations are shrinking to cut costs.
- Many companies cannot prove that their technology investments provide a positive return on investment.
- IT is expected to say "yes" to all business technology needs, but without the ability to say "no," the quality of the solutions suffers.
- IT managers, rewarded for being gifted technologists, suddenly find themselves in management positions without any training or resources to help support them in a people-oriented role. Nor have many been exposed to good IT leadership examples. Contrast that with a strong CIO, who knows he must be literate in the latest technology while also managing myriad relationships from vendors, to internal executives, to internal customers, and to their direct reports. The skilled CIO manages and leverages these relationships while allowing others to manage and leverage the technology. This type of thinking is alien to new IT middle managers, who tend to respond to crises by desperately returning to the skills that brought them success in the past.
- Companies tend to invest in IT leadership competency (for example, conflict management, negotiation, relationship management, transition, coaching, and change management) far less than in training for other skills. Send a CIO to an executive leadership retreat at Harvard and price is no object. Ask for permission for a middle manager to attend a five-day IT leadership workshop down the street, and you'll be asked to find a cheaper e-learning alternative to be done during downtime.
- IT practitioners are stressed and tired. Extended work hours and 24/7 virtual home offices, considered temporary during Y2K work in the late 90s, have become the status quo.

We wrote this book to help you grow the leadership skills you need to overcome challenges like these so you can achieve success in your IT organization. You'll learn why, when, how, and with whom to apply these new tools that will enhance the tools you already have. The first chapter will help you create a plan to best invest your reading time for maximum return.

Opportunities for Growth _____

After reading this chapter, the reader will be able to:

- Define IT leadership
- Use the alchemy metaphor to organize and identify personal characteristics that will make you a more effective IT leader
- Assess and build a plan to develop your own leadership abilities
- Use your own strengths and weaknesses to prioritize the time you spend exploring this book

Agenda _____

What is Leadership?

Alchemy: Turning Common Into Precious

Assessing Your IT Leadership Competencies

Navigating This Book

What is Leadership?

Leadership is a frustrating concept. Browse through any bookstore and you will see more titles on leadership than on most other topics in the business section. Obviously, people feel the need to learn more about leadership; they feel inadequate in the role of leader. On the other hand, many of these leadership books offer advice that is either trite, mystical, or has nothing to do with real leadership. How often have you picked up a book, read it, and then said, "Sounds great, but what am I supposed to DO?"

We believe leadership is the result of using one's role and ability to motivate and influence. Successful leadership involves managing one's self and relationships to move toward a specific business goal. We wrote this book to help IT people grow their skills, knowledge, and confidence to develop leadership in a real, practical IT context. Simply put, we'll help you avoid real horror stories like these:

- An IT person was laid off through a text message on his beeper while attending a large international conference in the same city as his own office.

- A woman asked for leadership advice after she was abruptly given the job of her boss, who committed suicide. She was not given any directions, training, or coaching.
- A five-year SAP project for a global pharmaceutical company has logged two deaths from heart attacks, large turnover rates, and illnesses.
- A woman hired by a software firm discovered that she could no longer work with the technical people on her team because they refused to communicate with her. Ironically, she was hired so that her communication skills would rub off on them. Her comment: "Is there any place in IT that I'll be able to work all of my skills?"

Exercise: Zoning in on Competencies

Take a moment and write a brief definition of IT leadership. List at least 10 competencies you'd expect from a great IT leader. Now, from those 10 competencies, select the three you consider most critical.

The IT leadership competencies described in this book were developed through two different research projects. The first, email-based effort asked 3,000 IT professionals to identify the top 10 competencies for IT leaders, and then asked them to choose the top three from the 10 most frequently identified choices. The second project involved an advisory panel of CIOs, IT middle managers, IT consultants, and IT researchers. The competencies these research efforts identified provide the basis for the chapters that follow. In addition, the advisory panel shared the following observations:

- "With speed so important, IT leaders have to be much more decisive when addressing rapid changes to technology and business drivers. They need to be more technically savvy and must be able to lead complex, diverse organizations."
- "IT leaders must thrive on the excitement and intrigue of the world of technology, dealing with people at all levels of the organization, planning for change (a contradiction for sure), leveraging the critical nature of technology for business, dealing with 'wild and crazy' users and vendors, being underappreciated, and almost always being blamed as the cause of any major mess-ups."
- "IT leadership tends to touch all aspects of the business, which makes the CIO leadership positions similar to CEO or COO in their breadth. Success as an IT leader is neither all strategic nor all operational. The true leaders of the IT industry have a strong focus in both areas and can

move between the 60,000-foot level and the 100-foot level. The need for a unique combination of people skills and technology skills is unlike other leadership positions in other business areas."

One panel member recalled:

"In the mid-60s, while working for a start-up IT venture, the general perception was that a 'manager is a manager is a manager,' and that someone who managed a light bulb factory could manage software development. That perception still exists in some organizations, but it's gradually becoming more widely appreciated that IT leadership is at least somewhat different than 'general' leadership.

"One difference has to do with the nature of the product of an IT organization. One of the most obvious differences has to do with the nature of 'tradeoffs' between schedule/deadline, budget, personnel resources, functionality, and quality when estimating a project. Over and over again I've seen non-IT-aware senior managers exclaim, 'Look, it's absolutely imperative that we have this new IT dot-com system finished in half the time you've estimated. So I'll give you twice as many people as you asked for and everything will be fine, right?'

"The other difference has to do with the nature of the work being performed. IT people are doing intellectual work, the ultimate result of which will be a bunch of invisible bits inside a computer. There are lots of other professions involving intellectual effort, but most of them result in a physical, tangible artifact. An external observer, such as the manager leading the effort, can look at the artifact at various stages throughout the project and derive a gut estimate of the degree of completion. It's harder to do that with software projects. Finally, software is one of the few professions where the 'assets' of the organization can walk out of the office at 5:00 p.m. with no guarantee that they'll return. The assets are not 'fixed.' Thus, the manager who leads by intimidation, fear, and bullying runs the risk that the entire project team will walk out."

Consider the differences between IT and other leadership disciplines:

- IT processes are unique to IT and the leadership must drive process improvement, including solution development, security, contingency planning, project management, and capacity planning.
- Strongly technical IT people tend to follow a certain behavioral model. Certainly, there are many exceptions, but a successful technical person

is often highly theoretical, good at detail work, comfortable working alone, driven by internal rules, and tolerant of conflict. This sets the stage for specific relationship norms and challenges between an IT leader and her team.

- The "why" of a business, organization, or team is critical for IT project prioritization. This is true in all areas of life and business, and is not unique to IT. However, IT organizations tend to not have shared vision and values, and are often unaware or removed from the vision of the overall enterprise. There may be visions and values on a sign on the wall, but IT troops typically find it difficult to internalize them.

In general, the tougher challenges of leading IT people are no different than those of leading other professionals. Getting the best out of people and having them work with each other to achieve a common goal requires the same skills whether you're leading a sales team or a technology group. The critical leadership skills cut across all parts of an organization. However, IT practitioners are a unique group of individuals with preferences and behaviors that may be different than those of other business professionals.

- IT leadership deals with a unique group of highly intelligent, technical people immersed in the innate unpredictability and chaos of technology.
- A great IT leader knows how to leverage the strengths she already has, and to surround herself with others to fill in the gaps. A great IT leader realizes that each of her people is unique, so she coaches them to leverage their own strengths as well. Therefore, IT leadership is about releasing the potential that is already there.
- Leadership development is a paradox. It must ultimately be practical and something that an IT leader can immediately do for others. However, to be able to "do," leaders must find quiet time to develop self-understanding. Leadership includes skills, knowledge, technique, and personal spirit.

In each chapter, you will read about basic concepts and techniques associated with each of the 10 competencies. The words SALT, SULPHUR, and MERCURY refer to the alchemy metaphor, which we'll describe in the next section. Each chapter will also describe intermediate and advanced techniques and advise when to use them. If a particular competency is a special challenge for you, use the intermediate and advanced techniques for future growth (or hire someone with that skill).

Finally, in each chapter you will be encouraged to do some journaling. While that process may seem frivolous and easy to skip, failing to journal may be surprisingly costly. If you truly want to achieve IT leadership success, pause briefly at these points and think about what you would like to accomplish. After all, you cannot achieve goals that you cannot quantify.

Next, you'll learn a little about alchemy, and why we chose this metaphor. We'll then give you the opportunity to assess yourself as a baseline using the 10 IT leadership competencies. Finally, we'll map out the chapters so that you can design a personal strategy for growing your IT leadership capacity.

Alchemy: Turning Common Into Precious

"Alchemy neither composes nor mixes: it increases and activates that which already exists in a latent state."—Franz Hartmann, late 19th Century alchemy historian, from his book, *The Life of Paracelsus and the Substance of his Teachings.*

As we completed this book, the United States is swept up in mystical mania with huge box office success for *Harry Potter* and the *Lord of the Rings.* In such a time of uncertainty, it seems natural to long for magic and mysticism. When it's clear that we cannot control the external events around us, we wish for a spell or potion to give us power. In the book by Peter Sacks, *Generation SX Goes to College: An Eye-Opening Account of Teaching in Postmodern America,* the author notes that our current cultural fascination with mysticism parallels the prevailing situation in the Middle Ages, when alchemy was at its peak.

You may think of alchemy as turning common metals into gold. That is the best-known part of it, although many other chemical reactions were also attempted. In a broader sense, alchemy was a philosophy that attempted to leverage what was already within common metals to activate something valuable. IT leadership is the same thing, and all IT managers have the innate capacity to be leaders. This book is designed to be the start of a process to activate that innate capacity through additional skills, knowledge, and motivation. Like IT leadership, alchemy was more about ongoing questions than about definitive answers. And, like all things of value, alchemy was really about the journey, rather than the destination. You'll find that IT leadership is very much the same.

We've divided the IT leadership competencies into three sections:

- Self-alignment—Who am I? What do I believe? What are my strengths and challenges?
- Working with others—How are we all different? How can I motivate and influence others?
- Integration—Given each leadership situation as unique, how do I customize to the need?

Figure 1.1 summarizes alchemy's three principles. *Salt* symbolizes crystallization, condensation, slow growth from within, and independence. We use this principle to detail the self-alignment of the leader. Unless you are clear about who you are, what you believe, and how you judge effectiveness, leadership will be purely an academic exercise. Self-alignment is the basis for a leader's prioritization, making it both the operating system that all leadership runs on, and the criterion for measuring success as a leader. While measuring leadership growth is difficult, we've included tools for setting measurable goals and tracking them. "SALT" appears next to the chapters addressing this topic.

Sulphur is the expansive force. When combined with other things, sulphur creates new results. Similarly, an IT leader cannot be a leader by herself; leadership is a collaborative effort. The chapters with "SULPHUR" focus on competencies involving the external expression of leadership to others. Like alchemy, the results will always be surprising. After all, as most IT managers have learned, people are not as predictable as technology.

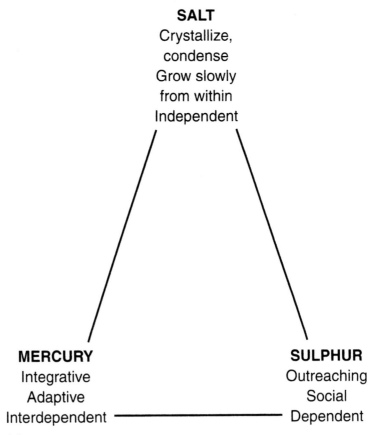

SALT
Crystallize,
condense
Grow slowly
from within
Independent

MERCURY
Integrative
Adaptive
Interdependent

SULPHUR
Outreaching
Social
Dependent

Figure 1.1
The three principles of alchemy. (Modified from Illustrations from *John French— The Art of Distillation, Book III.* http://www.levity.com/alchemy/jfren_3. html-39K-2001-02-14.)

Finally, *mercury* represents integration. It tempers the extremes of salt and sulphur, creating a unique result for each specific time and place. Similarly, IT leadership requires a unique reaction to each opportunity, depending upon the people involved, the history, the culture, the processes, the moods, and even the time of day. It is critical that IT leaders realize that what worked yesterday will not necessarily work today. Like mercury, IT leadership must transform itself and flow into the places available right now—but when misapplied, it can be a disaster. You'll see "MERCURY" with the competencies geared toward integration.

Exercise: Ranking Your Strengths

Take a moment and think about the three principles of alchemy: Salt/self-alignment, Sulphur/work with others, Mercury/integration. Rank these based on the strength of your competency in each area.

Many IT managers attend leadership workshops or devour best-selling leadership books only to return to work completely unchanged. Too often the experiences gained in a workshop with "the right answers" don't reflect the realities of the chaotic IT world. More worrisome are the learners who return with "the right answers," but are unable to practice the agility and flexibility needed for difficult situations.

We believe that the seed of leadership is in everyone. Each person has a unique ability to be the leader they were meant to be—something that's as true in IT as it is anywhere. Forcing yourself to look like somebody's ideal is stress-inducing and ignores your own natural leadership talents. Instead, we created this book to help you identify and leverage your natural leadership strengths while minimizing your weaknesses. One caution, though: If your primary attraction is power, technical reputation, prestige, or salary, and not the value of truly helping others, leadership may not be the right role for you.

Assessing Your IT Leadership Competencies

Look at the list of competencies in Figure 1.2. For each phrase under the main competency title, indicate whether you think your competency is High, Medium, or Low by writing an H, M, or L. Review each grouping of phrases and give yourself an overall assessment score for each of the 10 competencies, again using High, Medium, or Low.

SALT 1. Inner Leader—Self-Alignment

- Clarify and acknowledge that leadership comes from within the leader
- Understand the difference between leadership character and leadership persona, and apply this distinction to your own approach to leadership
- Identify your personal values, purpose, and vision, and explore their alignment with your actions as a leader
- Design a strategy for receiving honest feedback regarding your leadership style from those within your leadership sphere
- Build your own personal brand as a leader

SALT 2. Inner—Resiliency

- Assess your personal strengths and areas for development around the attributes of individual resiliency
- Adopt and maintain an empowered attitude in the face of adversity
- Create and hold a vision as a guide through uncertain times
- Build a flexible-thinking approach to challenges
- Utilize a process for effective decision making and establishment of priority actions
- Recognize and seize the opportunities hidden within challenging situations
- Balance the modes of "doing" in the present, planning for the future, and processing learning from the past

SULPHUR 3. Interpersonal and Team Skills

- Understand the essential nature of strong relationships for effective leadership
- Identify the key elements of healthy interpersonal interactions
- Develop strategies for building trust as the foundation of strong interpersonal networks
- Build skills for more effective conflict management
- Recognize and leverage the value of individual diversity

SULPHUR 4. Communication Skills

- Be clear as to the intentions of your communications
- Recognize the two messages comprising every communication
- Select the appropriate communications channel for sending messages

Figure 1.2
The 10 competencies of IT leadership.

- Manage interference for clear communication
- Strengthen your presentation performance
- Practice multiple levels of listening
- Employ reflective listening for effective leadership interactions

MERCURY 5. Coaching
- Motivating employees to high performance
- Coaching for development and improved performance
- Manage with appreciation/respect for diversity of individual values and needs
- Delegate tasks as needed and with awareness of employee development opportunities
- Select appropriate staff to fulfill specific project needs and responsibilities

MERCURY 6. Customer Orientation
- Understand and apply customer needs and expectations
- Gather customer requirements and input
- Partner with customer in gathering requirements, maintaining communication flow, and managing work
- Set and monitor performance standards

MERCURY 7. Strategic Business Acumen
- Demonstrate ability to ethically build support for a perspective you feel strongly about
- Holistic view—think in terms of the entire system and the effects and consequences of actions and decisions
- Operate with an awareness of marketplace competition and general landscape of related business arenas
- General business acumen—functions of strategic planning, finance, marketing, manufacturing, R&D, etc.

MERCURY 8. Project Leadership
- Build cohesive teams with shared purpose and high performance
- Set, communicate, and monitor milestones and objectives
- Gain and maintain buy in from sponsors and customers

Figure 1.2 (Continued)

- Prioritize and allocate resources
- Manage multiple, potentially conflicting priorities across various/diverse disciplines
- Create and define systems and processes to translate vision into action
- Maintain an effective, interactive, and productive team culture
- Manage budget and project progress
- Gather and analyze appropriate data, and input and manage "noise" of info overload
- Manage risk versus reward and ROI equations
- Balance established standards with need for exceptions in decision making
- Align decisions with needs of business and organizational/team values
- Make timely decisions in alignment with customer and business pace

SULPHUR 9. Creating and Actualizing Vision

- Gain new insights and different perspectives on vision as a process
- Learn and explore the power of compelling vision
- Apply vision as a management tool in an unpredictable world
- Create a business unit vision via a co-creation process
- Align business unit visions with the larger organization
- Enroll stakeholders in the business unit vision
- Convert vision into action
- Enact the leadership role of vision keeper

MERCURY 10. The Challenge of Change

- Clarify the distinction between change and transition
- Map the human journey of transition
- Assess the challenges of the transitional journey
- Manage your own personal leadership transformation
- Discover the essential components for successful organizational change
- Develop strategy for leading individuals with different change styles
- Build the skills necessary for leading change

MERCURY 11. A Plan for Action

ALL 12. Resources

Figure 1.2 (Continued)

If you'd really like to jumpstart your experience, ask your boss and/or a couple of your team members to offer their assessment of you. Remember, no one is perfect in all of the competencies, and it's critical that you understand your own strengths and weaknesses. Don't focus entirely on trying to fix the negatives. Instead, consider supplementing your weaknesses through collaboration with others.

Leadership is a complex, fluid undertaking. Each person has a unique need for leadership, and the context of that need will vary at any point in time. A leader must be able to adapt constantly to those needs.

Interestingly, your strengths are also your weaknesses. As people succeed, they tend to limit the competencies they bring to each situation to those that have been successful in the past. *The Last Word on Power* by Tracey Goss is a provocative book on this subject. Referring back to an earlier example, a middle manager promoted because of technical prowess will go right back to manipulating technology under stress, returning to the competencies that are most natural. An IT leader must remain mindful and alert to these tendencies. Look for overused competencies, and notice when you use them.

We've written these chapters on two levels. They provide technique, knowledge, and self-understanding for the leader, along with guidance for working with the team. Even if you discover that you are strong in a competency, briefly scan the chapter for that mindset to learn some new ways to grow that competency in your staff.

Navigating This Book

Figure 1.2 outlines the alchemy principles as they relate to each chapter. Chapters 2 through 5 focus on the SALT of IT leadership—working on self-alignment. This is an important starting place, and we encourage you to begin with these chapters. They provide a cornerstone for growing IT leadership competency.

Chapters 6 through 9 focus on the SULPHUR of IT leadership—working with others. There may be chapters about competencies with which you already feel comfortable, and you may want to prioritize your time here. Remember, you can use the techniques, or teach them to your team.

Chapters 10 and 11 focus on the MERCURY of IT leadership—working on creating a vision for your team, and helping them through the accelerating change and transition that defines the world today.

Chapter 12 focuses on creating your own Action Plan, helping you define concrete and measurable goals. As you read through the earlier chapters, you

might mark the location of Chapter 12, and jot down your ideas as they occur to you. It might be a good idea to share your finished plan with someone
else for reinforcement and accountability.

Chapter 13 details books, articles, journals, web sites, and other resources
that will help you continue your journey—and tell you how you can share the
details of your journey with us.

Summary

Bob Glass, editor of the *Journal of Systems and Software* and a prolific IT writer,
recently asked, "Aren't alchemists the quacks of the Middle Ages?" IT people
are often dismissed with the same sort of tone, and ridiculed with terms like
"nerd" and "bit head" while being envied for their salaries. Strong IT leadership will not only grow individuals who can meet business goals; it will help
to increase respect for the field.

You must enter this learning experience with an open mind. You already
have the competencies needed to continue to become a great IT leader. Now
you can gain the ability to increase your competency level beyond your current successes, enabling you to deal with the current challenges and complexity of IT work.

Leader Self-Alignment

We refer to alchemy as bringing together various essential elements toward the formation of something greater and more valued. The form of alchemy best known to most of us through history focused on the formulation of gold from other materials. Practiced primarily in the Middle Ages, this process always began with a base element, usually another metal. The creation process needed a foundation from which experimentation and discovery could begin. Your journey into leadership similarly needs a starting point.

Leadership grows from what already exists within the leader. This is where we begin to explore and discover our leadership selves. Remember the three principles of alchemy, and that salt is the contractive force in nature. Crystals form slowly as the material accumulates and builds over time. Discovering ourselves and gaining insight into our leadership strengths is also a contractive force. As we draw inward, we slowly accumulate "material" that develops into a stronger sense of self-awareness and self-knowledge, and will provide the base from which we'll create and grow the leader within us.

Opportunities for Growth _____

- Clarify and acknowledge that leadership comes from within the leader
- Understand the difference between leadership character and leadership persona, and apply this distinction to your own approach to leadership
- Identify your personal values, purpose, and vision, and explore their alignment with your actions as a leader
- Design a strategy for receiving honest feedback regarding your leadership style
- Build your own personal brand as a leader

Agenda _____

Being Leadership

Leadership Values, Purpose, and Vision

Leader Self-Awareness

Creating Your Leadership Brand

Being Leadership

We've all seen lists that attempt to quantify leadership; for example, "Top 10 Things Great Leaders Do." On those lists, you'll find items such as "articulate vision," "inspire performance," and "drive change." We identified one such list—the 10 IT leadership competencies from Chapter 1, "The Value of Technical Leadership"—as the basis upon which this book is built. Lists like these provide a good starting point for assessing our leadership because they define the role of leaders. However, knowing and performing those roles doesn't necessarily constitute leadership. Anyone can learn and apply the mechanics of inspiring others to perform. But effective leadership demands more than mechanics. It stems from *being* a great leader, rather than merely *doing* the things that great leaders do. And great leaders share the desire to continually grow in their leadership—that goal is critical!

Becoming a great leader requires developing and maintaining the qualities of leadership within the depths of our *self*. Leadership qualities begin within and expand outward until they are reflected in our actions. Through the curriculum of the Institute for Women's Leadership, an organization about women in leadership, Rayona Sharpnack helps participants develop what she calls their leadership "context"—who they are as leaders. In an interview with *Fast Company* magazine, Sharpnack notes that the *being* aspect of leadership is what enables breakthroughs in what people do and what they learn. Her approach is based on the belief that success is more likely realized by transforming the leader's mental framework rather than memorizing mechanics.

Executive coach Kevin Cashman defines leadership as "authentic self-expression that creates value." In other words, the leader's expression of who he is serves as the basis for his effectiveness as a leader (we'll talk more about authenticity later). Through its work with hundreds of leaders, Cashman's company, Leadersource, has identified several essential themes for exploring and growing leadership from within:

- As the person grows, the leader grows. The missing element in most leadership development programs is growing the leader by growing the person.
- Most definitions of leadership need to be turned inside out, moving from viewing solely through external manifestations to examining the internal source.
- Connecting leaders with their essence/character is central to effective executive development.
- Leaders who learn to bring their purpose to conscious awareness experience quantum increases in energy, effectiveness, and fulfillment.
- Those who integrate personal power and results power with synergy power accelerate their effectiveness as leaders.
- Leaders who work on achieving career/life balance are healthier and more effective.

In his book, *Leadership From the Inside Out* (Executive Excellence Publishing, 2000), Cashman differentiates between character and persona. When we lead from our being, and when our leadership actions are closely aligned with who we are, we are leading from *character.* Character centers upon our essential nature as a person and is rooted in our values. Conversely, *persona* is like a mask that we wear, or a role we play. When we merely follow a list of leadership rules without aligning them to our unique values, we create a leadership persona. While we may initially feel that there is nothing wrong with "acting the part" (and sometimes there isn't), we cannot maintain the illusion of being something we are not indefinitely. Eventually, that persona will crack, our "ruse" will be exposed, and our effectiveness as a leader will be undermined.

How do we get inside ourselves and explore whether or not the right stuff is there and can be expressed through our leadership actions? It requires the commitment to venture into the uncharted territory of self and create a map that will guide us toward authentic leadership.

Leadership Values, Purpose, and Vision

Authentic leadership is about leading based upon who we are, and requires that we know and understand ourselves intimately. We have all "lived with" ourselves and been conscious of our being, yet few of us ever direct time and energy toward knowing our authentic selves. Rarely do we take the time to reflect on how we define and live our personal values, individual vision, and purpose. Simply put, authenticity is the alignment of a leader's actions with his values as a human being.

Exercise: Epitaph of a Leader

Imagine that years into the future (many, we hope) you have passed on to the great beyond. As part of the process of passing on to whatever comes next, you have the opportunity to listen in on your own funeral ceremonies and eulogies. What would you hope to hear about yourself? Imagine two separate such ceremonies: one a gathering of family and friends, and one a collection of co-workers and colleagues. Summarize how you would hope each group would honor and remember you.

If you took this exercise seriously, with thoughtful reflection, each statement you've written represents a core value you hold. You may have to distill that value from the statement, but it's there. For example, if you thought a co-worker might say, "She was always willing to go out on a limb for others," the underlying value is being supportive of and loyal to people. Write down the personal values you just identified and add others that come to mind.

Personal Values:

Do your daily actions and behaviors reflect these values? Are any of the personal values you identified not being reflected?

Our values are the very essence of our being. They define who we are. Exercises like this (and another you'll encounter in Chapter 6, "Coaching") sometimes reveal that we are not living true to our values. Usually, this results from a lack of self-awareness or failure to become attuned to what we truly deem important. Being out of touch with ourselves can cause a great deal of stress. To become effective, authentic leaders, we need to get back in touch with our values and integrate them into our leadership role. This is the first step to leading from our *being*.

Our values provide the supports for our purpose and vision as a leader. Purpose answers the "why" questions (Why am I a leader? What is the ultimate purpose behind my energies and focus as a leader?) while vision focuses on the "how" (How do I focus my energies in ways that fulfill my purpose as a leader?), providing the path we travel in pursuit of our purpose.

What is the essential purpose of leadership? Exactly what is it we are here to do as leaders? The answers depend upon the nature of our IT leadership role and the circumstances surrounding it. John Kotter, author and former professor of organizational behavior at Harvard Business School, noted that leadership is about coping with change (Kotter, "What Leaders Really Do," *Harvard Business Review*, Dec. 2001). Perhaps you'll choose to focus your leadership purpose on Kotter's view; after all, IT is all about developing technological solutions that both manage and create change. Or maybe you'll discover more of a purpose in coaching the professional growth and development of your people. You might also choose to lead from the purpose of surveying the future of your work, defining a vision, and inspiring others to follow. Whatever your choice, defining your purpose is an individual act and you must connect with it independently to achieve effectiveness as an authentic leader.

Exercise: Defining Leadership Purpose

What does your leadership role mean to you? Why are you in your role, and what are you there to do? Revisit the definition of IT leadership you created in Chapter 1, "The Value of Technical Leadership," and write a brief, direct statement of your leadership purpose below. If it helps, begin by making a list of everything your leadership role encompasses. Such a list may offer insight into certain common denominators related to your purpose. Think about this over the next several days and see what emerges. Keep in mind that purpose is usually something almost beyond reach, never completely fulfilled. We never actually *arrive* at our purpose; it is something we are always striving for. For example, your purpose as a leader may be to leverage the creative energies of your people toward creating technological solutions to your company's challenges.

With a clear purpose we can now define the vision or path we'll follow in its pursuit. As authentic leaders, our actions must align with our values—we must "walk our talk"—so vision is also a reflection of our values brought to life.

Purpose may be grand and nearly untouchable, but vision should be more concrete, with solid, attainable steps. It makes us define how we'll choose to use our role as leader to fulfill our purpose—making it purpose in action. Outlining vision in limited timeframes helps us keep it real and tangible. However, given our world of rapid change and shifting circumstances, our vision must also be dynamic and flexible. (We talk more about vision in Chapters 3, "Resiliency," and 10, "Creating and Actualizing Vision.")

Let's explore how values, purpose, and vision work together. Suppose, as leaders, we've agreed that one of our values has to do with learning and growth. Behind this value is the core belief that all people have unlimited potential for growth, and therefore, unlimited potential for adding value to the organization. Suppose we have identified our purpose as supporting that growth and nurturing the contribution of the people we lead. As a vision for fulfilling this purpose, we might choose to implement one or more of the following steps:

- Get to know each team member individually to better identify their professional interests, strengths, and aspirations
- Facilitate a process for development planning as a way to encourage team members to identify development needs and grow professional skill sets
- Sponsor training sessions to help team members enhance their skills
- Provide regular, consistent performance reviews while improving your own coaching and feedback skills
- Create a safe environment in which team members can stretch their abilities (and fail occasionally) as a means of professional growth
- Personally model growth and a learning attitude

Values, purpose, and vision are the essential building blocks of our character and the source of our being as leaders. Authentic leadership grows from a clear sense of these human elements and carefully aligning our actions with what they represent.

Leader Self-Awareness

When you look into the mirror, what do you see? At first glance, you probably see yourself as younger, thinner, or more fit. It's hard to take an honest look at ourselves and acknowledge that we are not quite as young, as thin, or as fit as we would like to be. Being truthful with ourselves can be painful and it's often easier to obscure the truth and fool ourselves that we are just as we would like to be or need to be.

When we try to assess the alignment of our behavior with our values and vision, the same type of self-delusion often gets in the way. We talk a good game of being authentic, but do we really walk the talk? Does the image in the mirror of our minds truly reflect our behavior? How do we know? That depends upon our capacity for self-awareness. When we are not sufficiently "tuned in" to ourselves, it's easy to overlook behaviors that fail to align with who and what we say we are as a person and as a leader. Self-awareness tunes our personal radar to detect that kind of misalignment.

In 1995, psychologist and science writer Daniel Goleman wrote a book entitled *Emotional Intelligence: Why It Can Matter More Than IQ* (Bantam Books, 1995), which pinpointed skills that research indicates are essential to success in any facet of life. Collectively, those skills are known as emotional intelligence (EI)—one's ability to manage emotions and work effectively with others to achieve desired levels of performance. Goleman explained the theory behind the EI skill set and why emotional intelligence is ultimately more important for business success than intellectual intelligence and technical competence. Though the EI concept had been around for some time, the book launched a frenzy of interest in this topic as it relates to workplace performance. Goleman and his colleagues recently published *Primal Leadership: Realizing the Power of Emotional Intelligence* (Harvard Business School Press, 2002), which highlights the even greater importance of EI skills for those in positions of leadership. The EI skill set includes several components:

- Self-awareness
- Self-management
- Self-motivation

- Others-awareness/empathy
- Social or interactive skills

Self-awareness is the EI set's foundational skill, focusing on our ability to tune into how we're feeling about ourselves and our situation at a given point in time. A self-aware person consistently asks two questions:

- What is my current emotional state? What am I feeling?
- How does this emotional state affect my ability to achieve my desired performance outcome?

Some IT leaders may not be accustomed to connecting with their feelings in this way. ("I have feelings?") Others may feel that it's important to ignore emotions at work, or that to exhibit emotion is unprofessional. However, because emotions drive behavior (often in ways of which we're not conscious), emotional self-awareness is a critical factor for authentic, effective leadership. Leaders must be aware of their emotions and the resulting behaviors so that they can manage and direct their emotions toward alignment with their authentic selves and desired performance outcomes.

Consider a team leader about to confront his team about what he perceives to be a lack of commitment to a project. The team leader has been stewing on this for some time and his anger and frustration have finally come to a head. Lacking self-awareness, he goes into the meeting and explodes. What's the outcome? At best, there's a performance improvement that's been manipulated by intimidation and has created an underlying resentment throughout the team without addressing the real issues. At worst, an unmotivated, uncommitted team simply shuts down.

Contrast that with a self-aware leader who recognizes and acknowledges his anger. He assesses whether revealing his anger will help the team achieve what it ultimately desires: an understanding of the issues surrounding the perceived lack of commitment and a way to inspire improved performance. This self-aware leader is also able to recognize whether a forceful exhibition of anger is aligned with his leadership values and vision. He may then choose a more purposeful way to bring about the desired result.

It's important to note that the facets of emotional intelligence are not static, and can in fact be grown and nurtured. Developing and maintaining self-awareness takes effort and commitment. If we seek to lead from our being, from who we are and will be as leaders, we need to commit ourselves to this effort. We should recognize and accept the need for help from others. Self-awareness requires behavioral insight we probably won't be able to see for ourselves. Gaining this insight in an honest, authentic way means asking others for feedback and creating a safe environment so they can provide that feedback candidly. Many 360-degree feedback tools are available (such as the informal process we suggested in Chapter 1), and a good leadership development coach may also be helpful.

Exercise: The Three-Person Feedback Challenge

Identify three people who have had the opportunity to observe you as a leader, and ask them for some basic insights as to how they perceive your leadership style in certain general behavioral areas. Choose three people who will provide honest, open feedback, and create a safe environment for them to do so.

1. List three people from whom you will request feedback.
2. Plan your "invitation" strategy. Include an explanation of why you seek this feedback, what you hope to do with the feedback, why you selected them as someone to ask feedback from, and a statement expressing the safety and "no reprisal" nature of the process. You will also need to think about whether you would like to receive this feedback in writing, verbally, via email, or by another channel.
3. Identify maybe four areas of your leadership performance about which you would like to receive feedback and develop questions designed to elicit that feedback. You can use the leadership competencies list from Chapter 1 as a starting point. Sample questions might include:
   - How would you describe my general mood as a leader?
   - How would you describe my skills as a coach—supporting and inspiring performance?
   - How would you describe my team management skills?
4. Respond to each question yourself, both with an honest assessment of your own skills in each area, as well as a vision of how you'd like to be. You may choose to share these self-reflective responses with the others or simply keep them to yourself.
5. Once the feedback has been received, process the responses and compare them to your own self-assessment. Note the alignment or misalignment of perceptions. Begin planning for any needed behavioral shifts or actions.
6. Thank the people who provided feedback and inform them of any actions you plan to take as a result of this process.

Creating Your Leadership Brand

You're familiar with product branding. If we showed you a Nike "swoosh," you would know what that represented. If we said "Intel Inside," we would need to say no more. Product branding was a key marketing strategy throughout the 1990s and into the new century. Every successful product had a clearly established brand.

People also have a sort of brand in the "legend" that accompanies their name and represents how they are known in the world (or organization). A leader's brand might be about integrity, it might be about risktaking or vision, it might even be about the leader's transformation from a brilliant programmer to a highly effective manager of team performance. A brand is the common story that others tell about their leader.

Fast Company made branding the cover issue of their magazine a few years back. Management consultant Tom Peters wrote the cover article, which expresses the branding imperative. Peters claims that each of us needs to understand the importance of personal branding. His perspective holds that in business today our most important job is to serve as head marketer for the brand called "You." Each of us is responsible for shaping our own legend. This is especially critical for leaders.

What is your brand as a leader? What are you "known for" within your organization? How does your brand align with who you really are—your values, your purpose?

Remember the "Epitaph of a Leader" exercise? The eulogy you would receive from those with whom you work—particularly from those in positions under your direct leadership—describes your leadership brand. Product and people branding is a function of popular perception. Brands are legendary—and it takes effort and attention to create a legend. If legends are not authentic, people will see through them and the legends will die, yielding to more accurate brand perceptions. Brands are derived from the honest and consistent expression of values and purpose. If you discover that your leadership brand is not aligned with who you feel you really are, it may be time to get back in touch with those values and purpose and create a vision that expresses them more authentically. Do this, and do it well, and your brand will become legendary.

Summary

Effective leaders lead from who they are. Their leadership is an authentic reflection of what they value and how they connect with and live their purposes. Self-alignment begins with clarity of these personal elements. Each of us needs to seek knowledge and insight into the degree of alignment between who we believe we are and how we act and are perceived. Success as a leader comes not from doing the things that leaders do, but from being the leader that we are.

Lessons Learned

- Leadership stems from who we are, our *being,* not what we do. Effective leaders lead from their character/essence, not a false persona or leadership mask.
- Authentic leadership is leading from a clarity of and alignment with our personal values, purpose, and vision.
- Values are the core beliefs we hold about others, our world, and ourselves. These beliefs shape our purpose and vision as leaders.
- Purpose represents the "Why?" of our role as a leader. It defines our basis for existing in leadership. Purpose is something for which we are always striving.
- Vision represents the "How?" of leadership: How do we choose to live our leadership purpose day by day? Vision is purpose in action.
- Clarity and alignment of values, purpose, and vision with our actions as leaders often requires insight and feedback from external sources. Those we work with everyday are often the most accurate mirrors of how our behaviors are perceived. Seeking feedback from these sources is essential to exploring our internal leadership landscape.
- Leaders become "branded" by the stories and legends others tell of their leadership style. Authentic leaders work to ensure that their leadership legend is close to their true character.

Action Plan/Journaling

Take a moment to reflect on your own degree of self-alignment, and consider the following:

- What core values would you strive to honor more fully through your actions as a leader?
- How do your leadership actions align with your purpose and vision as a leader?

- Do you operate primarily out of a leadership character or persona?
- What is your perceived brand as a leader and how does that fit with your image of your leadership self?

Take a few minutes in your journal and describe yourself as you would like to be. What kind of personal and leadership self-alignment do you imagine yourself having in the future?

Finally, jot down some quick notes about the first steps you will take to grow into this competency.

Resiliency

The IT manager slumps into his desk chair, finally out of the meeting. All the hours that his team invested in the last month, sacrificing health and home, have just been wiped away with a new requirement. That project is now on hold, and the new business need is even more aggressive than the one it is replacing. There seems to be no end in sight to the uncertainty of the ever-shifting business landscape and the constant challenge and frustration that it brings. The manager lifts his head out of his hands. Leaning back in his chair, he weighs his options. He realizes that the new requirement makes perfect sense if the company is going to survive these tough times, it's just the dramatic degree of the change that is hard to take. He shakes his head and smiles despite himself. It's the nature of the business. He needs to gather his team and break the news. With a sigh, he gets to his feet and walks wearily out of his office, mentally reviewing something he recently read about the need to be resilient in the face of adversity.

Alchemy is the blending of base ingredients toward the creation of something new, something where the whole surpasses the sum of the parts. Resiliency is the same—a combination of abilities blended together into a competency package in which each element enhances the potency of the others. Each skill has its own stand-alone value, but when combined, they produce something truly remarkable. And in the face of today's IT challenges, something that's required for success.

Resiliency has evolved into something of a buzzword, thanks to a decade of unrelenting change moving at an incredible pace. Corporate restructuring, downsizing, mergers, sector booms and busts, accelerated product cycles, implementation of new technology—together, they add up to a faster, less stable world in which resiliency is a critical competency for survival.

Resiliency as a leadership competency aligns with the salt principle of our alchemy metaphor: It is an internal trait. Our inner strength and ability to manage the challenges and setbacks we face is key to our effectiveness as leaders. We must model resilience if we are to inspire and nurture it within others.

Opportunities for Growth _____

- Assess your personal strengths and areas for development around the attributes of individual resiliency
- Adopt and maintain an empowered attitude in the face of adversity
- Create and hold a vision as a guide through uncertain times
- Build a flexible-thinking approach to challenges
- Use a process for effective decision making and establishment of priority actions
- Recognize and seize opportunities hidden within challenging situations
- Balance the modes of "doing" in the present, planning for the future, and processing learning from the past

Agenda _____

Resiliency in our World of Permanent White Water

Kayakers' Rules for Navigating Permanent White Water
- Attitude
- Don't Look Where You Don't Want to Go
- Flex with the Flow

- Manage the Mess
- It's No Fun if You Don't Get Wet
- Eddy Out

Resiliency in Our World of Permanent White Water

Author Peter Vaill used the phrase "permanent white water" to describe the complex, turbulent nature of our world in his book, *Managing as a Performing Art: New Ideas for a World of Chaotic Change* (Jossey-Bass, 1989). It is an apt metaphor for IT. Running a white water river in a raft, canoe, or kayak is an experience that is at once exhilarating, frightening, thrilling, dangerous, and challenging. As you race along the river, unanticipated situations emerge in a blink and must be addressed instantly. You constantly make adjustments for the water's speed and direction, not knowing what lurks around the bend. If you don't keep pace, you'll get swamped.

Vaill applies the metaphor to the complex systems within which IT organizations operate, describing several characteristics of permanent white water:

- Permanent white water conditions are full of surprises
- Complex systems tend to produce novel problems
- Permanent white water conditions feature events that are messy and ill-structured
- White water events are often costly

We live in that white water world of change, experiencing those conditions nearly every day. Consider the following:

- The person driving your project just took a new job. Although the new project leader has not yet been assigned, you're still expected to meet aggressive project delivery deadlines.
- After a great lunch, you've finally gained the trust of one of your most important internal clients. Returning to your desk, you find an email from one of your colleagues to this person, blasting them for something that you know was just a simple miscommunication. There goes *that* relationship!
- One of the project managers working for you just confessed that his project is running at least six months behind. He's been afraid to challenge the added customer requirements because he doesn't want to be seen as being difficult to work with. He's hoping you will break the news to the customer.

Successfully navigating this terrain demands a certain mindset. Those who actually thrive in this world of permanent white water have a capacity for dealing with the challenges these conditions thrust upon them. Their capacity stems from a blending of perspective and skill—a combination of characteristics comprising the competency package of resiliency.

Resiliency is all in your head—literally. Think of it as a puzzle for which you already hold all of the pieces. The behaviors we characterize as resiliency stem from the ways we view the world. As we discuss attitude in the coming pages, we'll explore how each of us is capable of directing thoughts and world views. Through this capability, we can also direct our behaviors toward greater resiliency in a changing and challenging world.

Kayakers' Rules for Navigating Permanent White Water

As we think about white water, let's turn to kayakers as a source of navigational advice. Kayaks tend to sit low in the water, offering the perception of being one with the flow. River kayaks are individual crafts; though you may have company on the water, the experience is essentially one of you, your boat, and the river. (Because this chapter focuses on individual resiliency, the kayak is a better fit than a white water raft with its more team-oriented dynamic.) Using the kayaking metaphor as our model for moving through our white water world, we can apply a few kayakers' rules for thriving in a world of permanent white water:

1. Pack Your Attitude
2. Don't Look Where You Don't Want to Go
3. Flex with the Flow
4. Manage the Mess
5. It's No Fun if You Don't Get Wet
6. Eddy Out

Pack Your Attitude

Resiliency is an alchemy of elements: a combination of skills, perspectives, and personal stylistic traits. At the heart of this mix lies one essential ingredient: attitude. The thoughts running through our minds as we deal with the events of our lives (in other words, the way we "talk" to ourselves about the situations we encounter and the challenges they hold) make up our attitude. The power of attitude is evident as we consider our past experiences. At times, we were convinced we couldn't get the job done (or simply didn't want to exert the effort), and the end result reflected our diminished approach.

There have also been times when we "talked ourselves into it," approaching a difficult task positively, and once again the results were evident. Your potential for success is rooted in the power of your attitude.

There's a story about a man stopping by a Peewee League baseball game on his way home from work. Sitting down behind the dugout of the team out in the field, the man asks a boy about the score.

"We're behind 14 to nothing" the boy replies with a smile.

"Really," says the man, "you don't seem very discouraged."

"Discouraged?" the boy asks looking puzzled. "Why would we be discouraged? We haven't even been up to bat yet!"

Considering the world's complexity and the challenges that it poses in our struggle for some measure of accomplishment, it may be disheartening to realize that we actually control very little. All we can truly master is ourselves— our thoughts, feelings, and the ways in which we choose to view the world and its challenges. We struggle to channel what little we can control into the desired direction. Yet the potential of attitude rests within us, though its power is sometimes difficult to harness.

Dr. Martin Seligman, author and University of Pennsylvania psychology professor, defines optimism in the same way we define resiliency: our ability to recover from setbacks. Seligman's research suggests that some of us are born with a predisposition toward bouncing back from adversity, but the thought process that accompanies this behavior can be nurtured and developed within everyone. In other words, we can actually learn optimism. When we react to adversity, we are reacting to our feelings about that event, rather than the event itself. And while we may not be able to control what happens to us, we do have some control over our emotions. (See the references to emotional intelligence in Chapter 2, "Leader Self-Alignment.") When adversity strikes, how we think and what we choose to believe will determine how we feel and how we act (Seligman, *Learned Optimism*, Pocket Books, 1998).

Figure 3.1 illustrates the typical human process of reacting to unwelcome events.

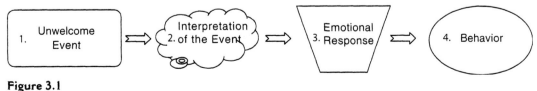

Figure 3.1
Bad news flowchart.

1. We all experience unwelcome events from time to time. Some examples might be:

   - The technology for which you're an expert is being phased out.
   - A key customer bypasses you, taking a complaint directly to the CIO.
   - Your team permanently loses two people but still needs to meet its project goals.

   Some are minor inconveniences, some are more dramatic—and some are downright traumatic! Yet the level of severity we place upon the event is entirely up to our interpretation.

2. We interpret every event, regardless of its depth or breadth, through the lens of our experience. Simply put, our past shapes our thinking on the present. Our thinking triggers factors such as the level of control we feel, the degree of struggle required to exert that control, and the ultimate return for engaging in that struggle. Our attitude determines how we talk to ourselves about the events we face.

3. Our interpretation of the unwelcome event begins to activate an emotional response. Emotions are conditioned responses based on our perceptions of situations. We may feel helpless, hopeless, and/or apathetic in the face of a challenge over which we perceive little control. High-impact personal events may trigger anger, fear, or frustration. In those cases, the event begins to exert control upon us and the results appear through our behavior.

4. With our emotions in play, it becomes difficult to manage our behaviors. Brain theory claims that highly charged emotional states such as anger, fear, or being overwhelmed send our brain into survival mode (commonly called the "fight or flight" mechanism). The brain directs our behavior to deal with what we perceive as a threat. The heart beats faster, our breathing quickens, and adrenaline is released into the bloodstream. Our now-supercharged blood races to our arms and legs to support this defense, so less blood is feeding our brain, impacting our ability to think clearly and control our emotions and the behavioral responses they influence.

How can we manage this chain of events? The key lies in the interpretation and how we "see" whatever issue may be obstructing our clear path to success. Choosing to see such issues as *challenges* triggers a different perception than seeing them as *problems*. Problems weigh us down, cause us stress, and force our hand. Challenges energize us and seem to be a test of our abilities—one for which we crave a victory.

How we interpret and think about the unwelcome events of life determines the choices we make. Within our thinking, within the attitude we choose to adopt, lies our power

Exercise: The Winning Interpretation

Select an unwelcome event from your recent past in which your response was less than resilient. Consider the interpretation you applied to the event, the emotional response it activated, and your resulting behaviors. Make a list of alternative interpretations—other ways of thinking or talking to yourself—you could have chosen. Follow each alternative interpretation through the emotional response and behaviors it would have triggered. Which alternative interpretation leads to the most favorable outcome? How would you describe the "winning" interpretation and its elements?

As we said, resiliency is a package of attributes, yet attitude is the one that makes or breaks the recipe. The first, most critical step along the path to resiliency is developing an empowering attitude. Fail to pack the proper attitude, and the white water will swamp you every time.

Don't Look Where You Don't Want to Go

You're on the white water river in your kayak. Despite the river's best efforts to unseat you with a raging flow and churning water, you're holding your own. You realize that you're actually enjoying the ride. You drop into a deep hole and dig in with your paddle to push yourself out the other side. As you rise back up and scan the terrain downriver, your heart skips a beat. About one hundred yards away (and closing quickly), the channel narrows and there is a large "strainer" (a.k.a. tree) down along the left—its branches reaching out like a net to snare you. There's a slim line of clear, smooth water flowing just between the tree's outer branches and the rocks lining the right bank. It's a narrow margin, but it's enough, if you can only tear your mind away from its focus on that tree!

Creating and holding a clear vision of our hopeful outcome in a challenging situation is a key element of personal resiliency. (See Chapter 10, "Vision"). When trying to avoid disaster, remaining focused on the doorway to disaster is a surefire way to find yourself in disaster. The trick behind *Don't Look Where You Don't Want to Go* is just that: Focus instead on where you *do* want to go. Lock in on a vision you do want to follow—one that avoids the disaster. Concentrate on that slim line of clear water between the tree and the riverbank, and you're more likely to travel that course.

In times of adversity, we often narrow our focus to the challenges before us. As we discussed earlier in this chapter, a range of negative emotions often accompanies adversity and tends to narrow our perception. We're not suggesting that you simply ignore the challenges; we're saying that it's important to find a way to broaden your perspective and take a more holistic view. Reconnecting with vision—our sense of what is possible—helps us to reconnect with our choices and redirect our focus in the right direction.

A hopeful vision provides light when circumstances seem dark. A vivid vision lends a tangible quality to imagination. An inspiring vision elicits strong connection and commitment from believers. In times of uncertainty and struggle, vision provides a hopeful direction, a real sense of something positive, and a dedication to persevere through the challenges.

The obstacles and challenges we're bound to encounter may be real dangers and warrant some attention. Yet we can't concentrate solely on them. By choosing our line along the river ahead and envisioning ourselves at each destination, we'll find our way through.

Exercise: A Vision for the Road Ahead

Scan the professional or personal road ahead of you and choose a challenge you expect in the near future. Create and outline a vision that will navigate this challenge so you emerge safely and securely on the other side. What do you hope for? What will it look like as it takes shape? What will it feel like as it unfolds and becomes real?

Flex with the Flow

We've defined resiliency as our ability to recover from setbacks and overcome the challenges of adversity. Given the uncertain nature of our world, the ability to solve problems and effectively deal with unexpected circumstances is a prerequisite for success. While attitude helps us to continue striving, and vision provides a sense of direction and hope, our ability to flex our problem-solving muscles is one of our most powerful resiliency tools. Flexible thinking, or applying creativity to our challenges, is a necessity in a world full of surprises. (For more on this topic, see the section on flexible structure in Chapter 9 "Project Leadership.")

Where does the creative process begin? As the term implies, creative thinking is a process that involves thinking differently: out of the box, along a new pattern, in different combinations and permutations. In order to apply creative thinking, you must first believe that you are capable of doing so. If you don't believe you have any creative ability, your creative process will be stymied. As any creativity guru or kindergarten teacher will tell you, the truth is that we all have the capacity for thinking differently; we merely need to look at challenges that way. IT professionals pride themselves on their problem-solving abilities, but rarely turn to this competency in situations unrelated to technology.

Consider a current or recent challenge. When you first ran up against it, where did your thinking process begin? More than likely, your process of seeking a solution began with a question like:

- How can we correct this system flaw?
- How can we enhance communication effectiveness between project teams?
- How can I get the kids to soccer and band practice while the van is in the repair shop?

Given that the creative process begins with a question, the trick to seeing different possibilities is to ask the right question. Frankly, the questions we ask often limit our thinking.

Consider the team of engineers called on to solve the problem of a tall truck lodged in an underpass. True to their profession, they began taking measurements and figuring extensive calculations. They debated about how to best apply the exact amount of force at the correct angle to free the truck. A small boy watching nearby finally turned to one of the engineers and asked, "Why don't you just let the air out of the tires?"

The degree to which we recognize possibilities is linked directly to the way our questions frame the challenges. Creativity is built upon a foundation of questioning—and the strongest foundation is one made up of several questions. Asking as many questions as possible from many different angles will expand your creative possibilities. Pose your challenge to yourself or your team as a question. Now pose it as a different question. Then again as a still different question. Exploring all the facets and interconnected elements allows you to see different perspectives on the challenge and opens the door to different solutions.

Peter Vaill suggested that permanent white water is full of surprises. In a world of frequent, unanticipated challenges, we need to maintain a high degree of flexibility in our approach to seeking solutions. Flexing with the flow implies applying creative energy to keep the boat afloat in the face of the obstacles our challenges create.

Manage the Mess

Resiliency begins in thought. It's demonstrated in behavior carried out through action or a series of actions. As we speak of resiliency in response to adversity or crisis, the question becomes: "How do we choose the most appropriate action in such situations?" How do we establish clear priorities for action in the midst of chaos?

Exercise: Imagine the Following Scenario . . .

You are driving down a lonely stretch of highway late one night when you come upon an accident. A car is overturned on the road. A second car with a smashed front end sits sideways, partially over the shoulder. Small flames are beginning to flicker up from under this car's hood. A wounded deer lies near the first car. As you prepare to stop, your headlights shine on a person dangling from the overturned vehicle, bleeding badly from a gash in the forehead. Glancing at the other vehicle, you see a person moving slightly in the driver's seat. The back door of this car is open and a small child is standing by the driver's door. You are alone, you have a cell phone, and there is no other traffic on the road. What are the first five actions you take?

How did you do? Did you come up with the correct five actions? Actually, it doesn't matter what you answered. We simply wanted you to make decisions in a chaotic crisis situation.

Think about the process you used. After reading the previous section's focus on questioning, you may have begun your process with a simple question: "What do I do?" It's the same question we ask whenever we're searching for an action in a situation filled with multiple options. The pressure-filled, high-stakes scenario we described here is not all that different in its need for fast decision making from the crises you may encounter in the workplace—and you probably approached it in much the same way you'd approach a crisis at work: by asking, "What do I do now?"

But in a high-pressure, chaotic situation requiring quick decision making, where does "What do I do?" mentally place you? It plants you right in the middle of the chaos, pain, fire, blood, guts, screaming, and yelling, with everything demanding your attention all at once. Being mentally in the middle of the mess means that it's all swirling around right in front of you, making it very easy to be influenced by the emotion of it all—and that's exactly where you don't want to be, at least until you have clarified your priority actions.

Recent studies on decision-making processes among emergency personnel—such as paramedics, firefighters, and police—suggest a different approach to choosing priority actions. Instead of "What do we do?," these emergency responders ask, "What's going on?" This simple shift of focus from self to scene makes a tremendous difference in the responder's mental capacity for clear, prioritized decision making.

"What's going on?" mentally places you on the outside of the scene rather than in the middle. Separation from the chaos and the associated emotion allows the responder to assess the situation, stay connected to top-level priorities, and choose the most appropriate course of action.

Of course, a significant amount of training helps. Emergency responders are highly trained professionals who understand the ramifications and interconnectedness of their actions, are grounded in essential priorities of preserving life and minimizing property damage, and have likely encountered similar scenarios.

However, that's quite similar to the pressure-filled decision-making scenarios you regularly encounter as an IT leader. You're a trained professional with years of experience in your field who understands the priorities of your role in the organization. You have weathered similar brushes with crisis in your professional history and you will weather future ones, too. The only factor remaining to be determined is how much pain and suffering you, your staff, and your customers will experience along the way. Though you probably cannot eliminate the pain and suffering caused by the situations, you can minimize them by making good decisions based on clear priorities. You can learn to manage the mess.

Exercise: Handling Crises

Make a list of five ways to remain on the outskirts of crises during your initial action planning, decision-making process. Example: Train yourself to list your action approach to crisis situations on paper as a way of forcing yourself to evaluate and prioritize options.

It's No Fun if You Don't Get Wet

If we're going to play the white water game, we need to admit one thing from the start: It's going to get hairy at times. We will encounter challenges and adversity along the way, and the journey will get difficult in places. Part of the experience of running the white water river is knowing that you're going to get wet. Several good dunks and a few scrapes come with the territory.

We can choose to try to play it safe. We can try to position ourselves so that we can sit out most of the rough water. Of course, we can never fully disengage ourselves, and that "safety" may be an illusion. Even if we find solid, safer ground, it carries a price of its own. We must make that choice, but our decision goes back to attitude—how we choose to see the challenges of our white water world. We can view the sometimes harsh conditions of white water as a danger or as an opportunity.

It's no fun if you don't get wet is the kayakers' rule that deals with being proactive. Resilient people look upon adversity as both an opportunity and a danger. While they don't ignore the danger, they choose to focus on the opportunity the challenge provides.

Some people exercise the "ostrich approach" to adversity and duck for cover at the first sign of trouble. These are the people who choose not to get wet, and in doing so, miss out on the fun and the opportunity.

What are some of the opportunities hiding within the dangers of the adversity we encounter? Of course, every situation is different and it's up to each of us to identify the opportunities for ourselves. It can be as simple as an opportunity to shine within the organization or a chance to spread and exercise our leadership wings. It may be an opportunity to demonstrate our commitment to a client, thereby advancing our partnership. Challenge may offer us the opportunity to test new approaches and create new solutions. Sometimes the opportunity lies in turning the danger on its head.

Resiliency is about bouncing back, about moving forward despite the ongoing struggle of navigating the white water. There's nothing that says forward progress has to be slow and painful. Taking the proactive approach may in fact offer a leap of forward progress. Rather than waiting for the wave of adversity to hit and then responding to the aftermath, proactive behavior anticipates the wave, adjusts before the impact, and rides its momentum.

Exercise: Challenge Equals Opportunity

Select a challenge you currently face. Brainstorm a list of five opportunities that this challenge presents. Be creative!

Eddy Out

It can be a rough ride on the river, especially as an IT leader. Navigating ourselves and guiding our organization through the white water requires a tremendous amount of energy, focus, and sheer guts.

An eddy is a calm place on the raging river, usually behind a large obstruction, that offers a safe haven or rest stop for a weary river runner. Kayakers occasionally "eddy out" to regroup, plan the run through the next rapid, make a quick review of their learning from the day, do a little scouting, or simply take an opportunity to catch their breath and celebrate their success. We don't often allow enough time for eddying out in our business lives.

The attention of performers in an organization is usually divided between three modes: operational, strategic, and reflective.

Most of us spend our time in operational mode, which is where we do what needs to be done: advancing the work of our organization, managing people, interacting with customers, and putting out fires. It's where we realize measurable achievement, it's what our customers look for, and it's what most organizations reward, so it makes sense that most of our attention is channeled here.

Strategic mode is where we divert some attention to looking ahead. We spend time planning, playing out possible operational scenarios, anticipating problems, being proactive in creating potential solutions, practicing continuous learning, and building our teams and organizational communities. Some of us are good at committing time at regular intervals to strategy, but many of us ignore strategic mode until the neglect creates an operational issue. That's a problem, because planning strategy under pressure tends to put us in survival mode, too focused on the "problem" to see the bigger, more strategic picture. (For more on strategy and vision, see Chapter 8, "Strategic Business Acumen" and Chapter 10, "Vision.")

Reflective mode involves looking back over the road we've traveled and considering the lessons we've learned along the way. We can do this individually or collectively, perhaps as a post-project review, a celebration of organizational culture and history, or a "how did we wind up in this mess?" session. Reflective mode typically gets little time and attention, though there is tremendous value in the process of looking back.

Eddying out is about creating space for strategy and reflection and recognizing the inherent value of each. Certainly, we need to focus our energies and resources on operational mode, which serves our customers and our organizations best. Yet we all know that failure to plan and failure to learn dooms us to repeat the same mistakes. In addition, frenzied paddling—the "doing" aspect of our organizational function—is simply not sustainable. By eddying out from time to time and investing a little attention in strategic and reflective modes now and again, we can relieve some of the daily frenzy.

Exercise: Eddy Out

Brainstorm seven ways to create more personal space for eddying out. With which three of these are you willing to experiment?

Summary

Resiliency is a true alchemy of skills—attitude, vision, creativity, crisis decision making, a proactive approach, and leveraging time for planning and learning—which blend together to form a critical leadership competency. Reflect on your abilities in each of these areas, maximize those in which you're strong, and seek enhancement for the less-developed abilities. Each of the elements is beneficial individually, but when bonded together, they are truly powerful.

Lesson Learned

- Thriving in our complex, fast-paced, and highly unstable world requires resilient behavior. The resiliency package includes several components that can be developed and strengthened with time and practice.
- Attitude is the foundation of resiliency and represents a conscious choice that each of us makes based on our interpretation of the adversity we face in life.
- Vision provides a sense of direction, hope, and a base of strength for perseverance. Focusing on where we wish to go will help us avoid some of the hazards along the way.
- Flexible, creative thinking is a requirement in a world full of surprises. Flexibility in thinking begins with (and can be limited by) the range of questions we ask in search for solutions.
- Resiliency is more than recovering from setbacks—it also has to do with discovering the opportunities hidden within challenging situations.
- We need to disengage from the journey every now and again to spend some time planning for the journey ahead and reflecting on the lessons learned from the path already traveled.

Action Plan/Journaling

In the next section, take a moment to reflect on your own degree of personal and leadership resiliency. Consider the following:

- Which of the five attributes of the resiliency package we explored—attitude, vision, flexible thinking, being proactive, eddying out—are your strengths and which need development?

- Choose one attribute that you regard as a strength and journal on how you might maximize that behavior and use it to its fullest potential.
- Choose one attribute you recognize as a development need and journal on how you might go about growing in this area. What would be the first five steps of a development plan for this resilient trait?

Take a few minutes in your journal and describe yourself as you would like to be. What kind of personal and leadership resiliency do you imagine yourself having in the future?

Finally, jot down some quick notes about the initial steps you will take to grow into this competency.

Interpersonal and Team Skills

Dr. Margaret Wheatley's provocative book on chaos theory as it pertains to organizational leadership describes our world as being made up not by atoms, but rather of relationships (Wheatley, *Leadership and the New Science,* Berrett-Koehler, 1994). Apparently, science has discovered that the atoms themselves do not build anything. The bonds between the atoms are the foundation of matter as we know it. It makes sense if you think about it—the pieces alone are nothing until they are placed in relationship with one another. The same concept applies to people.

As individuals, we are defined by our interpersonal connections with others. We are leaders, husbands, mothers, friends, colleagues, strangers, or even hermits due to our relationships with other people. Through these interpersonal interactions, we exist, and so do our teams and organizations. After all, organizations are communities of people defined by their place within the web connecting employees, customers, managers, suppliers, competitors, and many other interfaces. As leaders, we are also defined by interpersonal relationships. In fact, leadership *is* relationship.

Leadership is influence; it is directing the energies of others and supporting their growth toward personal and organizational goals. There is no influence in the absence of relationship, so without relationships, there is no leadership.

In our alchemy model, we apply the principal element sulphur to our exploration of interpersonal and team skills. Sulphur is an expansive force, expanding outward and combining with other materials to create new results. Leadership, the leveraging of interpersonal relationships within the team or organizational context, is about reaching outward to connect and combine our energies, our ideas, our visions, and our potential in the search for results.

Opportunities for Growth

- Understand the essential nature of strong interpersonal skills for effective leadership
- Identify the key elements of healthy interpersonal interactions
- Develop strategies for building trust as the foundation of strong interpersonal networks
- Build skills for more effective conflict management
- Recognize and leverage the value of individual diversity

Agenda

Interpersonal Skills for Effective Leadership

Essential Factors of Strong Relationships

Exploring Trust

Managing Conflict

Interpersonal and Team Effectiveness in a World of Difference

- Tuning in to Operational Differences
- Valuing Operational Differences
- Respecting Operational Differences

Interpersonal Skills for Effective Leadership

Leadership is about directing the efforts of our employees toward our organizations' goals. Interpersonal relationships are the vehicle through which we inspire performance in pursuit of these ends. While there are other ways to induce performance—like coercion, intimidation, and manipulation—

each carries a cost that we may wish we had not incurred when it comes due. Workers don't quit companies, they quit managers. Managers who rely upon "the stick" to drive performance may find themselves struggling with retention issues. Leveraging healthy interpersonal connections is the truest, most effective form of inspiration. While IT is not known as a center of relationship-oriented behavior, the energy and attention invested in relationship building is almost always rewarded through performance and results.

Essential Factors of Strong Relationships

Our bonds with other people form the matter of our lives. We each establish tens of thousands of interpersonal connections over time, and this rich experience teaches us a lot about what makes a relationship effective.

Exercise: Relational Effectiveness

Make a list of five people with whom you feel you have a strong, healthy, positive interpersonal connection. Review the list, think about these relationships, and make some notes as to what you see as the foundations of their effectiveness. Now think of two or three people with whom you struggle to create an effective interpersonal connection. What elements are missing from your interactions with these people that exist in your healthier relationships?

Healthy relationships include certain essential ingredients, among them:

- A foundation of trust
- A sense of caring or concern for each other's well-being and success
- Some common values and shared goals
- Respect and acceptance of the other, even during disagreement
- The ability to manage the inevitable conflicts that arise as a part of any relationship

Exploring Trust

Trust is the foundation upon which interpersonal relationships are built, and is essential for forming and maintaining effective relationships. Lack of trust can severely undermine effective interactions in supervisory, team, and customer relationships, making those relationships little more than transactions.

An exercise we use in some of our training programs explores the impact of trust upon group effectiveness. It involves a small team of people working together to arrange decks of cards in a sequence by suit and face value. Teams have a limited amount of time for this task and are in competition with other teams to sort the most decks in the allotted time. The teams are warned that they may have a saboteur in their midst—someone who has been instructed to secretly disrupt the group process and impede team success—but only some of the teams actually do (Workshops by Thiagi web site: *www.thiagi.com*, "Saboteur").

The outcome of this exercise usually plays out similarly. The teams that believe a saboteur is present take time to make accusations, argue, and double-check work—basically expending energy and focusing on distrust. Not surprisingly, they do not complete as many decks of cards as the teams who are working in a more trusting environment. In some teams, this lack of trust and its associated behavior is warranted—they actually do have a saboteur among them and inevitably this person's behavior reveals the hidden role. But the only sabotage impacting the teams without saboteurs is created by their own lack of trust. (For more on the impact of trust upon team and customer relationships, see Figure 7.3 in Chapter 7, "Customer Orientation.")

When we explore trust in the classroom, we ask how many in the room feel they are trustworthy. It's no surprise that every hand in the room goes up, but if that were really the case, trust should be a non-issue. The reality is that trust is a significant issue in teams and organizations, one that often undermines effective leadership. If everyone is trustworthy, why is this so?

If most of us are worthy of trust most of the time, trust then becomes an issue for two reasons: 1) Unconscious or thoughtless acts undermine existing trust between people, and 2) We are initially reluctant to risk trusting others.

How can actions undermine trust? Begin by exploring our own actions. As humans, we each occasionally act in thoughtlessly inconsiderate ways toward others—ways that may damage their trust in us. With the pressure to perform in a fast-paced world, it's a wonder that this doesn't happen more often. If we become aware that we have acted inappropriately to someone with whom we share and value a strong interpersonal connection, we must correct the situation through three steps:

- Connecting with some personal awareness of our act and having the willingness to reflect on its impact upon the other person. (See the section on leader self-awareness in Chapter 2, "Leader Self-Alignment.")

- Finding the courage to acknowledge that we may have behaved or acted inappropriately.

- Having respect and consideration for the other person so that we can communicate an apology and empathize with his or her feelings about our action.

We also need to realize that our act may have triggered a significant withdrawal from our joint trust account with this individual, and that withdrawal may need to be paid back over time. Suppose you're unable to make a meeting you had scheduled with an internal customer, and you forget to call and cancel. She expects you but you don't show up, leaving her to assume that you are not as concerned with her issues as you had indicated. You've just made a withdrawal from the trust account you hold with her. To repay this withdrawal and rebuild trust, you will need to demonstrate that you value the relationship and are interested in her concerns. It may take several positive interactions before you fully repay the withdrawal and restore the level of trust.

How can the unconscious acts of others affect interpersonal interactions? If we feel victim to something we perceive as inappropriate behavior, a lack of self-awareness on the part of that person may force us to return balance and harmony to the relationship by implementing effective conflict management skills. We'll talk more about these skills later in this chapter.

The second reason trust can be an issue involves our willingness to give trust. Trusting is a risk that exposes us, makes us vulnerable, and moves us a little more out of the realm of control.

Risk implies putting something *at risk*—exposing something to potential harm or loss. For example, trusting in someone else to follow through on a task for a project we lead may expose our perceived competence as a project manager or our very reputation to harm.

There is more to risk than loss, however. Every risk also holds the potential for gain. For example, delegating tasks to trustworthy staff members can bring rewards, such as less work on our own plate, a different perspective or approach to the task, or providing a development opportunity for a rising star performer.

While nobody wants to get burned, we need to perform a cost-benefit analysis of the trust-risk equation. Choosing not to trust carries a cost. Think about your own professional history—how motivated were you to perform at your highest level for someone who obviously had little trust in your abilities to deliver the desired results?

Exercise: Trust Assessment

Think of two people you have worked with in the past, one peer and one subordinate. Imagine delegating a task of high-level importance to each individual.

How do you behave with each of them? Are you concerned about the task and the individual's progress? Do you check in to see how things are coming along? Do you interject your thoughts, perspectives, and suggested approaches? Do you turn your attention elsewhere, fully expecting the task to be completed by the agreed-upon deadline? What is the basis for your behavior? How and why might your behavior differ between these two people?

Person One: Delegation Behavior: Rationale:

Person Two: Delegation Behavior: Rationale:

How do we measure trustworthiness? How would others score us on that equation?

Trust is based upon our opinion about a person with a given context, and may be shaped by several factors:

- Credibility—the degree of skill, knowledge, and experience we believe the individual has within the context for which we may offer our trust.
- Consistency—the degree to which we believe we can anticipate the individual's performance based upon past experiences.
- Communication—the degree to which ongoing information provides the confidence and reassurance we need to accept that our trust is deserved.

Exercise: The Trust Factor

As a leader, measure yourself against these three factors to determine the amount of trust you inspire from those you lead:

1. What level of credibility do you hold in the specific context of your IT leadership role?
2. How consistent are you in your actions and decision-making processes?
3. To what degree do you use communication as a means of building confidence and reassurance within your work team?

If there were one of these areas on which you could focus more attention and strengthen your performance, which would it be? (For more on this type of insight, see Chapter 2.)

If you recognize a lack of trust inhibiting the development of an interpersonal connection, identify the source of the shortfall. If you determine that you are reluctant to give trust, assess the risk involved. What is the loss you could personally experience by not trusting? What is the damage your lack of trust costs the relationship? What is the potential gain you could reap if trust is given and demonstrated worthy?

If you determine that the lack of trust originates with the other person, assess their rationale for not risking trust in you. Do you need to deal with problems from past interactions before the relationship can move forward? Will some act of trustworthiness encourage greater risk in trusting?

Trust is the cornerstone of interpersonal relationships. It is a fragile dynamic that exists between individuals and entities. Difficult to establish, easily shaken, and extraordinarily hard to repair once violated, trust requires care. As leaders seeking to leverage our employee and customer relationships to maximize performance and create new opportunities, we need to nurture trust.

Managing Conflict

Conflict management is much easier to write about than it is to accomplish. The emotion surrounding conflict often blinds us to alternative interpretations that could allow us to see a different perspective as to the source of the conflict and its resolution. (See more on event interpretation and emotional response in our discussion of attitude in Chapter 3, "Resiliency.") Openness about the root issues of conflict is needed to overcome what can otherwise deeply undermine relationships.

Communication is the key to managing conflict, and most conflicts result from insufficient or ineffective communication. (We'll focus more on communication skills in the next chapter.) While the ideal is to avoid miscommunication and therefore the conflict, once conflict emerges, communication paves the path to resolution.

As we noted, conflict often brings emotions into play. While emotions are sometimes warranted, they can inhibit effective resolution. You may recall from Chapter 3 that emotions trigger certain behavioral responses. In conflict situations, these behaviors follow the path of our individual conflict management style.

Each of us has our own preferred style for managing conflict, something that we've developed and perfected over time. The approach we use as an adult was largely formed between birth and six years of age. As young children, we experimented with the most effective strategy for having those around us fulfill our needs. These experiments led to the development of our conflict management strategy.

There are three basic conflict management approaches (with some individual variations):

Aggressive—This approach is characterized by a strong demand from the aggressor for agreement with his point of view or desire. In its extreme forms, this demand may involve intimidation tactics such as explosive anger, yelling, and other volatile behavior. An example is the customer who "blows up" at the service representative in order to get their change request expedited.

Passive—This approach is characterized by an individual "backing off" from the conflict issue and offering an agreement or giving in to the other's desire. The passive person has not entirely abandoned the fight, however, and will seek to meet his needs through a less direct approach. In the extreme, such a "back door" approach may involve some form of manipulation or passive-aggressive behavior. Typical passive behavior is exhibited by the colleague who reluctantly agrees to add more work to their pile but then secretly complains of overwork to other members of the team.

Neither of these approaches to conflict is truly effective. Neither resolves the conflict issue, though both may seem to do so temporarily. Through unexpressed feelings, damaged egos, and lingering unresolved issues, both approaches ultimately damage the relationships.

Our individual conflict management style falls somewhere along the continuum from aggressive to passive. Most of us are good at staying in balance and don't often stray to the extremes. However, there are times when we find ourselves behaving at the outer edges of appropriateness. During those times of stress and emotion, we need to move back toward the middle, toward the third approach: assertiveness.

Assertive—This approach is neither aggressive nor passive but employs the best of each. The assertive person expresses a position on the issue while neither demanding nor giving agreement. By approaching conflict this way, the assertive person creates space for exploration into and dialogue about the many perspectives that accompany conflict situations. An example is a manager who disagrees with the actions of a subordinate, expresses that disagreement, but then invites the subordinate to discuss it. An existing, healthy interpersonal connection built upon factors such as mutual trust, acceptance, and respect contributes to the effectiveness of this process.

The assertive style truly seeks honest resolution. If carried out effectively, all parties can move beyond the conflict, using trust, respect, and open communication to strengthen the relationship.

As we noted, conflict management is easier written than done. Remaining within the bounds of assertiveness and not straying toward the extremes of passive or aggressive behaviors takes consciousness and effort. The following tactics may help:

- Focus on the facts of the situation; be wary of acting on assumptions or behavioral observations that are open to interpretation.
- Use "I" statements ("I felt . . .", "I understood . . .") instead of "You" statements that tend to put people on the defensive.
- Seek to understand the other person's position before expressing your own. By demonstrating your willingness to listen, you encourage people to listen to you.
- Frame the conflict as a mutual challenge and express your willingness to explore creative win/win solutions.

Exercise: Assess Your Conflict Approach

On a scale from one to 10, with 1 being an extreme passive behavior and 10 being an extreme aggressive behavior, where would you place your typical conflict management approach? Under extreme conditions, which direction on the scale do you move? How does this vary in different situations, such as with the team you lead? With your boss? With your spouse? What strategies could you employ to take a more assertive approach to conflicts?

Interpersonal and Team Effectiveness in a World of Difference

One of the issues that may stand in the way of being effective interpersonally is the struggle that's sometimes involved when partnering with those who are different. Gender, cultural background, age, life experience, and operational style are all ways in which people differ. These differences generate different ways of seeing issues, of interpreting the same observations, of approaching challenges, of organizing tasks, and of setting priorities—and sometimes cause conflict between people. When you have a conflict with a customer, it may actually be a clash of styles. It can be difficult to maintain a healthy, effective relationship with those with whom we often butt heads.

How do we work together in such a world of difference? How do we avoid the clashes that are sometimes caused by differing perspectives and approaches? Taking three steps will help us work within these differences and will also help to build complementary partnerships and teams:

- Awareness—recognizing the operational differences that exist between people
- Appreciation—connecting with the complementary value these differences offer
- Respect—nurturing difference to maximize the value it creates

Tuning in to Operational Differences

Working effectively in a world of difference begins with an awareness of these differences and the ways in which they manifest themselves in individual behavior. We're all generally aware that these differences exist, though we often fall into the trap of making assumptions that others will view and interact with the world in the same way we do. For example, when we begin working with a new colleague, we might make the following assumption:

$$You = Me$$

This formula suggests our assumption that the other person is the same as we are and will behave and make choices as we do. Of course, it won't take long for us to realize that something is wrong with our formula. We discover that our new colleague is not seeing things exactly as we do. We scratch our heads in wonderment before realizing that we need to amend our original formula to:

$$You = Me + d_1 \text{ (where } d_1 \text{ equals one small difference)}$$

Now we're okay again with this new colleague—we can accept one small difference—and the partnership moves forward a bit further. But it doesn't take long before we realize that our formula is still not quite accurate. We amend it once more:

$$You = Me + d_1 + d_2$$

You can see where this goes. As we get deeper into our work with this new colleague, we discover far more than just two differences. The formula eventually becomes:

$$You = Me + d_1 + d_2 + d_3 + d_4 + d_5 \ldots$$

If we can learn to accept these differences, we'll be fine working with these new colleagues and on diverse teams. It's when we forget that the *d* in the formula stands for *difference* and begin thinking that it stands for *disability* that we set ourselves up for trouble.

Valuing Operational Differences

With some colleagues, we may discover that we are practically operational opposites—the list of differences appears to be infinite. It is hard to work with people who are that different. We tend to prefer to partner with people who are more like us, but that's not necessarily better or more effective in terms of perspective. This is where the value of difference and the need to appreciate that value comes in. Leveraging difference adds:

- Broader perspective
- Greater creativity
- Improved balance
- Diverse strengths
- Complementary skills

Imagine partnering with a colleague on a complex project. Suppose you are replacing a billing system or upgrading a network—something requiring vision, creative problem-solving abilities, highly developed logistical and detail management skills, and an intuitive sense of people. The project will require that you "manage" the customer and navigate a difficult political climate within the organization. We'll assume that both you and your colleague are experienced and talented IT performers. You've always enjoyed working with this colleague. The two of you just seem to click, perhaps because you come from similar backgrounds and share a common perspective and approach on this sort of project work.

Despite your years of experience and obvious talents, you know that you will have greater strengths in some of the project's requirements than others. Perhaps you are gifted in the vision, creative problem-solving, and interpersonal/political savvy aspects of the project. Your colleague's skills mirror your own, which leaves a gap in the detail and logistical elements that the project requires. The two of you may get along famously in your like-thinking approach to the project, but the project will suffer as a result of this gap.

Now imagine that you have foresight enough to recognize this gap and anticipate the trouble it may cause. You and your partner agree to bring in a third colleague, one with the detail orientation and logistical sense that the project requires. This person sees the world differently than the two of you. There may be some differences of opinion and style clashes, but it's important to weather them for the project's sake.

Respecting Operational Differences

Diversity is more than just difference. Diversity implies strength. In ecology, the term *biodiversity* (diversity of life) is a key indicator of the health of an ecosystem. We refer to places with significant biodiversity, such as rainforests and coral reefs, as being biologically rich. There is strength in diversity—if we can accept and leverage it.

As leaders, we must become comfortable with the challenges that operational diversity brings. We must grow beyond simple awareness that these differences exist, and move toward promoting a model where diversity adds richness and opportunity. Properly implemented and well-managed, diversity is a key element of overall effectiveness, especially in complex work, so we should consider the value of creating intentionally diverse teams.

Maximizing the complementary potential of difference requires awareness, appreciation, and respect. Awareness demands that we tune in to the underlying root of the other's "difficult" behavior and understand that it may stem from simple differences. Appreciation asks us to recognize that these differences bring value. Respect requires that we demonstrate our recognition of this appreciation through our behavior.

One technique for demonstrating respect is the application of the 60/60 rule, which stems from something my father once said to me. We were discussing his marriage to my mother, and he commented that marriage is a compromise. He clarified that he didn't mean a 50/50 compromise but rather a 60/60 compromise. It's not enough to just come together by meeting in the middle; each party in the relationship needs to be willing to go and give a little extra, an additional 10 percent. As we cross the middle ground in seeking to understand and accommodate the other person a bit more, we create common space where we can stand together.

The 60/60 rule does not imply that we must diminish our perspective or approach to tasks for the other's benefit. We each bring value to our interactions, and the other people need the strengths of our perspectives and the gifts of our approaches as much as we need theirs. Rather, the 60/60 demonstrates our appreciation for difference and our recognition of the value inherent in it. It is identifying the complementary in what could otherwise be conflicting. Through this level of awareness, appreciation, and respect, we reap the rewards of living in a diverse world.

Exercise: Valuing Differences

Think of someone with whom you sometimes struggle to partner effectively. Explore this struggle from the perspective of operational differences—how likely is it that your challenge stems from a difference in perspective and approach? How does this individual's approach to tasks and view of challenges differ from your own? Setting your own operational preferences aside for the moment, what value can you recognize in this other individual's operational approach? How could you exercise the 60/60 rule in your next interaction with this person?

Summary

The strength of our relationships gives strength to our leadership. We exist as leaders only within the context of the interpersonal connections we build and maintain with others. Trust is the foundation of these relationships. Conflict management skills enable us to weather the interpersonal storms that appear from time to time in every relationship. Awareness, appreciation, and respect for differences further our abilities to leverage the diversity that exists within our teams and organizations. They are the critical skills for fostering relationships.

Lessons Learned

- Leadership is enabled through interpersonal relationships. Leaders only exist within the context of their relationships with those they lead.
- Trust is the foundation of effective interpersonal connections. A relationship without trust is merely a transaction.
- Credibility, consistency, and communication shape trust.
- Communication is a key to managing conflict, and an assertive communications approach is most effective for conflict management.
- There is strength in individual difference. Leveraging this strength requires awareness, appreciation, and respect.

Action Plan/Journaling

In the following section, take a moment to reflect on your relational and interpersonal skills as a leader. Consider the following:

- How do you build and leverage trust as the foundation of your interpersonal effectiveness?
- How do you characterize your conflict management style and how effective are you at resolving conflict before it damages a relationship?

- To what degree do you seek to leverage the power of difference within your sphere of leadership?

Take a few minutes in your journal and describe yourself as you would like to be. What degree of interpersonal effectiveness do you imagine yourself having in the future?

Finally, jot down some quick notes about the first steps you will take to grow into this competency.

Communication Skills

In the previous chapter, we explored how relationship is the building block of effective leadership. In this chapter, we'll explain how communication is the lifeblood of interpersonal relationships and how effective communications is essential to effective leadership. That doesn't mean that leaders must be oratorical giants or sublime writers, but knowing the dynamics and application of interpersonal communication is a critical ingredient of effective leadership.

Communication is leadership's vehicle for reaching out, tapping the expansive nature of the alchemy principle of sulphur. Applied in a specific way at the right time and in the right amount, sulphur is a catalyst that triggers a reaction to bring about the desired result. But when applied inappropriately or without due consideration, sulphur can be explosive. Communication is much the same: Applied appropriately, it is a powerful leadership tool; used unconsciously, it can be a leader's undoing.

Opportunities for Growth _____

- Be clear as to the intentions of your communications
- Recognize the two messages within every communication
- Select the appropriate communications channel for sending messages
- Manage interference for clear communication
- Strengthen your presentation performance
- Practice multiple levels of listening
- Employ reflective listening for effective leadership interactions

Agenda _____

Communication Intentions

Communication Basics

- Messages
- Channels
- Interference

Leadership and Communication

Presentation Skills

Listening Skills

- Levels of Listening
- Reflective Listening

Communication Intentions

Interpersonal communication should be an intentional act. When you consider the times when unintentional communications created trouble for you, this point becomes more salient. We communicate to accomplish a specific purpose and that purpose must be clear if the communication is to be effective.

Think of intention as the heart of the communications interaction. Ask what you intend to achieve through the exchange. As communication interactions occur between two or more people, there may be multiple intentions at play. Alignment or at least disclosure or discovery of these multiple intentions is essential for effective communication.

There are five basic intentions underlying most communication interactions:

- Informing—to share information or insight
- Persuading—to influence a perspective on an issue
- Understanding—to create common understanding of an issue or perspective
- Deciding—applying a combination of informing, persuading, and understanding to facilitate a choice between action options
- Inspiring action—applying a combination of informing, persuading, and understanding to initiate and drive a desired action

Consider a typical communications interaction between IT and its customers. A customer sends an email informing IT of a system glitch. IT corrects what seems to be the problem but fails to inform the customer of its effort. The frustrated customer calls the IT manager to report that his system still isn't working properly and that he has received no response from IT. The manager, wondering what's going on, calls the system techs. They throw up their hands thinking that the problem has already been solved. The reality is that the customer didn't supply complete information in his initial communication and IT corrected the wrong problem, because it was working in a communications vacuum.

In this example, the process is about trying to receive (and provide) good customer service. The context is one of limited communication exchange fueled by mistrust and frustration on both sides as a result of their previous encounters. This history has created communications interference based on assumptions: IT believes that the customer has no clue whatsoever and the customer believes that IT couldn't care less about his needs. This communications interaction falls flat because all parties failed to focus on the intention of the interaction—fixing the problem—and didn't communicate in the right way to fulfill this intention.

If communication is to be effective, it must be carried out with the intention in mind. As we'll discuss in this chapter, there is a range of communication approaches, styles, tools, and channels. The intention of our communication helps us choose the appropriate communication means for maximizing effectiveness.

Communication Basics

In any basic communications workshop, the presenter introduces a diagram that captures the elements of the typical communication interaction. The diagram typically includes a sender and a receiver, with the sender sending a message and the receiver responding in turn with a feedback message. These messages can be sent back and forth via a variety of media or channels—face-to-face verbal, phone verbal, written text on paper, fax, or email. Often, a box drawn around this diagram represents the context or situation within which the communication takes place. Typically, the next element added is a series of wavy lines or scribbles drawn between and around the sender, receiver, and their respective messages. These lines represent interference or things that inhibit the effective exchange of messages. The diagram is similar to a basic data communications model in which two computer systems are networked, because communication flow between humans has the same basic elements and considerations.

Messages

Every communications message we send, whether verbal or written, has two components: the content and the feeling. Content is the "what," the core or intention of the message we're sending. Feeling is the "how," referring to the way the message is packaged. The packaging of the message affects the interpretation of its content. For example, consider this question:

Why did you do it that way?

Read the question aloud as if you were asking it with curiosity. Now read it aloud again as if you were asking it to someone who had just taken a stupid approach to a simple task. Notice the difference? It's the same content packaged in a different feeling context, the same "what" delivered via a different "how."

When confronting a project management team about its failure to meet customer requirements, the "communicationally-challenged" IT leader might say something like, "If we don't get our act together, heads will roll!" Naturally, this draws a particular behavioral response from the team. How would the team respond if the leader had instead said, "We're not doing the job in meeting our customer's needs. What's it going to take for us to be more effective here?" The content message is basically the same—addressing the problem of meeting customer requirements. The feeling message is vastly different and will achieve different results.

Messages are influenced by a combination of three factors:

- The words we select in expressing the message
- The tone of voice we use in doing so, either spoken or implied in our writing
- In face-to-face communication, our body language

Figure 5.1 shows the relative importance of each of these factors upon the message's clarity.

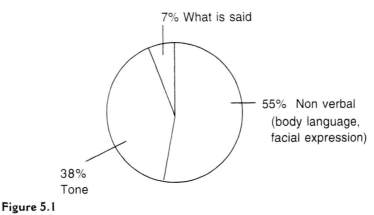

Figure 5.1
Factors affecting clarity of messages.

As you can see, the actual words we choose have the smallest influence upon the message. Tone of voice influences the message significantly more. And, depending on the context of the communications exchange, body language such as facial expression and body posture weighs in as the greatest influence. Body language is mostly a consideration for face-to-face interactions, though you're probably aware that smiles and frowns can also be "heard" through phone lines.

Our intention drives the content of our communication messages. To fulfill the intention, we need to be aware of how we package the message, and therefore influence the receiver's interpretation of it (based on the feeling component revealed through tone of voice and body language). These factors are easier to manage when we are clear as to the intention of the message.

Channels

We can send messages through a variety of communication media or channels. With a nod of thanks to technology, we have more channels available to us today than ever before. The most obvious include face-to-face communication, written communication (including email), and telephone.

Any method of communication can serve along a continuum from formal to informal. The context of the communication and the audience receiving it determine the place along that scale of formality at which our communication should fall. Face-to-face communication can range from a casual exchange of information between two colleagues to the more formal, persuasive delivery of a proposal to a top-level management group.

Written communication also has degrees of formality. Email tends to be IT's preferred communication channel. However, the convenience and casual ease of email as a written form of communication makes it somewhat dangerous. Many people are careless with email communications, over-looking the intentions of their messages and sending thoughts that can easily be misinterpreted. Unless carefully crafted, email lacks a clear feeling message, so the reader must apply her own tone of voice interpretation to the words. If the receiver's tone doesn't match the sender's, this can create problems.

Recognizing that communication is an intentional interaction, we should select a communication channel that either supports or enhances fulfillment of the communication intention. Be aware of the needs of your intended message, both in content and in feeling, and choose the channel which best serves those needs. Make an intentional choice between popping off a quick email, picking up the phone, or walking down the corridor for a face-to-face interaction. *Know your audience* is one of the most basic guidelines for effective communication. The insight you have into your audience—your relationship with them, their preferred communication style, their current state of readiness for your message—will also help you determine the most appropriate channel for communicating your message.

Interference

Remember those wavy lines and scribbles cluttering the communications diagram? They represent all of the interference we battle in accurately delivering our communications messages. There is more interference in our world than ever before. It takes many forms and can originate from the sender, the receiver, or within the environment of the exchange:

- Assumptions—beliefs we hold about the other or they hold about us—i.e., the assumption that the receiver is aware of what we're discussing or their belief about the degree to which we know what we're talking about.
- Time pressures—taking the time to express our message clearly and in the right way, and allowing the necessary time on the other end for receiving and processing the message.
- Mental models—the unconscious interpretations held about the situation being communicated on: our mental map of the situational landscape.
- Differences of style—misalignment between the communication needs of the receiver and the approach of the sender. (For more on communication styles, see the section on influencing in Chapter 8, "Strategic Business Acumen.")

- Noise and distraction—environmental and psychological factors that distract and inhibit the message from being sent or received accurately.

There are others that can be added to this list, but the central point is that we are attempting to communicate effectively despite many barriers to doing so. Maintaining simple awareness of these communication inhibitors allows us to make better choices about our communication approaches. Consider these questions:

- What underlying assumptions may be at play here? How can we test their validity and clarify or correct them if necessary?
- Is this the right time for this exchange? Are there time or environmental factors that will inhibit the effectiveness of this communication?
- Are we working from opposing or limiting mental models on this issue? How can we expose our mental models and create common understanding?
- Who is my audience for this message and to what degree am I considering his or her communication style needs in my approach?

The nature of life in the IT world places a tremendous strain upon effective communications. With more crises to manage, the technology infrastructure of your organization and/or customers' organizations to support, and the accelerated pace overall, IT communication interactions are subject to more interference than those in other parts of the company. The Catch-22 is that at the same time these factors push us to accelerate performance (fight fires faster), effective communication requires us to slow down and be more intentional. When the system is down and the customer is screaming, speeding up may only fuel a greater crisis through miscommunication. Performance and response are actually enhanced when communication is carried out carefully—being clear in our messages, selecting the appropriate channel, and managing the noise of interference.

Exercise: Feedback Skills

Imagine yourself preparing to deliver performance feedback to a member of your IT staff. Overall, this individual has performed well, though you do need to call attention to some areas in which improvement is required. As with any feedback process, this exchange may be a bit awkward and may make both of you uncomfortable. Given what we've discussed, consider the following questions.

- What is the core intention behind this communication interaction? How can you ensure that this intention is communicated clearly?

- In its simplest form, what is the main content message you seek to deliver here? How does that content need to be "packaged" such that it is received as intended?
- What communication delivery channel would you choose for delivering this feedback message? How does this choice support the clarity of your intention?
- What interference may be encountered in this exchange? What steps can be taken to eliminate or minimize these factors?

(See more on feedback skills in Chapter 6, "Coaching.")

Leadership and Communication

As a leader, you carry an additional responsibility for clear, intentional communication. From your position of leadership, your words tend to "speak louder" than those of others within the organization. As a business leader, you may also find yourself in situations where high-level, business-critical communications are underway, such as processes for:

- Communicating vision
- Enrolling new customers
- Assessing customer needs
- Addressing customer concerns
- Inspiring the performers who work in our unit
- Redirecting employee performance through feedback processes and coaching
- Plotting strategy with other business unit leaders

In addition to competency in the communication basics, leaders need enhanced abilities in two other communication areas: presentation skills and listening skills.

Presentation Skills

Presentations can take many forms; there is no set way for designing and delivering them. The same basic guidelines that apply to all communications apply here as well, with some additional considerations. First, some communication skills become even more important in a presentation:

- Acknowledge your intentions, understand the purpose behind the presentation

- Consciously design the delivery of both the content and the feeling components of your message
- Know and adjust to your audience
- Help the audience recognize their connection to your content
- Apply the appropriate presentation approach (channel) for content delivery
- Manage interference, both environmental and psychological

Unlike everyday or casual communication, presentations involve a more structured process. Think back to grade-school essays and you'll be reminded of the normal structure. Effective presentations often follow the same flow as a well-written essay and for good reason—it's a format that most people are comfortable with and it works. That format includes three basic parts: the introduction, the body, and the conclusion. Presentations need all three for coherent flow.

The introduction is where we spell out the reason for the presentation and why the audience should care. "Tell them what you're going to tell them" goes the old adage. As you may recall from writing essays, some sort of "grabber" is often a good technique for capturing interest and attention. Steer clear of the cliché about starting every presentation with a joke. While that can be effective, if the joke is forced, irrelevant, or poorly told, you may have to struggle to regain your audience. Stories, quotes, bold statements, related facts and figures—all serve well as grabbers. The introduction also sets the tone for the presentation so it is here that your feeling message should be introduced carefully.

You'll present the content in the body. Here again, the essay model applies: package the content into coherent pieces connected by transitions that link it all together. Remember your intention for the presentation. What are you hoping this content will do? Inform? Persuade? This is where the consideration of appropriate delivery mechanisms or channels becomes important. IT people tend to lean on presentation technology, but that may not be the most effective method. Is the content best served by a facts and figures-style lecture, through the use of PowerPoint or overhead slides, with some sort of interactive group process, by a story or metaphor, or even some combination of all?

It's important to open the presentation on a strong, clear note, and just as important to end this way. In the conclusion, you wrap up all of your content, summarize ("tell them what you told them"), and help the audience understand its next action. Memory research indicates that people remember the first and last things you tell them most vividly. If that's true, the conclusion gives you one final, powerful opportunity to drive your message home.

Perhaps conducting an effective presentation sounds formulaic—almost scientific. Yet it's also an art, and there's no right or wrong that covers every case. Each presentation you create will differ depending upon many variables—how you relate to your content, who your audience is, the circumstances of the presentation, your own style, and how you choose to reveal that style that particular day and time. You'll have to determine your own right blend of art and science. As leaders, our abilities in this area will become part of the essential mix: our alchemy.

Exercise: Presentation Improvement

Think of a time when you made a presentation that was less than successful. Using what you've learned in this chapter, generate a list of things you could have done differently to improve your performance. What points will you keep in mind in creating future presentations?

(For more effective presentation skills, see the material on customer presentations in Chapter 8, "Strategic Business Acumen.")

Listening Skills

For some, effective leadership communication may suggest an image of grabbing a bullhorn and shouting directions. Indeed, there are times—during crises, for example—when this approach may be appropriate. However, everyday leadership communication relies upon a style that's the fundamental opposite of the bullhorn approach. It's grounded in the leader's ability to listen.

After all, leadership is about connecting—connecting with the people who we lead, connecting with the customers whose needs direct our efforts, and connecting with the business landscape in which we carry out these efforts. Tuning in to these connections requires a keen ear.

Communication is a two-way interactive process. Yet much discussion of communication focuses on the sending of communication messages. Communication may begin with the sender and her intended message but pivots upon how that message is received and processed. Effective communication is built upon a foundation of listening and receiving, not just expressing.

IT people tend to be great problem-solvers, but often jump to solutions too quickly. For example, they sometimes ignore much of what the customer says beyond the initial statement of the problem. Improved listening skills would go a long way toward solving future headaches of misunderstood require-ments, poorly aligned fixes, and redundant work processes.

Levels of Listening

Earlier, we stated that intention is the heart of the communications interac-tion. Quality listening begins with the receiver recognizing her own personal intention around the interaction—in other words, why the message carries significance to her—and her struggle to connect with the intention of the sender. Each of these elements is influenced by an internal conversation on the part of the listener.

The first rule of listening is *Stop Talking*. You may laugh, but this is not as obvious as it seems. When someone is communicating a message to us, we need to stop talking so we can listen. But even though we may stop the physical act of verbal expression during that time, often we continue to talk to ourselves inside our heads and merely go through the motions of listening.

"They have a good point, but they've failed to see this side of the issue" or "I don't have time for this now. I've got to get this other work done" or "This person is truly clueless!" are all examples of the internal talk that sometimes takes place while we're acting as listeners. Effective listening begins with the authentic pursuit of understanding, and internal chatter diminishes our abil-ity to do that. Listening takes place at three levels:

- *Level One listening* is a focus on self—Why should I care? What's in this for me? How do I respond to this? Level One listening is not deep lis-tening. It's not about understanding, but more about rebuttal and self-interest. Without awareness and effort, this is the level of listening most of us use most of the time.

- *Level Two listening* is a focus on the other person in the communication interaction—Where are they coming from? What are they truly ex-pressing? Level Two listening is about connecting with the senders and their intention in communicating their message. Listening at this level means tuning out our own internal talk and concentrating on under-standing the other. Many of our leadership roles, including coaching performance, building relationships, co-creating vision, and assessing customer needs require this level of listening.

- *Level Three listening* is a focus on the global aspects of the communica-tion, the intangibles surrounding and affecting the interaction. What is this person not saying that is important here? What is the level of urgency that I sense from this person on this issue? Level Three listening in-volves an intuitive sense of the environment both within and around the speaker. Our capacity to tap into this global awareness strengthens our ability as listeners, enhancing our effectiveness as leaders.

For leaders seeking to connect, achieving understanding in communications is critical. Fulfilling this critical requirement means listening intentionally—momentarily tuning out our internal talk and exerting effort toward truly hearing the message as intended by the sender.

Exercise: Intentional Listening

Begin to notice the degree to which you engage in internal talk while listening to others. In an upcoming meeting or other future communications interaction, catch yourself mentally "talking back" to the speaker and tune in to how this affects your ability to listen with the intention of understanding. Concentrate on listening intently and notice any difference in the level of understanding you achieve, the quality of interaction and connection you experience, and the general effectiveness of the exchange.

Reflective Listening

Listening is a mode we choose. It's an intentional act supported by specific behaviors and awareness. Effective listeners are operating primarily at Listening Levels Two and Three—focusing on the speaker, his intention for the expression of thought, the feeling message in which his content is packaged, and the global issues surrounding the communication interaction. It's not that Level One Listening is never appropriate, it's just a different mode and comes to play in a different sort of interaction.

How do we know when we're being listened to? Effective listeners:

- Provide eye contact
- Maintain an interested and open body posture
- Encourage the speaker with both verbal and nonverbal support (nodding of the head, motion of the hands, verbal acknowledgment—"Yes," "Uh huh")
- Use "door opening" questions to reveal a safe environment for and sincere interest in the interaction
- Ask genuine questions to gain deeper understanding of the message sender's perspective (as opposed to questions that shut down or rebut the sender)
- Reflect back their understanding through summary and empathy

We have all applied these behaviors as listeners, sometimes consciously, sometimes not. With awareness, these become automatic when we activate our deeper listening modes. The last item on the list—reflecting back with empathy—often requires some practice before it can be applied comfortably and genuinely. Poorly delivered, empathy can come across as fake and insincere, sending the wrong feeling message in response to the sender's initial communication.

There is a difference between simply summarizing and applying empathy. Summaries are fine when the message is primarily content (such as factual information) containing little or no expression of feeling on the part of the sender. Summarizing allows us to demonstrate our having heard and understood the content of the message as delivered. As a requirement for effective listening, empathy enters when an expression of feeling is present in the message as well. A summary is not enough. We may understand the content of the message, but without empathy we fail to acknowledge the more important feeling aspect of the message and the person delivering it.

Empathy is about reflecting back to the sender your understanding and nonjudgmental acceptance of their position or perspective, without regard to your agreement or disagreement with that position or perspective. Empathy is a powerful, important interpersonal relationship skill, because it's the primary means by which we express caring and connection.

Empathy is expressed as a listening skill that represents our ability to tell the sender our understanding of the emotional and psychological charge their message carries for them. This doesn't require advanced mind reading ability; through their communication, the sender always gives clues as to what is happening emotionally and psychologically for them. These clues come in the form of specific word choices, non-verbal facial and bodily expressions, and what is left unsaid but nevertheless lingering in the air. With awareness and a conscious effort to apply Listening Levels Two and Three, such clues may be readily noticed without mind reading.

Understanding is crucial to the empathetic response, but empathy goes further. Simple understanding is not enough; there is also the need to express the caring that is critical to the relationship. That caring is demonstrated in the nonjudgmental acceptance of the other's emotional/psychological state (the other's feeling message) and can be shared through a statement that says in effect, "I can understand how you might feel that way." This statement must be made even if we might feel or respond differently in the same situation. This is genuine acceptance, allowing the other to sense validation in their feelings, and it is the most significant intention behind the interpersonal interaction. It's also the ultimate connection you can create with others as a leader.

Exercise: "Practicing Empathy"

Consider this scenario and draft an empathetic response to the communication interaction described:

You are meeting with one of your team members for a status update on a project you're overseeing. The project has been moving along nicely; it is thus far on target with regard to budget and delivery time frame. As your staff member makes his report, he allows that he hasn't made much progress since last week's update. While he clearly accepts responsibility for the slip in progress, he shares that the past week has been a tough one for him. You "open the door" by asking about his week. He goes on to describe the discovery of a serious illness in the family, a car that has been in the shop for three days, and the numerous "fire fights" he has been paged to respond to due to glitches in the server. It is obvious that he is feeling overwhelmed and emotionally drained. How would you respond with empathy?

(A sample response appears at the end of the chapter, after the Action Plan/Journaling Section.)

Summary

If leadership is relationship, communication is the primary tool we apply to leverage that relationship toward the performance and result we seek. Effective leaders are effective communicators, understanding and applying the basics of communication, influence through presentation, and the power of listening.

Lessons Learned

- Communication must be an intentional act. There are five basic communication intentions: Informing, Persuading, Understanding, Deciding, and Inspiring Action. Communication effectiveness requires intentional awareness.

- Every communication message contains both content and feeling components. Our words, our tone of voice, and our body language influence these components. When the content and feeling messages misalign, the feeling message is usually accepted as the real intention behind the communication.

- There are many different channels through which we communicate. Selecting the appropriate channel for our message is important for the clear expression of our intention.
- There are many forms of interference that can inhibit effective communications. These include assumptions, mental models, time pressures, differing communications styles, and noise/distraction. Awareness and management of these factors is essential for effective communication.
- Leadership carries a responsibility for being clear and intentional in our communications. Leaders may require enhanced abilities in presentation skills and listening capacity.
- Conducting effective presentations is both an art and a science. The science requires knowledge of presentation structure and flow, and can be likened to writing a good essay. The art allows for the creative use of our own personal style in accommodating the variable circumstances of our presentations.
- Listening is foundational to effective leadership.
- There are three levels of listening. Level One focuses on self. Level Two focuses on the other in the interaction. Level Three focuses on the environment in which the communication is taking place. Effective listeners function mainly in Levels Two and Three.
- Reflective listening is a process by which we demonstrate our understanding of a communication message we receive. It includes both summary and empathy. Empathy is the expression of both understanding and acceptance of the communication sender's feeling message. Empathy is a critical skill in the building and maintenance of strong interpersonal relationships, an essential component of effective leadership.

Action Plan/Journaling

In the following section, take a moment to reflect on your communications effectiveness. Consider the following:

- How would you describe your style as a sender of messages?
- How would you describe your listening style?
- How does your communications style support your leadership role?
- What communication behaviors do you exhibit that get in the way of you being effective as a leader?
- What three communications behaviors would you seek to alter to strengthen your effectiveness as a leader in your organization?

Take a few minutes in your journal, and describe yourself as you would like to be. What kind of communicator do you imagine yourself being in the future?

Finally, jot down some quick notes about the first steps you will take to grow into this competency.

Sample Response to Empathy Exercise   Consider this scenario and draft an empathetic response to the communication interaction described:

You are meeting with one of your team members for a status update on a project you're overseeing. The project has been moving along nicely; it is thus far on target with regard to budget and delivery time frame. As your staff member makes his report, he allows that he hasn't made much progress since last week's update. While he clearly accepts responsibility for the slip in progress, he shares that the past week has been a tough one for him. You "open the door" by asking about his week. He goes on to describe the discovery of a serious illness in the family, a car that has been in the shop for three days, and the numerous "fire fights" he has been paged to respond to due to glitches in the server. It is obvious that he is feeling overwhelmed and emotionally drained. How would you respond with empathy?

Sample Response:

"You *have* had a tough week! I'm sorry to hear about the illness in your family. It sounds as if you're a little overwhelmed at the moment. I can understand you feeling that way. What can I do to help; and what can we do to get the project back on track?"

As described in the chapter, empathy needs to be authentic, so whatever response you choose needs to be in your own "voice." However you voice your empathy, there are several key "do's" and "don't do's" that support empathetic responses:

- Do reiterate some of what you heard from them—"You *have* had a tough week!" This reinforces that you were listening fully.
- Do express your concern about their situation—"I'm sorry to hear about the illness . . ." This reinforces your caring about them as a person.
- Do make a summary statement of the expressed feeling message—"It sounds as if you're a little overwhelmed . . ." This lets them know that you understand where they're coming from emotionally/psychologically.
- Do demonstrate some acceptance of their feelings—"I can understand you feeling that way." This provides validity to those feelings.
- Avoid making "autobiographical" statements such as, "When my car broke down it really wrecked havoc with my life too!" Though this may seem an expression of "I can relate," it may be construed as minimizing

their experience somewhat and makes the assumption that your situation was the same as theirs.

- Do offer to help, but only if the offer is sincere. It is actually enough to express empathy without offering assistance.
- If the issue being faced is one that you are somehow connected to—joint ownership and responsibility for a project for instance, a statement such as "What can we do . . .?" helps remind the other that they are not alone without removing responsibility from them.

Coaching

Leadership is about recognizing the untapped potential within those you lead and nurturing that potential to fulfillment. It is about supporting the growth of others as we model the growing process within ourselves. Leaders juggle the roles of boss, evangelist, guidance counselor, parent, servant, disciplinarian, best friend, and worst enemy. Leadership is about adding value to your enterprise, and in this chapter we'll focus specifically upon using your abilities as a leader to inspire the value-adding performance of others. The alchemy principles of salt, sulphur, and mercury categorize the facets of leadership, and you'll learn how to apply their equivalents—self-understanding, working with others, and integration through coaching (a critical focus tactic for leaders).

Opportunities for Growth _____

- Define and quantify the coaching role you play for your staff and peers
- Apply a template to begin a coaching engagement

- Help others develop measurable, achievable, pragmatic goals
- Leverage assessments for those you coach so that they can better leverage their own strengths and minimize their own weaknesses by identifying areas of potential growth
- Deliver effective feedback

Agenda _____

What Is Coaching?

Coaching Language

Beginning the Exploration

Writing Meaningful Goals

Leveraging Assessments

Giving Respectful Feedback

- Redirection Feedback
- Reinforcing Feedback

What Is Coaching?

Many IT managers shy away from coaching, usually because they mistakenly believe that coaching is therapy, and they don't feel qualified as therapists. They're afraid that coaching may uncover psychological problems that they won't be able to manage.

Yet the people working for these managers crave someone to connect with. They would like useful and non-judgmental suggestions from others. This combination of IT managers who are afraid to coach and IT staffers who are hungry for feedback can limit the growth of IT capacity.

The first step to resolving this situation is to clarify the coach's role. A coach provides support, not therapy. Simply put, therapy looks back, coaching focuses on going forward. The coaching you do with your staff should focus on present challenges and future opportunities. If issues from a person's past do emerge in the coaching process, you should proceed with caution, because additional support may be needed. If the employee appears to need help with past situations (for example, a challenging family relationship), it's prudent to refer the person to a therapist. In addition, coaches should avoid bringing up work problems from the past because that meant they weren't addressed in a timely manner. Focus on the present—or at least the very recent past and future.

Performance coaches car. be either internal or hired from outside the organization. External coaches have the advantage that they don't work with you or for you, so they have no reason to influence your behavior. An external coach can remain neutral as you make personal choices, and can stand up to you when you avoid something you need to address.

The role of an internal coach carries other challenges the external coach doesn't face. As a leader of the person being coached, you care about the behavioral goals and are not neutral about the behavior you expect from your staff. You can help an employee set appropriate goals, but if she makes choices that are not consistent with the corporate strategy and values, you're responsible for encouraging her to rethink her behavior. And, if she fails to reach behavioral alignment, you must take action as the leader. Internal coaching is not a neutral position because you're responsible for moving the employee toward the company's goals. Often, these two purposes coincide.

At this point, we should clarify the difference between coaching and mentoring. Coaching is a limited-term, skill-specific development role that focuses on behavior. Mentoring implies a longer-term, future-focused, career-guiding kind of relationship. A coach offers performance feedback based on observation, while a mentor offers advice based on the wisdom of experience. An internal coach in IT will focus primarily on behavior, but may find times when mentoring is more appropriate.

As you begin coaching your staff, finding your own coach may be helpful. Working with a coach not only allows you to learn more about coaching, but also helps you model the type of growth you'd like to see in your staff.

Coaching is something like a mirror, and it's generally wise to reflect back on what you think the employee has said. Encourage more exploration through active listening (see Chapter 5, "Communication Skills") with carefully designed, probing questions. If asked what you think about something, always turn the discussion back to the person with a phrase like "I'm not sure. What do you think about this?" After all, coaching is focused on the person being coached— not on the coach. If you're talking more than 30 seconds, you're no longer coaching; you're telling. Being a leader and boss naturally involves more telling, but an effective coaching role demands that you spend the vast majority of the time listening. A talented coach doesn't tell an employee the answers. Instead, she asks the questions that enable the employee to discover the answers.

Exercise: Coaching Success

Consider the situations that have led you to play a coaching role with your staff. An example might be a team member with a performance problem. List three to five of these situations below. Be as specific as you possibly can. Next to each situation, rank your success.

High   the coaching situation was extremely successful

Neutral the coaching situation was partially successful

Low   the coaching situation was not successful

Figure 6.1 describes coaching based on a three-phase maturity model, which will help you identify both the starting spot and the end goal for each unique individual. The three steps are:

- Awareness
- Performance improvement
- Transformation

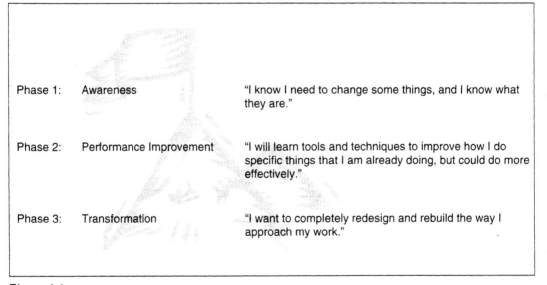

Phase 1:	Awareness	"I know I need to change some things, and I know what they are."
Phase 2:	Performance Improvement	"I will learn tools and techniques to improve how I do specific things that I am already doing, but could do more effectively."
Phase 3:	Transformation	"I want to completely redesign and rebuild the way I approach my work."

Figure 6.1
Phasing into coaching.

Awareness is where a person starts when he is unaware of the gaps in his behavior. Identifying trouble areas is the focus of coaching here. Performance improvement follows awareness, when the person is ready to change behaviors. Transformation occurs when the person is ready to make drastic change. Most coaching begins with the awareness stage and usually ends with performance improvement. While transformation is valuable in the right setting, that intensity is not needed for most situations.

As you'd expect, transformation takes a greater time investment for both parties than simple awareness. And while the potential return on the investment is greater when you progress through transformation, the risk of failure is higher, too. No matter what the goals, both parties must agree on them from the start. Later in this chapter, we'll share ways to help the people you coach create appropriate development goals that are unique to their situation.

Exercise: Adjusting Your Performance

Return to the list of situations you created in the last exercise. Think back—what level of maturity was appropriate for each situation—awareness, performance improvements, or transformation? Were there common expectations of the starting and ending places? In retrospect, does this explain your perceptions of success or failure? In any of the situations, were your goals for maturity aligned to (or too far apart from) the individual's goals? What would you do differently with that knowledge?

Coaching Language

The language you use as a coach communicates your true feelings about the person. Remember to serve as a mirror, using these guidelines:

- Avoid directing the discussion
  Symptom: "No, that's the wrong goal."

- Avoid analysis and interpretation
  Symptom: "Yes, I know which part bothers you the most!"

- Describe the future in the present state
  Symptom: "What will your relationship be like?"

- Push to the end result, not just the next step
  Symptom: "Is promotion what you want in the end?"

Beginning the Exploration

To ensure consistency and progress, we recommend that coaching occur four times a month for one hour each meeting. Initially, four sessions should be scheduled at a time. This gives the person you're coaching the chance to reflect on what he learned in each session and time to do his homework. At the end of each cycle of four, both you and the person you're coaching can determine whether to go on from there.

Honor the one-hour limit to show respect for the other person's time (and your own). This is very difficult because it demands that you stay mindful of the time without being distracted. Coaching in a private meeting room or office with a very visible clock is an excellent way to keep both parties aware of the time.

Starting your initial coaching sessions is always a bit awkward since it is an unfamiliar relationship. To minimize the discomfort, request some groundwork before you begin. Ask the person you're coaching to complete a behavioral and values assessment, and review it with him (see assessments later in this chapter). This gives you a neutral starting point, which enhances mutual trust so that both of you notice strengths and opportunities.

Figure 6.2 provides a flowchart for the progression of coaching activities. The coach begins by asking questions about why he asked for coaching now, and listens to what the employee finds enjoyable and what he finds frustrating. This information helps determine goals for improvement. Once you have reviewed the assessments and established trust, begin setting goals.

1. Ask the person why he thinks coaching is useful (even if he didn't choose it). Share why you think it's important only if there is a disconnect.

2. Ask the following questions. They should be answered in a work context, relating to behaviors, opportunities, feelings, training, etc.

   - What are some things you now have and want to keep?
   - What are some things you don't already have but want?
   - What are some things you now have but no longer want?
   - What are some things you don't have and don't want?

3. Ask the employee to think about a time when he was really happy and engaged at work. In many cases, this will be difficult for people who have never thought this way. Be patient and give the person time to think. Ask him to embellish on the previously asked questions.

4. Ask him to think of things at work that really frustrate him. This will probably be easier for most people because those underlying problems typically trigger the need for coaching. From these answers, help him to start a very rough list of goals, and ask him to complete the list for

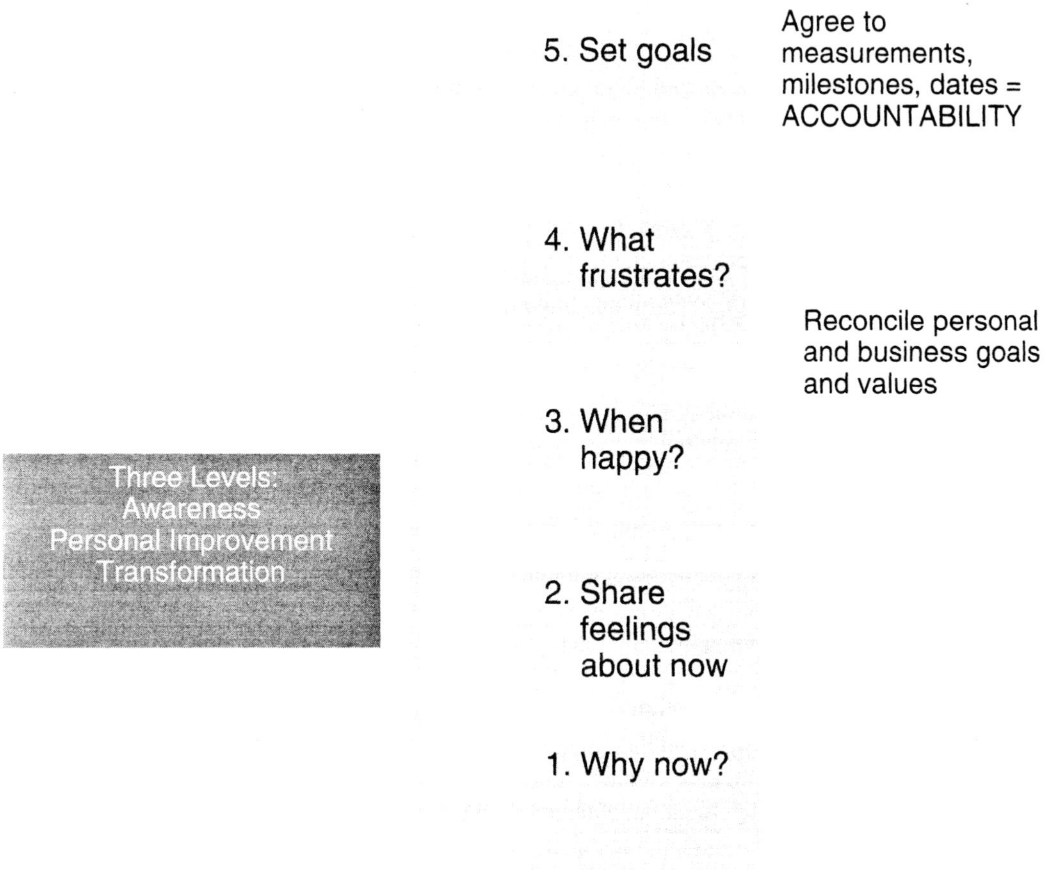

5. Set goals

Agree to measurements, milestones, dates = ACCOUNTABILITY

4. What frustrates?

Reconcile personal and business goals and values

3. When happy?

Three Levels:
Awareness
Personal Improvement
Transformation

2. Share feelings about now

1. Why now?

Figure 6.2
Taking people from where they are to where they can go.

homework before the next session. Use the goal-setting material that follows to help focus his goals toward balance and achievement so you can create a "coaching agenda."

5. Ask him to clarify how he will know that he has met the goals (measurements), and discuss what interim success would look like. Encourage him to read the goals at least once or twice a day. Ask him to pick the one goal he would like to work on first (although he may need to address a couple of prerequisites first). As he progresses, use the measurements and interim successes to show signs of improvement.

Remember that the priorities of the employee's goals may change over time. He may occasionally enter a coaching session with a specific business issue. Help relate that issue to the original goals, and work through it. You may need to set some new goals, but a truly effective coach is flexible. Often, the journey is one step forward, two steps back. He must admit his mistakes, because this will prove to the people he works with that he is serious about improvement.

Coaching ends when the goals of the coaching agenda are met; coaching should build self-sufficiency rather than create ongoing dependency. The question always returns to "Why did you come in here in the first place?" Was that need met? Were the goals met? Have you acquired enough skill and technique to grow independently? These are the questions both of you can apply to recognize when a coaching relationship has fulfilled its purpose.

Exercise: Willing Participants

Make a list of people on your team who would benefit from coaching. Now identify whether the situation merits an external coach, or if you can coach that person yourself. Finally, come up with a strategy for suggesting that this person begin a coaching experience. How will you sell it to the individual without offending her? What specific behavioral goals will you share with her as a leader? What specific outcomes would you like to see?

Coaching effectiveness can be measured by looking at the four "Ss."

1. Speak the Truth

   Coaches must speak the truth to the best of their knowledge. Opinions and interpretation will not be effective in this setting.

2. Suspend Judgment

   It's almost impossible to avoid interpretation, and two people can interpret the same conversation in widely different ways. The question, "Did you get the report done?" spoken out of concern for the other's stress level, can be interpreted as, "What is taking you so long?" Replace interpretation with "options" thinking, always looking for multiple interpretations. Teach the person you're coaching how to notice his or her own interpretations by modeling this behavior.

3. Stick to the Facts

   Restrict and return the discussion to facts only, and avoid sharing your own personal feelings or hearsay. Although you will often discuss both the facts and the feelings of the person being coached, you must suspend judgment in order to listen effectively. This is essential for maintaining trust and openness.

4. Have Self-Respect

   A coach needs self-respect to have the strength to suspend judgments and feelings. Coaching is about the other person, not you, and successful focus on the person being coached requires a coach to be secure.

Writing Meaningful Goals

Goals are an essential aspect of coaching because they provide both parties with a way to:

- Determine the right "first step"
- Measure ongoing progress to encourage momentum
- Identify when a goal is met
- Know when a goal has changed or is no longer relevant

Setting goals isn't easy. Many people have given up hope at work, and will have trouble with a question like "What would you like to be if you could have anything?" Dreaming your goals takes a bit of practice. Coach people to think of goals as being fluid. Though some goals may stay quite stable over time, others may become inappropriate or undesirable. This is completely normal and necessary, and does not indicate faulty planning. The ability to build new goals quickly is a characteristic of resiliency (Chapter 5).

The first step in setting goals is to brainstorm a balanced list of desires. This is critical because setting goals along only one dimension (for example, to double your wealth) without establishing balancing goals (for example, to spend time with your family) can create undesirable outcomes. Consider the categories in Table 6.1.

Table 6.1
Setting Balanced Goals

Category	Example
Work: tasks that you do	Learn how to use MS Project
Work: people you seek to influence	Get along better with my boss
Work: career goals	Get a promotion
Family	Become a soccer coach
Health	Drink more water
Friends	Spend Friday nights with friends
Hobbies	Learn to garden
Spiritual	Spend an hour meditating each day
Financial	Save 10% of my income per month
Home	Remodel the kitchen
Stuff you own	Buy a new car

More than one goal is normal for each category, but it is best to have at least one. Notice that the examples are relevant, but general. More words need to be added to these goals, to make them measurable. Measuring success would be difficult if your goal was "Get along better with my boss." A more measurable goal might be "I will meet with my boss once a week for 15 minutes to review the projects in progress and her goals for that week." Goals should be concrete and measurable, and aggressive but achievable. If you don't believe that you can reach a goal, your performance will inevitably prove you right.

Table 6.2 shows some of the same rough goals converted to finished goals.

Table 6.2
Goals: From Rough to Realized

Learn how to use MS Project	I use MS Project to manage my projects so that I know at all times their status in terms of time, money, and resources.
Get along better with my boss	I meet with my boss once a week for 15 minutes to review the projects in progress and her goals for that week.
Get a promotion	I have an MBA so that I have a better chance of being promoted.
Become a soccer coach	I am a soccer coach for my daughter's team so that I can spend more time with her.
Drink more water	I drink eight 8-ounce glasses of pure water a day.

The goals are written in present tense, as if they have happened. This style of goal writing is called an affirmation or intention. You always set goals in your head, both positive and negative. Remember times when you have said something like, "Oh, I hope I don't have a bad day at work again today," and you did? Our goals create the reality upon which we focus, and we move toward goals unconsciously. By taking control of your goal setting, you can change your results—and by writing and rereading intentions, you coach your own brain into thinking that the change has already occurred. Your brain reacts to the world as if your intention is reality.

Coach the person to read over his intentions once in the morning when he first gets up and once at night before bed. Doing this for just a week or so will create results.

Exercise: Set Goals

It is impossible for you to help someone set goals if you haven't already done that yourself. In Chapter 1, "The Value of Technical Leadership," we asked you to prioritize your competencies and set goals for what you would like to get out of this book. You are halfway through this book and now know a great deal more about yourself than when you set those initial goals. Using Table 6.1 as a guide, construct a set of intentions for yourself, covering all aspects of your life. Do not limit yourself to the categories we've provided, and feel free to write as few or as many as you wish. Keep these goals in your PDA or on a little piece of paper so that you can read them once in the morning and once at night, or anytime you have a moment. Add a task to your to-do list reminding you to reflect on your progress one week from today. You'll like the results.

Leveraging Assessments

As we mentioned earlier, using assessments to determine individual value and behavioral preferences can make coaching more effective. The person you're coaching takes the assessments before coming to the first session, reviews his results prior to the meeting, and reviews them with you during the first session.

Assessments reveal that each of us has individual values, interests, and attitudes that we use daily to make decisions and prioritize how we will invest our attention. These beliefs filter reality for us, and help us decide where to invest our focus and time before we actually apply our behaviors.

Two of the most effective assessments are the DISC assessment and the PIAV (personal interests, attitudes, values). Other assessments such as Myers-Briggs, Social Styles, and Hermann Brain Dominance can also be used. Ask your HR department for a recommendation. In this example, we'll show you how to use the DISC and PIAV assessments to jump-start a coaching relationship. First, we'll examine the values, then the behaviors. As outlined in Table 6.3, there are six personal interests, attitudes, and values (PIAV) that help us understand a person's priorities.

Table 6.3
Values: The PIAV Assessment

Value	Passions	Motivated by
Theoretical	Solving problems Objectivity in all areas of life Identifying, differentiating, generalizing, systematizing Intellectual process Discovery, understanding, ordering Pursuit of knowledge, identifying truth and untruth Knowledge for the sake of knowing	Rational, analytical, and objective discovery, problem solving
Utilitarian	Practicality in all areas of life Surpassing others in attainment of wealth Utilizing resources to accomplish results Gaining a measurable return on all investments Creative application of resources Producing goods, materials, services and marketing them for economic gain Capitalism	Money, ROI
Aesthetic	Practicality, appreciation and enjoyment of form, harmony and beauty Enjoyment of all senses Subjective experience Understanding feelings of self and others Self-realization, self-fulfillment, and self-actualization Creative expression Appreciation of all impressions	Subjective things, feelings, harmony and personal fulfillment (not discomfort)
Social	Investing self in others Selflessness Generosity of time, talents, and resources	Ideas that help others, harmony

(continued)

	Seeing and developing the potential in others	
	Championing worthy causes	
	Improving society and elimination of conflict	
	Appreciation of all impressions	
Individualistic	Leading others	Increased power or position, using strength to strengthen others
	Achieving position	
	Advancing position	
	Forming strategic alliances	
	Attaining and using power to accomplish purpose	
	Planning and carrying out a winning strategy	
	Tactics and positioning	
Traditional	Understanding the totality of life	Rules to live by, causes, systems, beliefs, principles
	Finding meaning in life	
	Pursuit of the divine in life	
	Following a cause	
	Living consistently according to a "closed" book	
	Converting others to their belief systems	

Clearly, a person with a strong interest in the theoretical is going to have conflict with a person for whom theoretical is the least important value. In many cases, the inability to collaborate can be attributed directly to a values disconnect. Once individuals learn the values of others, they can better understand actions that are inconsistent with their own.

Table 6.4 shows the descriptions of the four behavioral components known as DISC. The values determine what is important to a person, while the behaviors are how that person implements action toward what is important. Like values, the strengths and weaknesses of these behaviors contribute to workplace success. In fact, carefully aligning these values and behaviors to a job helps an individual find the role that is best for her at a company. Figure 6.3 shows how they interrelate.

Table 6.4
Behaviors: The DISC Assessment

Dominance Characteristics	Behavioral Style
Results oriented	Act or speak before thinking
Desire to win	~~Impatient~~
Fast paced, ability to make decisions quickly	Create fear in others
Willingness to state an unpopular view	Too high risk
Risk taker	"Juggle" too much at once
Argumentative, quick to challenge	Quick to anger
	Interrupt and will not listen
Influence Characteristics	Behavioral Style
Creative problem solver	Talk about thinking
Enthusiastic, natural optimism	Lose track of time, often late and hurried
Humorous	Abandon position in conflict
Funloving	Disorganized
High contact ability, trusting of others	Overly trusting
Ability to make others feel welcome or included	Overly optimistic, often superficial
Steadiness Characteristics	Behavioral Style
Tenacity for order, stability, and closure	Possessive of things
Need for secure situations	Too low risk
Great listener, calms and stabilizes others	Hold a grudge
Good planner, natural ability to organize task	Too agreeable
Able to mask emotions	Resistant to change
	Too indirect when communicating
Compliance Characteristics	Behavioral Style
Follows rules	Require too much data
High expectations, quality conscious	Hard on self
Able to solve complex problems	Too low risk
Organizes and analyzes; willing to dig for information	Make excessive rules
Natural systems developer	Too critical of others
	Have analytical paralysis

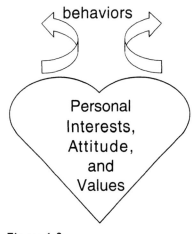

Figure 6.3
Behaviors and attitudes are related.

Coaching helps people to capitalize on their strengths and those of their team. For example, if I'm very detail-oriented but not comfortable in an interpersonal setting like a meeting, I might volunteer to assemble the reports and presentation, but ask someone else on my team to present them in front of a group.

Giving Respectful Feedback

If you're also the supervisor of the person you're coaching, you'll have to give and receive feedback in ways that maintain the integrity of the relationship but fully address real issues.

Think of feedback as "navigational information," designed to help people navigate performance situations, and substitute "reinforcing" and "redirecting" as forms of feedback in place of the emotionally charged terms "positive" and "negative/difficult." In Chapter 11, "The Journey to Change," you'll learn about an obstacle course activity in which blindfolded people making their way through a behavioral obstacle course need "sighted" coaches to provide them with feedback that either reinforces their path or redirects them to a better path. Everyone needs some navigational help now and again. In this section, you'll read about:

- Redirection Feedback
- Reinforcing Feedback

Redirection Feedback

It's easy to avoid giving difficult feedback. Nobody enjoys being the bearer of bad news. Believing that feedback is bad news prevents it from being useful, but letting someone know about behavior that is interfering with productivity is imperative for improvement. Not telling someone that they are behaving poorly when it is impacting business is a disservice to everyone involved. Think of giving feedback as something you do to help. Redirecting feedback is a better mental model than difficult feedback. Not giving feedback makes your day easier at the expense of someone else.

We know this is easier said than done. Many people avoid giving feedback because they do not want to hurt someone else's feelings. In reality, they don't want the person to get mad and hurt their own feelings. It takes courage to help someone else grow, and that's what respectful feedback requires.

Effective feedback should be limited to facts. Avoid talking about your feelings or those of others. Feedback should be given as soon after the occurrence of the "fact" as possible. Keep the focus of the language on how you perceive the situation, using "I" instead of "you" whenever possible, which keeps the conversation from coming across as judgmental. Seek first to understand. Your interpretation of the situation may not be complete, so allow the person receiving feedback the opportunity to share his or her side of the story before you share your own. The techniques you read about in Chapter 4, "Interpersonal and Team Skills," pertaining to conflict management may also be useful here.

Here's an example of a poor opening feedback statement:

> "You are really bugging the people in customer service. You better stop making them so mad. This is the same problem we have had over and over with you." (Unclear behavior—what does bugging mean? Followed by a threat, then bringing up old news without any specifics. And who is "we?")

Here's another example of a poor statement, illustrating how some people try to put themselves or others down to cushion the feedback:

> "I am not sure I should be telling you this, and I hope you won't get mad, but I don't think those customer service people like you very much, although I know they are really idiots and it's probably their fault."

Compare those two examples to this version, which contains factual, current data, the "I" language, and seeks to understand.

"I would like to talk with you about your relationship with the customer service area. Two of the staff in that department called yesterday and said that you were rude to them on the phone. What do you think happened?"

Reinforcing Feedback

IT people often find it difficult to give others positive feedback. This may seem surprising, but complimenting a co-worker can seem like you are buttering her up for something you need. The guidelines described here keep positive feedback from becoming "brown-nosing." The use of the "I" language, facts, and specifics are critical. Make a habit of "catching people being good" because as much learning occurs by reinforcing good behaviors as it does from constructive feedback. Here are two examples, starting with a poor approach:

"Umm, I just wanted to let you know that you are doing, um, a good job, I mean, it is really a good job."

Contrast that with:

"That report you presented yesterday was extremely well done. I especially liked the summary at the beginning and end, and the way you kept your remarks concise and to the point. Thank you."

Notice the power in "thank you." That simple phrase is underused in IT organizations.

While coaching is not the best setting for a leader to receive feedback from the person you're coaching, it may happen. Demonstrating that you can receive feedback effectively will help your staff's ability to receive feedback. When appropriate, redirect any feedback you receive in a coaching session, and set up time for talking about this outside the coaching agenda.

Receiving feedback well is important for your own growth as a leader. In *Servant Leadership*, author Robert Greenleaf says that receiving requires a humble spirit. Those who have the capacity to receive, value, and leverage feedback are very strong leaders. Here are some additional tips for receiving feedback:

- Most people aren't skilled at giving feedback. They will express feelings, not objective assessment. Listen through the emotion for facts that may have merit, remaining as neutral as possible.

- Feedback is perception, not truth. Use feedback for learning about how others perceive you as the starting point for more research.
- Appreciate and acknowledge the time and courage it took to provide feedback.
- How you respond determines what kind of feedback you'll receive in the future. Say "thank you."
- Reflect on why receiving the feedback was positive or negative, so you can use the knowledge in the future.
- Balance span of responsibility and span of control. Some feedback will be about things you can't change, and you must say that when it is true.
- Entering into this level of dialogue is a significant achievement. Congratulate yourself!

Here are some practical ways to focus your thoughts so that you keep your cool while receiving feedback:

- Take notes to keep busy and stay open.
- Let the person finish. Do not interrupt, no matter how long the feedback goes on.
- Ask for specific examples.
- Do not defend yourself. Focus on questions rather than debate and defense.
- Thank them for their honesty.

Summary

Each person receives coaching from a different starting place. As you learned in Chapter 4 and throughout this book, each person has unique strengths and challenges. In addition, each has a different transition velocity—how fast one can transition after experiencing change. Transition velocity is about resiliency, which you read about in Chapter 3, "Resiliency."

The challenge of a leader as coach is to uncover what the unique starting place is for each person, understand his unique transition velocity, and then move each from *where he is to where he can go*. There is no checklist or process to move all people to the same ideal place. There are coaching checklists and techniques, but the steps and techniques will be different for each situation. Each coaching candidate and experience is different.

Lessons Learned

To orient yourself to your role as coach requires the following:

- A coach must be able to clearly understand the role. Coaching is not therapy and in a business setting it's not about the person's personal life. An IT leader must learn to coach an employee's behavior toward the goals of the department (and ultimately, the business) through the employee's self-discovery as the coach mirrors the discussion.
- Using good coaching language creates the groundwork for an effective relationship.
- Writing meaningful goals is the first step. Coaches teach their charges how to write goals that are measurable and achievable.
- Leveraging goals—both writing and reviewing—helps a person achieve goals and progress along the way.
- Assessments, like the behavioral DISC and the attitudinal PIAV, provide a neutral view that allows a coach to help the person set growth goals consistent with her personal needs and the needs of the business.
- Assessments are useful to help a person better understand who she is and who she wants to be.
- Giving respectful but constructive feedback is important for IT leaders, who are not in a neutral role.
- Honest, factual feedback, both positive and negative, is necessary for personal growth.
- To be a coach means to listen and to mirror, helping another create a path to her own success.

Action Plan/Journaling

In the following section, take a moment to reflect on your own coaching capacity. Consider the following:

What did you learn from this chapter?

How has what you read related to your work experience?

Of the capacities required for coaching in this chapter, which is your strongest?

What is your greatest area for improvement?

What will you do differently going forward?

Take a few minutes to describe yourself in your journal as you would like to be. What kind of coaching abilities do you imagine yourself having in the future?

Finally, jot down some quick notes about some first steps you will take to grow into this successful coach.

Customer Orientation

While aligning the IT organization to the customer is one of today's most common IT goals, actually accomplishing it is rare. Like alchemy, customer orientation involves a mix of methods and techniques. Practicing customer orientation requires adjustment in both the leader's self-understanding and relationships. In this chapter you'll learn how to analyze your feelings about your work with your customers. That's important because customer relationships are the key to alignment. Once you understand those relationships, you will learn to build a plan to move toward alignment. The techniques alone will not create customer orientation, but paired with the right relationship, the techniques can accelerate and maintain the alignment.

Mercury represents the alchemy principle of adaptation. Successful IT organizations adapt to their customers. Since IT is the vendor, and the business people are the customers, IT must adapt to the needs of the business, rather than the other way around. Unfortunately, IT often requires its customers to jump through hoops to get the solution support they need. Business customers don't see IT as adaptive; instead, they often view it as a roadblock—and who wants to be aligned with a roadblock?

Customer service is not a new field; in fact, companies spend a great deal of money on customer service workshops. Still, many IT practitioners do not see customer service as useful. After all, they don't think they have problems with their customer service (although they can clearly explain how others in their group do). They cannot relate to most customer service training materials, which are typically written for call centers or geared to external customers. IT work is equally stressful, but more complex, because customer desires are not always known or possible. That can make IT resemble that roadblock, or just be the bearer of bad tidings.

Poor customer service can thrive in this situation. IT leaders need to acknowledge this and allocate time not just for PR but also for "public *customer relations*"? Because internal IT organizations feel reluctant to toot their own horns, nobody ever hears about IT successes—just the failures. Can you imagine a customer calling to say, "Thanks for having the network up and running today." Because bad news is the only news, the relationships between IT and its customers are negatively impacted. The large IT consulting companies, who are the competitors of internal departments, spend a great deal of time and money on PR. No wonder internal customers often bypass IT and contract with these larger and flashier companies.

Customer orientation is imperative because the ability of an IT organization to adapt to a customer-centric philosophy will determine its ability to help the overall business compete. Honoring the customer is also the best defense against the threat of outsourcing. Remember that IT exists only because it is integral to the operations of the overall business. It has no merit standing alone.

Opportunities for Growth _____

- Define your customers, product/service, and your organization's competitive advantage
- Build trust for effective customer interactions
- Define your customers' service values, and evaluate your ability to meet them
- Determine and leverage the communication required for a specific audience
- Improve your ability to gather complete and accurate business and technical requirements

Agenda

Manage and Leverage Customer Needs and Expectations

- The Role of Trust
- Value Market: Helping the Customer's Customer
- Monitoring Customer Orientation

Gather Customer Requirements and Input

- Ask Better Questions
- Interview Customers
- Group and Meeting Techniques

Manage and Leverage Customer Needs and Expectations

Exercise: Who Are You?

Before beginning the material that follows, please answer these questions:

What is your product?

Who is your customer?

What value do you provide to your customer?

What competition do you have?

Compare your answers to those in Table 7.1—which came from IT staff attending one of our Service Orientation workshops.

Table 7.1

Profiling Your Company

Question Asked of IT	Common Answer
What is your product?	LOTUS Notes
Who is your customer?	Any one who uses LOTUS Notes
What value do you provide to your customer?	LOTUS Notes
What competition do you have?	No one

After listening to these responses, we asked the students these questions:

- Did the customer call and specifically ask for LOTUS Notes?
- Would the customer consider any other technology?
- How does LOTUS Notes help the customer's business?
- Does anyone else (internally or externally) know how to provide the LOTUS Notes support you provide?

Now consider the actual reality of their situation shown in Table 7.2.

Table 7.2
Reality Check

Question	Actual Answer
What is your product?	Provide the ability for people to share documents and mail easily.
Who is your customer?	People in the company who need to share documents and email.
What value do you provide to your customer?	Help them communicate more quickly and effectively, reducing staff redundancy, which reduces cost.
What competition do you have?	The customer's own IT expert, outside outsourcing firms, and IT consulting companies.

Anyone who thinks her job is to deliver a specific software package like LOTUS Notes behaves differently toward the customer than does a person who believes that her job is to help that customer communicate more effectively. Before customer orientation can be improved, some deeply held, historical assumptions must be challenged. All members of an IT team must answer the simple questions in Table 7.1 consistently and with a common voice.

Many frontline IT staffers hold technology-centric views of their role. Often, that's because their leaders, who model accepted practices, also hold these beliefs. In many cases, the leader used to be a frontline IT person who had been indoctrinated with these beliefs. To align an organization to the customer, leaders must shift their own beliefs and then help their people challenge theirs.

How can you create this change? Leaders must deal with the whole problem of customer orientation, not just the easy fixes. The first step is to get the team to challenge their flawed beliefs through group workshops or facilitation. While this creates awareness, incentives must also be changed. The compensation of all IT employees should be tied to customer survey results, and 360-degree feedback should include key customers. Even more important, the leaders must be the first to attend the workshops, include customer feedback in their performance review, and be held financially accountable for the survey results. When IT organizations fail to create customer orientation in their ranks, it's usually because they have chosen to exclude the leadership from the efforts, signaling to the staff that the initiative is a facade.

This doesn't mean that the customer is always right or that the IT people should do everything customers want. After all, IT is responsible for implementing technology solutions for the good of the business, not the good of any individual. Any customer who is not moving in a direction that will increase revenue, avoid cost, or improve service should be challenged to rethink his or her strategy. However, that challenge must be issued using effective communication skills (see Chapter 5, "Communication Skills") that don't create animosity. Maintaining effective relationships through trust and integrity is a critical element when building strong customer collaboration.

The Role of Trust

Trust is bidirectional, with both of the people in any relationship deciding whether to trust the other. Many things influence this decision: past experiences at working together, the effectiveness of the communication, and any preconceived notions about each other from company history. If either party demonstrates a lack of trust, it influences the reciprocal trust from the other, and trust that's been broken is extremely difficult to rebuild. (See more on trust in Chapter 4, "Interpersonal and Team Skills.")

Figure 7.1 is a systems thinking model that shows how this dynamic occurs. To read this diagram, notice that the lowercase "s" means same, and the lowercase "o" means opposite. The arrows indicate a cause and effect relationship, rather than a linear progression (like a flowchart). For example, as the variable performance of IT increases, customer trust increases, because customers have seen success.

An opposite influence appears as the trust of the customer in IT increases—there's less nagging of the IT consultant. Continuing with this loop, as a customer trusts an IT provider, there's less need to micro-manage every aspect of their work together. The customer begins to grant the IT staff the autonomy to do what needs to be done, allowing the IT consultant to act with agility-creating performance. As performance improves, the customer feels

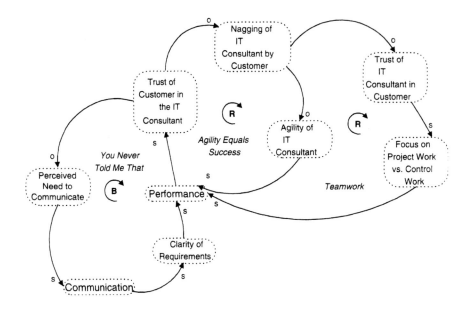

Figure 7.1
The trust dynamic.

that his trust provided a payback, so he trusts even more. Notice the far right loop, in which customer trust in the IT consultant changes the consultant's behavior, allowing him to minimize project control work and maximize value-adding activities. These are positive reinforcing situations.

But if something impacts performance—some external problem like a faulty software upgrade from the vendor—the customer may perceive that the IT person perhaps should not have been trusted. With less trust, the customer decides to check up on the IT person a bit more, which sends signals of mistrust. Both parties are now focused on watching or avoiding the other, so project work suffers, and performance decreases. It's a self-fulfilling prophecy. Notice how the same loop can reinforce in either a positive or negative direction, impacted by the change of only one variable. This phenomenon also makes intervention simpler, because fixing the problems may require influencing only one variable per loop.

The customer chain of experience in Figure 7.2 illustrates an everyday example of how this cycle could happen. Customers judge their relationships with IT through their interpretation of critical moments of truth—small contacts like emails, voice mails, or saying "hi" in the cafeteria. Most of us don't

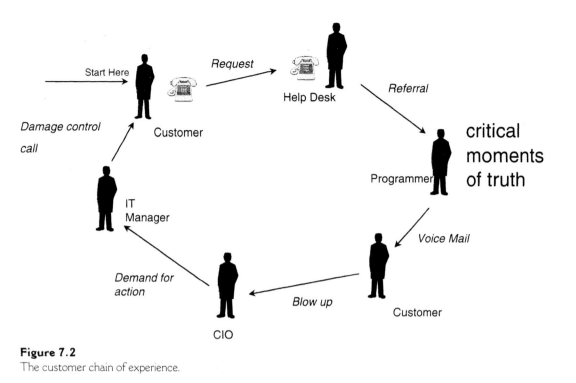

Figure 7.2
The customer chain of experience.

think twice about these moments and don't invest a lot of time thinking about doing them well. An IT staff person at a software company might explain the chain this way:

> "The customer called the Help Desk with a question about a problem with the new release of the billing software. The Help Desk contacted me as the programmer, and I worked 14 hours straight to fix the bug. I installed the change at 3 a.m. In the same fix, I made a slight change to a report that had been asked for by someone else earlier. At 4 a.m., I called the customer and left a voice mail that the fix was in. The next morning the customer called the CIO screaming about the lack of responsiveness of IT and that not only was the problem *not* fixed, but an important report had been screwed up."

We can all feel for the poor IT staff member who spent all night working to meet the customer's need. From the customer's perspective, the critical moments of truth were the initial call, a voice mail, and then the call to the CIO. There were no other points of contact, which is a problem. Adding an IT supervisor into this situation might have prolonged the pattern. The CIO might call and scream at the IT supervisor. The supervisor would then talk to the programmer, but make comments about how stupid and sensitive the customer was, agreeing with the programmer that no one really appreciates IT. Yet the customer has a different perspective of the same incident:

> "I called the Help Desk early Thursday morning when I noticed that the new billing software was not calculating the adjusted city tax correctly. At this point, I stopped all billing (which costs the company approximately $10 million a day). When I came in Friday morning, there was a strange voice mail left in the middle of the night from someone who said only that the fix was in—no name or phone number. I resumed the billing cycle, and saw that the calculation appeared to be correct, but it was showing up on a different part of the bill now, which would confound our customers. It was obviously not tested by anyone on my team. I decided to run our summary reports as I tried to contact the Help Desk again, and to my surprise, found that the headings on one of the reports were all shuffled. I was furious—IT was costing me hours and hours, and the company millions of dollars. I decided the only thing to do was call the CIO directly."

Notice the different perceptions of reality. The IT staff member:

- Dedicated heads-down time, including staying up all night, to meet the need of the customer.
  REALITY: Dumb mistakes are made when you stay up all night. Many of these occur because there is no one else around to ask questions about the situation or test your work.
- Tried to work quickly, and skipped testing.
  REALITY: Testing is never optional. Testing is customer service.
- Made additional fixes at the same time, minimizing rollout costs.
  REALITY: Doing work that meets other requirements without training and/or communication may first appear to be a mistake to the customer.

The customer:

- Stopped billing to avoid re-running or billing the external customer incorrectly.
  REALITY: The Help Desk was not told this. The priority of this request was unclear.
- Felt that IT didn't do anything; there was no sense of urgency.
  REALITY: IT was working on it.
- Claimed that the production reports were wrong.
  REALITY: The production reports were reformatted based on another area's needs.

Both sides are guilty of a lack of communication. (See more on intentional communication in Chapter 5.) There are many ways this situation could have been improved, including:

- The IT staff member could have created trust initially by calling to find out the priority of the problem, communicating to the customer how long it was taking, calling again when it was fixed, then making sure someone was there to help when the customer restarted billing.
- The new report requirements could probably have waited, but the customers should have been consulted to determine if that was a good idea.

Different communication styles and needs can often drive this type of disconnect. Here's an illustration of that. A manager in a workshop asked for help. He said that he had been creating large status reports for his boss, complete with color graphs and charts, and his boss didn't seem happy. They were not communicating well, and the manager was concerned. He planned to spend the entire night building an extensive PowerPoint presentation about his project status. I knew that this manager was the type of person who liked written and visual communication and I guessed that the boss was not. What the manager was doing was delivering his message the way he would have liked to receive it, not the way the boss liked to receive it. Even worse, he planned to go more dramatically in the wrong direction that very night. I suggested that before he invested all that time, he stick his head in and tell his boss quickly and succinctly how the project was going. He did that and it worked. Each customer is a different individual with diverse needs for communication style and frequency.

Exercise: Glimpsing the Other Side

Consider auditing the Critical Moments of Truth. Do you have a set of guidelines for proper email use? For proper voice mail responses? Have you checked the voice mail of your direct reports to see how a customer would feel leaving a message? Have you called your own? Watch your staff go to lunch or walk through the cafeteria. Do they make eye contact? Do they speak to the business people? Do they ever invite them to lunch? Are all your IT people sitting in a corner at the back of the cafeteria, hunched over, laughing at something or someone? How can you get your people closer to their customers?

Value Market: Helping the Customer's Customer

In *Working Knowledge,* authors Tom Davenport and Laurence Prusak describe knowledge management as a value market. This is applicable to IT, since IT

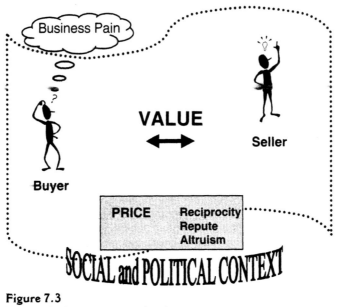

Figure 7.3
Viewing the business as a marketplace.

gets knowledge to the right people to increase revenue, avoid cost, and improve service. It's helpful to think of an IT organization as the seller of a service and think of the customers, whether external or internal, as the buyers. Viewing the business as a market helps redefine behavior. Figure 7.3 illustrates this metaphor.

The Seller is responsible for delivering something of value that the Buyer wants. There is an even exchange; the Seller provides the value, the Buyer provides a fair price. The price does not always have to be money; it can be the other things listed in the figure and discussed below.

IT is providing a service, and expects something in return from the buyer/customer. This might be budget and salary dollars, but IT people also expect prestige, respect, gratitude—or even just being thanked. Sadly, though, the only time IT usually hears from its clients is when something is wrong.

It is important to understand the "deal" of the market. IT provides technology solutions to the business area, and in return is paid for the value of those services through budget and labor dollars. No favor has occurred, and the accounts are not out of balance. No one owes anyone anything after an equitable transaction. Waiting for the thank you from the customer is not rational. If you compare it to a retail situation like Starbucks, the people taking the money say thank you, not the other way around. The IT people should be thanking the business client for the business. Adopting such a mindset will dramatically alter the relationship you have with your customers.

Continuing this value market metaphor, frequent communication about the customer's need is the only way that the Seller (IT) can stay in touch with the Buyer (the internal or external customer). In sales, this is called "Relationship Selling." Relationship selling is expensive because of the large time investment. Amplifying the difficulties, building relationships with customers is not something that many IT people feel comfortable doing. If you use the value market analogy, though, relationship building is a critical marketing effort that's necessary for generating future goodwill and successful projects.

The leader models this sales role when she positions herself as the customer advocate. Relationships between IT and customer areas focus on "getting mine" when the leader from the IT area is not in constant contact with the leaders of the customer areas. Investing in the customer relationships is paid back when a rough project issue comes up. Through a strong leadership example and performance goals reinforced through review, IT staff can learn to build relationships with their customers.

IT people who avoid conflict are often pressured into making unattainable estimates for customers. Giving a "best case" promise makes things easier in the short-term, but creates more risk of ultimate failure. IT staff must learn to under-promise—which allows them to over-deliver—and their leaders must support them. Save overtime work and long nights for times when the business really needs it.

Consider the following checklist for IT leaders and staff in creating a customer partnership:

- Model good customer orientation behavior. Do not accept anything less from your team.
- When there is a problem, spend more time, not less, communicating.
- Use jargon minimally or not at all.
- Adapt your style to each unique customer (see Chapter 5).
- Listen actively.
- Ask lots of questions—help the customer explain his need.
- Become an internal (and polite) skeptic. Do not jump to the solution in the middle of the customer's sentence. Delay new judgment, interpretation, and technology conclusions.
- Understand the customer's world and context.

- Use prototypes (screens, reports) to help the customer figure out and explain his need.
- Clarify the customer's expectations whenever decisions are made.
- Set mutual milestones and measurements.
- Say no when you need to.
- Don't use the word "but." Substitute the word "and." Example: "But that operating system isn't stable enough" becomes "And since that operating system may not be stable enough, we'll have to do a little more digging."
- Use "I," not "you." Example: "I need help understanding that billing exception" versus "You need to tell me more about that billing exception."

Exercise: Max Out Communication

Who are the influential customer managers you need to stay in contact with? How long has it been since you last spoke to them? How do you think they feel about you and your team? Come up with a strategy for improving your customer communication.

Monitoring Customer Orientation

People value and invest attention into what is measured. If the IT organization's customer orientation is not monitored, it will not happen. Measuring this is challenging.

A CIO from Canada offered a small checklist for IT project managers to review, representing "Project Health Assessment." This checklist included some expected questions, such as, "Do you feel like the scope is changing?" "Do you feel like you may miss a future deadline or budget goal?" However, the most impactful question was, "When was the last time you talked to your customer?" He felt that if the answer was "more than a week," the project was in serious trouble.

The easiest measurement of customer orientation is done through regular customer surveys and focus groups. A broad initial baseline survey creates a point from which to measure, along with numerical data that can be watched for changes. Has the average response time gone up or down in the last six months? Are the customers aware of the status of their projects? Do the customers feel like their IT contacts are honest with them? Once an up or down trend is noticed, other techniques must be used to uncover why the change has occurred.

Focus groups with important customers from multiple areas and levels can be used to develop a better understanding of cause and effect. Individuals will have very specific and sometimes unique opinions about what is right or wrong, but some actionable concerns will be heard again and again. For example, in one set of customer focus groups, the IT customers mentioned frequently that it was assumed that they would come to meetings at the IT building, and that IT never volunteered to attend a meeting at the customer location. A large IT consulting company would always go to the customer— so should your team.

At a project (value market transaction) level, each team must carefully assess the success of the initiative after it is over. The lessons learned from the project, when they include a focus on improving relationships, will create improved future project success (see Chapter 9, "Project Leadership"). Projects are the place where customer relationships are made or broken. The sign of a great leader is when these individual relationships remain strong without the leader's intervention.

Exercise: View Damage Both Ways

Remember the most recent time you were called in to do damage control? Write a brief summary of the situation from your team's perspective. Now, write another summary of the situation from the customer's viewpoint. Finally, think about your behavior during the incident. What could you have done differently?

Hold each individual IT staff member accountable for service behavior. Put criteria and goals in everyone's performance review process. Measure, coach, and provide incentives based on achieving goals consistent with the defined strategy of the department. All too often IT organizations say service is important, and even throw a couple of workshops at it, but never do the work that will create a truly systemic change.

Gather Customer Requirements and Input

According to the dictionary, "analysis" means to break a whole into its parts to find out its nature. Customer requirements are an example of this. Essentially, a requirements document requires breaking the business need down into parts that are understandable, and then capturing them in a document so that people can work in parallel on the solution. The complexity occurs because the requirements change as the business people and the IT people work out the parts. Business changes while the project progresses also affect the requirements. Requirements are defined in the dictionary as "order." In IT, we sometimes delude ourselves into thinking there really can be order.

Most IT projects are plagued by poorly understood requirements, changing scope, bad estimates, and glitches. Doing a better job in defining the requirements throughout the project has a crucial influence on project success. This is an evolving process, one that continues throughout the entire project. Requirements ebb and flow—influenced by communication, the people involved, the business climate, the market, the technology, the cost, and just about everything else.

IT leaders can teach their people to clarify the roles when gathering requirements. The IT analyst must learn, listen, seek to understand, and help the customer break the whole into its parts—something customers are often too close to the business to do easily. It is not the IT analyst's job to create requirements without the customer's knowledge, or to prioritize the parts without the customer's input.

Customers must dedicate the time to explain what is needed and decode the business area for the IT person. They shouldn't decide which technology solution will be best or how long it will take to implement. Figuring out who owns the requirements is a critical first step, and IT analysts may want to talk to people they don't immediately think of as customers, among them:

- Steering committee members
- Business area team members
- Business area managers
- Vendors
- IT support staff responsible for the current technology
- IT security and network experts
- IT staff previously working in this business area

The IT analyst plays the role of a detective. The business person is bringing clues disguised as "the problem." Many of these clues are probably symptoms of a larger problem, and many projects have been started on the wrong foot by jumping to solutions too quickly. IT leaders and the analysts who work for them must learn to delay judgment and seek out all of the clues.

The symptoms typically indicate one or more of four problem causes (Table 7.3), remembered through the mnemonic STEM.

Table 7.3
Four STEM Problems

System	The existing technology is preventing the business area from meeting its business goals.
Training	The people in the business area do not have the skills or knowledge to use the existing technology.
Environment	There is something in the work area that is hindering the proper use of technology, such as interruptions, noise, lighting, clutter, a mean boss, etc.
Motivation	The business staff is resisting something, and is not motivated to use the technology correctly.

Let's assume the customer has said that the current payroll checks are all wrong. There are four general possibilities, and the real problems will likely be a combination of these. Table 7.4 shows how this could be true.

Table 7.4
Root Causes

System	There is a bug in the software somewhere or the printer is jamming the checks.
Training	The business staff using the software is not trained in the software.
Environment	The company has just hired 1,000 new people, and the payroll employees are working tons of overtime. They are not attentive when entering the data like they used to be because they are tired.
Motivation	The payroll clerks are worried that a strike is pending.

An IT project can help meet the needs of the System (software, hardware) problems, and may have the ability to help with the Training problems, but the Environmental and Motivational problems can never be completely solved by using only technology. Many IT projects fail because technology (easy to see, easy to count) is thrown at a complex problem that cannot be solved with hardware and software. An example would be trying to implement an extensive call center system without improving the way the customer representatives deal with the external customers on the phone.

Ask Better Questions

IT people, whether leaders or technical experts, love to solve problems, and they are good at it. However, this desire to solve problems often leads an IT person to ask questions that:

- Lead the witness and suggest a solution
- Focus on technology-related issues
- Filter out relevant people and cultural issues

Here are some tips for constructing good questions, whether you are asking via email, voice mail, or face-to-face:

1. Seek a general picture of the issues. Example: "What do you think the issues are?"
2. Seek background (clues). Example: "How long has this been occurring?"
3. Seek details. Example: "Will you give me an example of how this impacts your business area?"
4. Seek feelings. Example: "How critical do you feel this problem is?"
5. Seek causes. Example: "What do you think is causing the reports to be late?"

These five categories of questions are represented in Figure 7.4. The order of these questions is intentional. The progression allows the customer to think through the obvious, starting at the big picture, move through feelings and details, and eventually identify suspected causes. It is likely that the causes identified by the customer are either partially correct or incorrect, but it is important to listen and evaluate each perspective. By asking the same type of questions to multiple customers in the same order, you can gather and synthesize clues—and it's easier to deduce the true problem when the same general questions have been asked during all interviews.

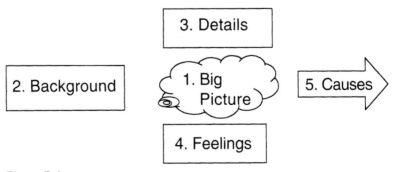

Figure 7.4
Problem-solving questions.

The five categories of questions are excellent for developing an initial understanding of the problems. When creating an IT solution, two additional phases of questioning become important: Setting the Scope (see Chapter 9) and Exposing the Detail. Good questions to ask to set the scope are:

1. What will the solution do for you?
2. Why is that important to the business?
3. Where will the information needed by the system come from? Who will receive information from the system?
4. Describe the elements of data that will be kept by the system.

These are powerful questions. In question 1, you are asking the client to describe the processes that the technology solution will handle. You are asking people to talk about what they are most comfortable with, which is their own work. The second question ensures that there is a strong business need. It also helps you troubleshoot possible funding challenges, which can be a consequence of an unclear business sponsor. The third question defines the boundaries of your technology solution project. Who provides input? Who receives output? Finally, the last question is the start of the data (or object) architecture, the most stable building block of a business technology solution.

Even more important is that the IT interviewer can use some answers to validate the completeness of others' answers. For example, if one of the answers to question 1 is "Print payroll checks" but "payroll check" data is never discussed in question 4, the results are not yet complete. The questions provide a simple validation check.

When seeking detail in later phases, each of the questions gets drilled down farther. What are the subprocesses? What events trigger system transactions? How will the keys of the data "chunks" be referenced? Most IT analysts are pretty good at asking these questions, but often create problems by asking them too soon. It is critical to capture the Big Picture before narrowing the path to the detail.

Interview Customers

As a leader you must coach your people on the best way to interview customers. This is an IT competency that is not included in most computer science or technology degree programs. The questions that are asked are not the same kind as you would ask in a job interview, which is most IT staff members' only other experience with interviewing. There should be no tension or competition.

Each decision about whether you call the customer on the phone, email the customer, or leave voice mail sends a priority to the customer. For example, if one customer is emailed and another is interviewed through a face-to-face meeting, you have inadvertently shown which customer's time is most valuable. Teach your staff to be mindful of these subliminal messages.

Some thinking is necessary before an interview, especially if the process feels a bit uncomfortable. Remind yourself that your job is to gather everything the customer says, not to debate it, agree with it, argue about it, or interpret it. A successful interview results in information passing from the customer to you.

Before the interview, do a little homework: What are the current primary issues in the business area? What role does this person play? Schedule time together and carefully honor that time. Don't just show up unannounced, and don't run over. Go to the customer's location, and set positive expectations for the meeting by sending the questions you plan to ask in advance so that the customer can be prepared. A few tips follow on how to open up the conversation, watch your body language, close the interview, and follow up.

Try using some non-work-oriented opening lines. It's natural to rush into the interview questions if you are a little nervous. Avoid that by planning to talk about a couple of other less important things to build rapport. The weather or movies may work, but it's better to know something about what is going on, for example, "How is that new rate filing going?" or to ask a question about something in the office: "I see you're a golfer." You can feign interest, but that will be obvious, so develop a genuine interest in connecting with people and putting them at ease.

While interviewing, remember the following:

- Avoid jargon. Speak the customer's language when possible.
- Slow down. Focus on listening. If you can't write and listen, stop writing.
- Never criticize or correct. Never finish sentences or interrupt.
- Never talk for more than 30 seconds. It's not about you.

There are two final questions that always get you lots of additional information:

1. What did I forget to ask you?
2. Who else do you think I should talk with?

Use these questions to pursue any areas the customer feels you need to know about. Schedule interviews with any people the customer suggests you talk with.

Promise to rewrite your notes and get them back to the customer within a short period of time for review. The quicker you do this, the better the results.

Remember to interview multiple people who have different perspectives. For example, the supervisor of a call center has a completely different perspective than the people on the phones. Remember that people tend to have poor memories, incomplete knowledge, and may exaggerate their own role. Wait to hear something from three or more people before judging it as fact.

Group and Meeting Techniques

IT leaders and practitioners spend a great deal of their productive time in meetings, where they often find themselves in charge. These meetings are critical moments of truth, and the customer is most likely to measure the respect of the IT staff through their behavior in these personal encounters. That's why it's important to know ways to maximize the benefit from each group meeting.

Orderliness Counts   Set rules of order for the meetings, especially if you will meet with the same people often. Here are some we particularly like:

- Start on time, end on time.
- Give lots of short biological breaks—at least one per hour.
- Encourage people to trust that when it's time for them to contribute they will know what to say. Ask them to avoid rehearsing what they will say in their head while others are speaking, since it prevents them from hearing what is being said.
- Be mindful of self-talk. Ask people to quiet the little judgmental voice in their own head, and show them how to challenge their own interpretations.
- Ask genuine questions. Are you asking because you really want to know, or are you asking to look good, to show others how smart you are, or to trip somebody up?

Seating   Seating is also something that can be used to your advantage.

- If you think the meeting will involve a lot of conflict, remove the tables and sit in a circle of chairs. Physical barriers provide safety for people who want to speak with anger.
- If you know there are two people who will be in conflict, sit them next to each other and next to you. Physical presence to you and to each other will control the expression of their anger.
- If you know there will be people at the meeting who are intimidated but have very valuable contributions, sit them beside you so they can respond to you instead of talking across a large group of people. They will feel more comfortable responding.

To get people to sit where you want them to, use nametags at the assigned spots if you don't know the people. If you do know them, nametags will not be taken as a positive. An alternative is to put materials that you want them to have on specific chairs.

A Common Goal   A common challenge to an effective meeting is the lack of a shared outcome. Each individual may have a different view of what he or she is being asked to contribute and why. For example, a boss may be having an informational meeting to present a decision that she has already made. Without clearly articulating what she expects of the participants, she may get lots of feedback about the decision from people who do not know that the decision is a done deal. Long term, this will discourage active participation, since the boss will be less than receptive to the feedback when the decision is final. Consider the spectrum in Figure 7.5 based on techniques in Peter Senge's *The Fifth Discipline Fieldbook*.

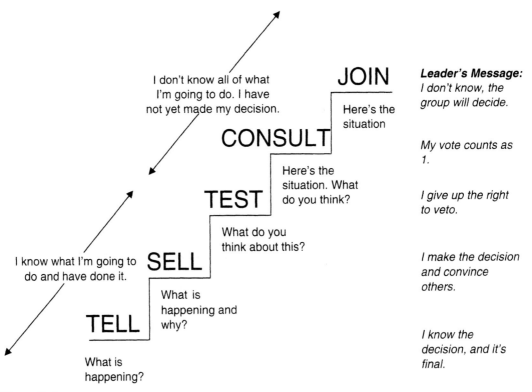

Figure 7.5
Meeting objectives.

As Figure 7.5 illustrates, the spectrum moves from Tell, where the decision has already been made, to Join, where the group will make the decision together. Moving up the stairs, the purpose of the meeting ranges through Tell, Sell, Test, which each start with a decision made by the leader, and to Consult and Join, which start without a decision. Notice the left-hand column indicates what the leader is thinking when she calls each kind of meeting. Tell will take the least amount of time, while Join takes the most.

A leader should choose the purpose based on the situation:

- When there is a lack of time, don't do Consult and Join, which are the most time-consuming.
- If the overall objective is technical quality, Tell and Sell don't make sense. In this case, the leader does well to involve the technical experts on her team.
- If the decision requires commitment of the team, Join is the best approach. This way the team will be able to operate without the leader if necessary, since it has buy-in to the approach.

Exercise: Productivity Check

Think back to your last meeting. How productive was it? Did you achieve the hoped-for outcomes? What was your purpose for the meeting? What do you think the participants thought the purpose was? How would you improve this meeting if you were able to have it again?

Ineffective meetings come up often in project post-mortems as the single largest waste of time in projects. These dysfunctional meetings burn salaries while creating distrust, and stifle collaboration. Ironically, effective meetings are often identified as the *strongest* predictor of a successful project during similar post-mortems. Meeting ground rules are not enough to guarantee effectiveness. It is important to find out early what the purpose of the meeting is.

The leader will have to be strong and avoid letting her ego be bruised by the participants. This is especially difficult when you have meetings with the same people over and over again. Just like family members, you will know all their tricks, history, and foibles—and they will know yours. It is very easy to focus on the negative before the meeting even begins.

Exercise: Admire the Enemy

A simple mental exercise that helps you prepare for meetings with people who threaten you is to look for something in each person that you admire.

This may take a few minutes, since it may not be your natural thought pattern about this person. Think about this admiration during the meeting whenever you start to follow old patterns. Think about how this person's behavior and ideas are sane from their perspective. Realize that we are all different, and we all add value to every collaborative experience.

Finally, learn to keep your meetings safe and non-competitive by modeling effective meeting behavior yourself. It is tough to break old habits, and it will take a couple of times before people transition to the new approach. Consider mixing up the techniques you use during the meeting, just to keep boredom and old patterns from breaking through. We recommend Michael Michalko's book *Thinkertoys* as a source for facilitation tools.

Brainstorming   Brainstorming is a good technique for generating out-of-the-box ideas in quantity. It is useful when the solution needs to be different than anything ever done before. It is not useful for building consensus or creating a single solution. After brainstorming, you will need to use a convergent technique to come to consensus (like the Nominal Group Technique described below).

Most IT people are not comfortable with brainstorming in a business meeting. The normal business behavior is to critique ideas the minute they are revealed. This limits the effectiveness of a brainstorming session if the facilitator cannot control it. Here are some tips:

- Critique is not acceptable. The goal is quantity, not quality. All ideas are gathered and logged in front of everyone, without discussion (except to clarify the idea). Make this rule clear from the start, and have a humorous way of catching people breaking the rule. For example, we use a small toy dinosaur named Negasaurus that roars. Whenever someone critiques someone else's ideas or their own, they are given Negasaurus, either by the facilitator or whoever currently has possession.
- Time the experience; let everyone know in advance how long the session will take, and stick to it.
- Use a metaphor to generate new thinking. For example, "How will our new system be like a new can of tennis balls?"
- The facilitator cannot contribute actively. She should focus on ensuring even participation as well as neutralizing negative verbal and non-verbal feedback.

A strong facilitator will set the stage and keep people open to crazy ideas. If people are not laughing, they are not brainstorming. The facilitator can prime the pump with a few really crazy ideas right at the start.

Delphi Technique   This is an educational research technique that adapts well to email. It is useful when the facilitator needs to pinpoint the feelings of people before a sensitive face-to-face meeting.

Email a set of questions with a numerical range response to the participants individually (without revealing who else the email went to). An example question: "How critical are the new system changes to your daily work, select 1 (not critical) to 5 (most critical)?" Average the results of each question, and resend them to the participants without any names. Ask them to re-answer, with comments. Resend the next set of results with the comments. Limit this technique to two rounds or so, before it becomes obvious that the recipients are dividing into camps. This helps everyone have common expectations about the existing thoughts before a face-to-face meeting.

Nominal Group Technique   This technique is useful for face-to-face meetings that have a history of conflict. It can be used when the meeting is falling apart, or it can be planned ahead for a meeting at which you anticipate there will be trouble. A single question is placed on the flip-chart, and each person has a set amount of time (say, five minutes) to respond to the question, each in his or her turn. A person can pass, but they can't exceed their time limit. In addition, nobody else can speak until it is his or her turn. People can use their time to ask questions of others or clarify their own ideas. This technique ensures that every player is given equal opportunity to be heard.

This technique demands a strong facilitator, since the people who would otherwise monopolize the meeting will still try to control the floor. Calmly explain the rules, and return the floor to the rightful owner—or use a fun technique like Negasaurus.

Talking Stick   This is a physical addition to the Nominal Group Technique. Based on Native American traditions, an object (a pen, a marker, or you can actually make something more symbolic) becomes the Talking Stick. You can talk only when you are holding the stick. An interesting use is to sit in a circle and put the Talking Stick in the middle. When you have something to share, you must first pick up the stick. When you are done, you place it back in the middle (do not let people pass it directly to another). This slows the discussion, and forces everyone to think clearly about what they are going to say. It also helps people listen more completely to others. Don't use this technique for extended periods because it will get tedious, and don't be surprised when people who often monopolize meetings get frustrated with the slowness. In general, the benefit of this technique is that it limits the communication of these very people.

Summary

The alignment of IT and their business customers is challenging but not impossible. Alignment does require a systemic approach and a concrete plan. Recognizing existing customer perceptions, thinking of the value market, and managing communication effectively are all prerequisites of strong customer orientation.

Lessons Learned

To orient your IT team to the customer requires a strategy of multiple, parallel steps:

- Model the customer behavior you want your team to adopt. Words are not enough.
- Define your customers together and be clear what the value market is. Use this definition to determine what should be monitored as you improve your teams and your own customer orientation.
- Be aware of situations where trust is jeopardizing communication from the customer to IT or from IT to the customer. Coach the participants through a strategy that will rebuild trust. Treating people as if they are trusted can go a long way toward creating trust.
- Customize communication to the unique needs of each customer. This includes both the delivery of the communication and the frequency. Ask customers how they prefer to receive communication if you don't know, and encourage your people to do the same.
- Practice asking better questions. Seek a general picture, and then move on to feelings, details, and suspected causes. Avoid "leading the witness" by jumping to conclusions.
- Stop "winging" interviews with the customer. Take the time to plan an approach, which shows respect for the value of the customer's time and builds mutual expectations.
- Practice group and meeting techniques that enhance the productivity of face-to-face meetings. Continue to grow your meeting facilitation toolkit to keep people engaged and energized, and consider hiring a professional facilitator for very important meetings.
- Being an IT leader means running an internal team as though you were running an external consulting company. The customer is queen. Build processes to become the customer's advocate, not adversary.

- Demand customer-centric behavior and settle for nothing less from your staff. Coach, mentor, and persist. Take valuable staff with less natural communication competency and partner them with people who have more customer orientation.

Action Plan/Journaling

In the following section, take a moment to reflect on your own customer orientation abilities. Consider the following:

- Talk often about expectations and trust. Expect solid customer relationships and you will achieve them. Watch out for the putdowns or negative jokes that feed distrust.
- Learn and teach how to treat each customer as unique with unique value to the business.
- Continue to collect techniques and tips for your team for effective interviews and meetings.

Take a few minutes in your journal and describe yourself as you would like to be. What kind of customer orientation processes and techniques will improve your effectiveness?

Finally, jot down some quick notes about some first steps you will take to grow into this successful customer advocate.

- Who is your most difficult customer right now? What services do you provide to this customer? What value does this customer want from your team?
- How might this customer's perspective be sane?
- What activity could you do that would both begin to build trust with this customer as well as symbolize to your team how important your customers are?
- What other steps will you take to engage your team in adopting a customer-centric philosophy?
- How will you share the techniques in this chapter that could be helpful with your team?

Strategic Business Acumen

IT organizations exist as part of a larger company, and the work done by IT teams is important only when it helps the larger business increase profits. IT professionals forget this, preferring to view IT as a means to its own end. Yet developing business acumen creates a stronger IT leader—a leader who, like the alchemy principle of mercury, can adapt her competencies to each situation, then integrate and align them. As you learned in Chapter 7, "Customer Orientation," lack of customer orientation can make it nearly impossible to align IT with the business. Orienting yourself and your organization to the customer is the prerequisite to developing strategic business acumen.

IT can only contribute to the good of the business when it understands the business of which it is a part. Technology expertise is not sufficient until it is mixed with a concise strategy. Business acumen demands the ability to build and sell an IT vision, plan strategically, grow and nurture a network of advocates, and decode complex business problems. These activities create a strong return on IT investments.

Strategic business acumen is an IT leadership imperative, because the ability of an IT organization to truly align with the rest of the company determines its ability to help the business compete. It also improves the job security of people in IT, protecting them from outsourcing. IT exists only because the business needs it. It has no merit standing alone.

Opportunities for Growth

- Build and use a vision to prioritize works
- Apply Scenario Planning to the creation of an actionable strategic plan
- Improve your ability to sell ideas and influence others, including persuasive presentation techniques
- Apply Systems Thinking to fully explore and attack a complex business problem
- Build intensional networks to grow your business knowledge and power

Agenda

Strategy = Clear Vision

Planning: Scenario, Strategic, and Contingency

Influencing: Selling Ideas

- Receptive Behaviors
- Expressive Behaviors
- Indirect Influencing Behaviors

Conflict Resolution

Systemic Thinking for Problem Solving

Building Intensional Networks

Strategy = Clear Vision

It is impossible to know enough about the technology and business to lead your team. There are two ways to cope with this challenge. The first is to avoid the unknown and cling to your existing technical knowledge. This kind of ineffective IT manager will force her group to continue building systems in older technology (such as RPG) when newer software would create stronger solutions.

The second more productive approach is to manage the scope of the information that you need by filtering it through your organization's vision. That vision gives you the criteria for determining what type of business and technology knowledge you need to acquire and to what degree. It should drive your hiring and staff development activities. It also helps you develop a strategy to find other internal or external resources with the information you need. As you will learn in Chapter 10, "Vision," vision is a critical factor in IT team or organization alignment.

You will learn more about this in Chapter 10, but here are some simple approaches. One is to gather a group and ask members to describe the vision of the organization using three verbs and one noun. This technique is an abbreviated version of a process from the book *The Path* by Laurie Beth Jones (New York: Hyperion Press, 1998). Here's an example. Suppose you ask a Help Desk organization about its collective vision. It eventually settles on the following statement (three verbs, one noun):

"Enable, support, and learn from clients about the technology infrastructure"

The first verb speaks to the need to grow the expertise of the clients (who could be in or out of IT by this definition), so they can do more themselves. The second verb, support, is the obvious choice for a Help Desk. Notice also that this definition includes learning from the customers to help future clients.

Where should this leader focus when building strategic business acumen? She should become very familiar with how the business areas use technology and their organizational visions. She should be proactive, by learning about projects just beginning or now underway, so she can ensure that the Help Desk is prepared for the changing technology infrastructure. To do this, she'll need to build a network of people in the other business areas with whom she can communicate regularly. She should stay in touch with high-level business leaders to strengthen their trust in the Help Desk—trust that will often be threatened by outages outside the Help Desk's control.

Living the vision requires an understanding of the value proposition (see Chapter 7, "Customer Orientation"). Who is the customer? What price (time, money, and other resources) is this customer willing to pay for products and services? Who plays the role of the broker in making this happen? Clearly defining the buyer, seller, and broker roles also helps to define the scope of the knowledge the IT leader needs.

Most important, learning about the business through networking (and politics) requires a mindset change for most IT leaders. Building strategic business acumen is real, credible work. It is not brown-nosing, selling out, or wasting time. Building a knowledge base around the overall business is a critical component of a leader's role. Few IT managers have been rewarded for doing this; instead, they're accustomed to rewards for independently implementing technology. That's why they often regard spending time with the customers as "not really working."

Exercise: Vision Statement

Using the preceding Help Desk example as a model, revisit the following questions about your organization from Chapter 7:

Who are your customers? Are they internal? External? Both?

What product or service do they buy from you?

What value do you add that makes you the preferred "vendor"?

Who is your competition? What value do they add that you do not?

Now, using these answers, construct a statement of vision for your organization using three verbs and one noun (and whatever additional words you need to make it clear).

Finally, consider what your customers believe your vision to be. Are your vision and their perception aligned? What can you do if they are not?

Planning: Scenario, Strategic, and Contingency

Effective leaders know how to have a flexible plan—and today's business world demands both the flexibility and the plan. Effective leaders do not tie their egos to the plan; they know that the plan is temporal and are prepared to abandon the current plan and adopt a new one when needed. To novices, this may appear to be chaos, but a flexible structure is a key attribute of an effective IT leader. Chapter 3, "Resiliency," deals with the importance of flexibility, and Chapter 9, "Project Leadership," has more information about creating project plans with flexibility.

IT people learn in school that the programmer's solution can be defined using if/then/else constructs. Failure to solve the problem is simply a lack of logic and intelligence. When promoted to leadership roles, many IT people take this same approach to planning. Not only does it force the IT leader into choosing a single, quick solution, it also creates a tendency to ignore any signs that the choice was not right. In other words, the ego of the chooser gets tied to the solution of the problem (in this case, the plan).

A better way is to devote time, at least once a year, to building a set of four future states (scenarios) with your team. By telling the story of these four future states, teams begin to see how the actions they take on a day-to-day basis can influence any one of the scenarios to happen. Psychologically, the participants experience the negative emotions of the less favorable scenarios, helping them to notice events and activities that might lead to these situations. By being open to the signs, they can react more quickly. Tim Galway's *The Inner Game of Work* (New York: Random House, 1999) provides similar examples that focus attention on critical indicators.

Royal Dutch Shell anticipated the oil embargo of the 70s and grabbed market shares when most of its competitors were still in denial. Often missing in this corporate legend is the fact that the oil embargo scenario was just one of Shell's scenarios. One participant sheepishly admitted that had he chosen only one of the multiple scenarios to study, he would have chosen wrong as well.

The benefits of scenario planning include:

- As project teams discuss future states, they create a shared vision.
- "Group Think" can kill a project, with group optimism being a dangerous example. Scenario planning forces teams to consider—not avoid—what they hope will never happen.
- Each individual on a project team influences the future of the project with his or her beliefs and assumptions (called Mental Models in Peter Senge's book *The Fifth Discipline*, New York: Currency/Doubleday, 1990). Discussing future states unveils inconsistent mental models within the team.
- Denial can be comfortable, but not for a project team. Forcing teams to face up to the possibility of trouble in the beginning makes it more likely they will plan for it and recognize it early should it occur. Brainstorming glitches before the project strongly influences the way teams build their project estimates. Instead of estimating best-case completion (see Chapter 9), they estimate more realistically.
- Project glitches trigger reptilian emotions, sending project members into fight-or-flight mode. Physiologically, the blood flow to the brain is rerouted to the heart and appendages so people don't think well. Many bad project decisions have been made because of emotional reactions to a business problem. By working through some of the emotion in the scenario planning sessions, individuals are more likely to respond rationally when surprises occur.

After the four possible futures are defined, the team can choose a strategy that steers toward the desirable scenario. The team may initiate some pre-emptive activities to guard against the negative scenarios. Where that's not possible, the best strategy is to create high-level contingency actions.

Normally, this type of session occurs when an organization needs to re-view its own beliefs and examine where it wants to be in the future. It is great for teambuilding and for clarifying vision. Some examples of use might be:

- Centralization of merged IT organizations
- Who is IT and who will it be?
- How will IT maintain the service levels if the job recruiting gets more difficult?
- What will we sell in the future?

Here's a checklist for how you would facilitate this type of session, with a Help Desk example:

Using a Post-It™ brainstorming technique, ask participants to answer the question, "If you are at a party, and someone asks you why you work where you do, what would you say you value about the organization?" Ask each person to put one idea on each Post-It and collect them quickly (keep it anonymous). Group them together and review them with the team.

1. From this brainstorming, two values will float to the top as most im-portant to the group. Assume the Help Desk participants chose two values of customer service and scope of service.

2. Vary these two (high/low) across four quadrants representing four possible futures. Figure 8.1 shows the two values varied over a quad-rant. There will always be a "Nirvana," with both values strong, and a "Hell," with both values absent. Many of the interesting discoveries occur in the other two less-obvious scenarios.

3. Depending on time, work on each quadrant at a time in teams or as-sign a quadrant to each team to work on in parallel and report back. Here are the guidelines:

Step 1: Describe what this future would be like as "A Day in the Life." Pre-tend you have come in to work and you are in this scenario. What is it like? Here are the topics for the participants to consider: people, processes, stan-dards, organizational structure, technology, customer, iinternal culture, products, and services. This should take about one hour or so. Figure 8.2 shows a sample idea for our Nirvana scenario.

Step 2: Ask them to return to their brainstorming. Switching marker colors, add the events that would have to occur between now and then to get to this future. Figure 8.3 shows a sample event for the scenario.

# Nirvana	# Hell
High customer service	Low customer service
High scope of service	High scope of service
High customer service	Low customer service
Low scope of service	Low scope of service

Figure 8.1
Four scenarios.

Nirvana

High customer
service

High scope of
service

"Our customer is always right—whatever they say we do—
no questions asked. I was going to work on some R&D work
today, but I immediately dropped that to work on a new
customer request."

Figure 8.2
Nirvana scenario.

Nirvana

High customer service

High scope of service

"We switched to complete hourly charge back, so now customer demand is followed with real money. Unfortunately, no one funds infrastructure and R&D directly, so that has fallen aside."

Figure 8.3
Events leading to Nirvana scenario.

4. Debrief the presentation of all the stories. Ask each participant:
   - Where do you think you are now? Where are you going? Where have you been? Why do you think that? How can you measure it?
   - What external events do you anticipate in the next several years? An external event is one you cannot control; for example, a failing economy, a gas shortage, a brand new type of computer, or a large government regulation. Which quadrant would weather these events best?

5. Action Plan: Help the teams create a summary of lessons learned from the discussion of the possible futures. As a group, develop a critical path with action items, dependencies, and owners. Don't let participants leave until they are sure what the next step is.

Exercise: Using Quadrants for Values

Try this exercise for your own team. Come up with two values that are important to your team. Vary them along the four quadrants as previously explained. Describe what each quadrant would look like, and then what events would have to happen between now and the future to get there.

What did you learn? Where do you think your team is now? What would it take to get your team to the desired scenario?

Scenario planning is a powerful tool that shouldn't take more than a couple of good, deep days. The final outcome should be a clear definition of the desired future scenario, where the organization is now, where it will go if it does nothing, and what can be done about it. This final piece becomes the strategic plan. You can document assumptions through the scenario stories and establish milestones to monitor actual results before things get too far down the road.

Strategic planning involves converting the lessons learned from the scenario planning into a project plan. This includes tasks, dependencies, estimates, resource allocations, and milestones—the basic components of any plan (see Chapter 9). The finish date of this project plan is the beginning of the next planning cycle, or a negative scenario that will demand a new strategy. The strategic plan is usually the one that is communicated to customers and staff because it's more pragmatic than the scenario plan.

The scenario plan is something useful for managing the expectations of both customers and staff. It takes a brave but good leader to share the likelihood of serious challenges before they happen. As we noted earlier, contingency planning falls out of scenario planning. At least three of the four scenarios will be undesirable, so you'll need to develop proactive tasks to avoid these futures, or reactive tasks to deal quickly with undesirable events.

Oliver Markley, Professor of Future Studies at University of Houston at Clear Lake, discussed the need for 360-degree vision in a *Fast Company* interview. He believes that 360-degree vision comes from paying attention to the trends going on in the world, and applies the acronym STEEP to tracking trends:

S - Social

T - Technological

E - Economic

E - Ecological

P - Political

He adds an additional analysis to the front end of projects and scenarios, using "premortems," and suggests that you:

- Gaze into the crystal ball six months (or more) ahead.
- Imagine that the outlook is not so good and the project is failing.
- Ask "Why?" and explore the causes.
- Plan to avoid/minimize/overcome these issues before they unfold.

There are different levels of investment and intensity in creating plans, and it's easy to fall into "Analysis Paralysis." A plan is useful when well thought out, concise, and timely.

Exercise: Looking STEEP into the Future

Using Oliver Markley's process, think about future trends that may impact your team.

S - Social

T - Technological

E - Economic

E - Ecological

P - Political

What can you do to prepare your team for these possible futures, or to avoid these possibilities?

Think of a critical project for which your team is responsible. Gaze into your own crystal ball, and imagine that the project is failing. How could that be? What could have happened? Now determine which actions you can take to avoid or react to the events that would create failure.

Influencing: Selling Ideas

In *Exercising Influence* (Berkeley, California: Barnes & Conti Associates, Inc., 2000), B. Kim Barnes describes how to align people by using influencing skills. She defines influence as a precise form of communication exercised with the intent of getting something done through another person or group. You can use these techniques to influence the people on your team and your customers.

Barnes writes that, in this time of drastic change, leaders must learn to consciously choose specific behaviors that achieve successful results. She divides influencing behaviors into two categories: direct and indirect. Figure 8.4 provides a breakdown of both categories.

There are two types of direct influencing behaviors: expressive and receptive. Expressive behaviors send your ideas toward others. Receptive behaviors invite others to send their ideas to you. IT leadership requires both. Indirect behaviors are only used as a last resort. A balance between expressive

Two influencing behaviors: Direct and Indirect
Direct influencing behaviors are Receptive and Expressive.

The Receptive behaviors include:

- Inquire
- Listen
- Attune
- Facilitate

The Expressive behaviors include:

- Tell
- Sell
- Negotiate
- Enlist

Indirect influencing behaviors include:

- Disengaging
- Disarming

Figure 8.4
Categorizing behaviors.

and receptive behaviors is essential under most conditions, especially in times of stress. Examples of each type of behavior follow, along with ways to determine which influencing behavior is most appropriate for each situation.

Receptive Behaviors

The receptive behaviors include:

- Inquire
- Listen
- Attune
- Facilitate

Inquire: Ask Open-Ended Questions or Draw Out   Phrase questions neutrally to learn about the other's issues, needs, or fears. Set aside your judgment and replace it. If you hear something that seems relevant, learn more about it. Don't take offhand remarks at face value. Don't assume that the first response reveals the underlying issue. Use patience and ask questions that go deeper. Pay attention to nonverbal behavior. Leave some silence after you ask to allow the other time to give a thoughtful response. Allow the other time to "vent" if necessary before you respond.

Listen: Check Understanding or Test Implications   You learned a great deal about listening in Chapter 5 "Communication Skills." Here are some others listening tips that will help you influence others. Let the other person know what you understood her to say by paraphrasing. Be open to correction. Make educated guesses based on nonverbal signs or a logical extension of the other's concerns and ask if what you suspect could be an issue. Always state the implication as something that a reasonable person might think. Never put words in the other's mouth that might make her sound wrong or stupid. Use both Inquire and Listen behaviors:

- When someone is behaving in a way that seems uncharacteristically hostile, stubborn, or withdrawn
- When someone responds to your legitimate request with sarcasm or irritation
- When someone expresses anger toward you that seems excessive, given the situation
- When someone gives a flippant answer to an important question
- When a rational discussion suddenly escalates into open conflict

Attune: Identify with Others or Disclose   Step into the other's shoes. Imagine what it would be like to be in her position. See yourself and your behavior from the other's point of view. Have the courage to make yourself a little vulnerable by acknowledging anything that you can honestly say was wrong, inappropriate, or ill-timed about your own actions or behaviors. Be open about your motivations. Use Attune behaviors:

- When someone who is showing signs of stress denies that she is having a problem
- When you think others, especially direct reports, need to know that it is normal to be uncertain, stressed, or fearful
- When you realize that you have behaved in an unproductive way and want to acknowledge your mistake and the impact it may have had on another
- When you want to empathize with others' feelings or fears

Facilitate: Clarify Issues and Pose Challenging Questions   Once the issues are on the table, you can begin to facilitate a problem-solving discussion. State your understanding of the other's issues, which keep her from moving toward resolution. Ask the other for ideas about how you can resolve the issues together. Encourage new and creative options. Generate many options and ideas before you close on any of them. Use Facilitate behaviors:

- To help someone think through how to deal with a conflict or stressful situation
- To help move the discussion toward resolution whether you are a direct or third party to the conflict

Expressive Behaviors

The expressive behaviors include:

- Tell
- Sell
- Negotiate
- Enlist

Tell: Express Needs or Suggest   It is important to let the other party know what you want, need, or are concerned about. You will want to find a way to get these issues on the table without implying that the other party intends to do you any harm. Use Tell behaviors:

- To express your own needs for understanding, forgiveness, and other intangible things
- To give direct and targeted (to the person and the problem) suggestions to someone who seems hesitant to make a decision
- To recommend a fair solution (one that will seem obviously fair to all parties) to a problem situation in which you are directly involved

Sell: Offer Reasons or Refer to Shared Values/Goals   Logical reasoning is often ineffective in conflict situations, but you may be able to "sell" the other party on a solution that allows you to achieve a common goal together. This will work only if your solution does not cause the other party to lose something important. This requires trust between the parties, or the participation of a third party that both trust. Use Sell behaviors:

- When you want to remind conflict participants of their common interests and align them toward a solution. Other common interests can help balance interests that are in conflict.

Negotiate: Offer Incentives or Describe Consequences   If you know about the other party's wants, needs, or fears, you may be able to offer

an exchange; a "quid pro quo." You will give something in exchange for the other party offering you something of equal value. In a conflict, trade-offs may be tangible or intangible. "I can accept this if you will change that," or "I will do this differently if you will change the way you do that." The incentives or trade-offs may be directly related to one another, or unrelated, but of equal value to the parties. The goal is for each party to feel "whole" as a result of the exchange. The consequences of not resolving the conflict must be clear to all parties—and may be stated as long as you do it in a matter-of-fact and non-threatening way. Use Negotiate behaviors:

- Early in any conflict over resources rather than getting involved in unproductive disputes
- Any time you become aware that vested interests are in conflict

Enlist: Envision and Encourage   Expressions of optimism or hope that you will reach a fair and equitable solution can be encouraging early in the discussion. Your behavior must reflect that hope. Whenever it is possible to frame the other person's actions or words in a way that supports this positive vision, do so. You want the other person to "sign up" to this optimistic view of the situation. You can encourage him to work with you in finding a solution by reminding both of you what you value about the relationship. Use Enlist behaviors:

- When you want to encourage someone who is feeling uncertain or stuck
- When you want to help people see a positive future—one that is optimistic but realistic
- When you want to refocus others on your own positive vision

Indirect Influencing Behaviors

Indirect influencing behaviors include:

- Disengaging
- Disarming

Disengaging   The most important of the indirect behaviors in managing stress and resolving conflict is disengaging. It is extremely useful in de-escalating conflict situations. Managing your own behavior under conditions of conflict requires that you know when to take a temporary step back. This may take the form of a short break or a longer postponement. Let the other person know that the disengagement is temporary and that you will re-engage at a time when you feel that you can be more productive. Never say that the other's behavior is a reason for disengaging. That is likely to provoke defensiveness and a further escalation. Use Disengaging behavior when:

- You or the others are experiencing or demonstrating high-stress behavior
- A conflict suddenly escalates and people are behaving unproductively
- The discussion bogs down and people seem withdrawn or uninvolved

Disarming   Sometimes, particularly under stressful conditions, you will find yourself engaged in unproductive battles over unimportant things, putting relationships under strain. At times like that, simply acknowledging that the other person has a point and that you can live with his solution may be appropriate. Use Disarming behavior when:

- You realize that you are getting involved in a conflict over something that doesn't really matter very much to you. Let it go.

These behaviors can help during any period of great uncertainty. Fear, stress, and conflict are normal reactions under such conditions. At the same time, it is important to note whether any employees require additional help. Reactions that continue over a longer period of time than expected or are severe enough to have a strong impact on productivity and morale may require professional help. Your company's Employee Assistance Program (EAP) should have a plan for helping employees with more serious problems.

Exercise: Influencing Behavior

Think of an individual on your team that you have trouble influencing. Which influencing behavior(s) do you normally try? How successful have they been? Using the material in this section, what are other influencing behaviors that you would like to try? Go through the same thought process thinking about a significant internal or external customer.

There is a model from the fields of Neuro-linguistic Programming (NLP) and Accelerated Learning that is useful when influencing others. The research (Lou Russell, *The Accelerated Learning Fieldbook,* Jossey Bass, 1999) shows that people prefer to receive information in a combination of three ways:

- Visually—through seeing
- Auditorially—through hearing
- Kinesthetically—through doing and/or emotion

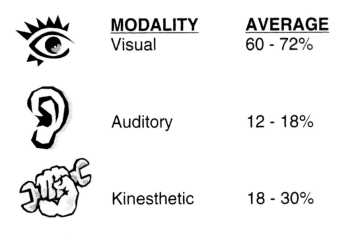

	MODALITY	AVERAGE
	Visual	60 - 72%
	Auditory	12 - 18%
	Kinesthetic	18 - 30%

Figure 8.5
Preferred ways to be influenced.

Figure 8.5 shows the breakdown of preferences across the general population in the United States. Notice that the vast majority of people you will influence probably prefer information to come to them visually. This means they will understand more clearly if you can show them visually that you are either listening (reflective) or explaining (expressive). Often, this is best accomplished through body language and expressions. Be aware of what you are doing. Crossing your arms or legs is an example of body language that communicates a disconnect. Instead, attempt to match the behavior of the other person.

Exercise: Figuring Out Preferences

Using Figure 8.6, guess what your intake preferences are. Think again about the team member that you have trouble influencing. Observe his behavior, and guess what his intake preferences are. It is very likely that they are the opposite of your own. Knowing this, think about ways you could temporarily adapt your behavior to mirror his style, increasing your own ability to influence him. Does he need you to speak less, but draw more pictures? Does he need to draw while you are explaining?

Modality	Eye Movement	Word Usage	Other
Visual	Upwards	I see I can picture Take a look	Dressed in matching colors
Auditory	Straight out	I hear you Listen to this Sounds good	Pauses while responding, rhythmic/measured speech
Kinesthetic	Downward	I get it Let's do it Cool!	Emotional, moving at all times

Figure 8.6
Intake preferences.

It's easy to identify someone's intake preferences. Different preferences exhibit behaviors that allow you to adjust your communication based on these clues. Figure 8.6 illustrates some of these. Of course, people can have many combinations of preferences. They may have an equal need to have visual and auditory communication, or may even need all three. Every person can receive communication using any or all of the preferences. However, people receive new information most effectively when you deliver it the way they most easily receive it.

As you learned in Chapter 5, you will tend to influence using the modality that you prefer, based on the assumption that everyone else is just like you. Often, a communication disconnect occurs not because of the content of the message, but because of the misinterpretation of the delivery of that message. The best influencing occurs when you can show someone, tell them, and help them feel positive about the request. That way, you've covered all the channels.

Conflict Resolution

You learned about conflict in Chapter 4, "Interpersonal and Team Skills." Even with the best techniques there is no way to avoid conflict entirely. Conflict often has tremendous benefits, among them innovation and collaboration. IT is complex, which naturally creates misunderstanding and conflict. Many IT leaders feel uncomfortable and unprepared when faced with conflict, and will avoid it out of fear that it will permanently destroy relationships. In fact, relationships require conflict to evolve, because it creates the change needed for innovation and flexibility. An IT leader who avoids conflict cannot truly lead. Here are some additional tips for conflict situations:

- Use the term "I," not "You." Consider the difference between:

  " You are not making me happy" replaced by

  "I am not happy."

- Stick to facts rather than interpretations or feelings. Consider:

  "This report is the worst I've ever seen" replaced by

  "There are 15 typos in this report."

- Stick to the current conflict. Consider:

  "I'm also mad at the decision you made last year" replaced by

  "I'd like to talk about what happened today."

- Resist mediating a conflict between members of your team until you are asked. Do not intercede without asking for permission to do so.

Systemic Thinking for Problem Solving

When issues get complex and the fixes don't seem to work, it's time to use something besides brainstorming. Systems Thinking (ST) is a powerful technique that allows teams to define the entire problem blamelessly so that a thorough solution plan can be implemented.

Every individual's view of the problem is sane, given his or her data. Yet when combined, those sane views can create insanity. It isn't anyone's fault; it is the fault of the complex but often-accidental system. In this case the word "system" means the variables and influences. Simple questions like, "Why are our projects failing to meet their budget and time goals?" usually cannot be answered with a simple response. Likewise, the solution will have to be complex and systemic if it is to have an impact and address all parts of the system. Quick fixes often fail because they focus on just one part of the problem, rather than the problem as a whole.

In *The Fifth Discipline,* Senge states that today's organizations must adjust, grow, and evolve to survive. Senge says the key is to become an organization that can learn—both from successes and failures. One of the competencies necessary for that is ST—a technique for analyzing and modeling the causes and effects of complex problems, and separating them into manageable pieces so they are better understood before fixing them. ST is best used on the types of issues that keep reappearing despite everyone's best efforts, such as:

- Why are our project skills lacking?
- Why is project management training ineffective?
- Why is it difficult to get IT to collaborate with its internal customers?

The best way to see how ST can help you learn more about a problem is to look at an example. Figure 8.7 is an ST model that is answering the question, "Why is project management training ineffective?" It looks overwhelming, but each loop represents one story (or one perspective). This model is called a Causal Loop Diagram. It reflects the story of the specific group of people involved in creating this model, so for that reason it may not necessarily represent your story. It is the truth as this group perceives it to be.

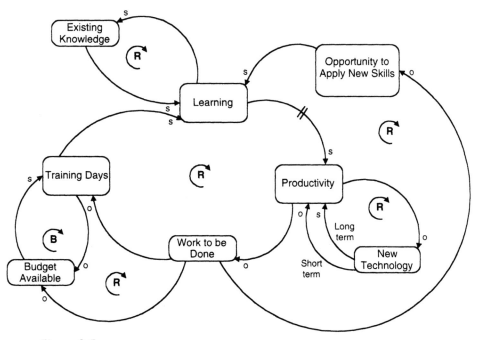

Figure 8.7
The Causal Loop model.

One of the strongest benefits of ST is that it reveals the Mental Models (assumptions) of the participants. In fact, most of the learning that occurs happens in the analysis and creation of the model, not in completing the model. The conversations in building the model will create a strong, shared vision that will allow the team to own the improvement.

To show you how to read this type of model, review the center loop starting with the variable "Training Days." First, you will read the story, then learn how to read the symbols. The story is that the more training days there are, the more learning that occurs. Workers who are learning become more productive. Productivity means that the backlog, or work to be done, decreases. Since work pressures have been lessened, there is more time for learning, and the cycle begins anew.

Here's how to read the model, starting in the same place. As Training Days increase, so does Learning. As Learning increases, Productivity climbs after a slight delay (the double lines). The small "S," in both cases, means that the variables vary in the same direction; for example, as Learning goes up, Productivity goes up. That leads to a decrease in Work to be done, because everyone is working better and smarter, which in turn increases time on Training. This is called a reinforcing loop; it will continue to move in the direction it is going (get better or worse) if left on its own. Notice that this loop can actually be read negatively or positively. Practice reading the loop again to see what happens if Learning decreases. A reinforcing loop spirals up or down depending on the direction of any one variable, which influences all the others. In fact, to correct a reinforcing loop that is spiraling the wrong way, pressure can be applied to whatever variable you have the leverage to influence.

The reinforcing loop is affected by other loops, which keeps it from getting too positive or negative. For example, as Training Days increase, Budget Available drops. The small "O" means that the variables vary in different or "other" directions; as Training Days go up, Budget Available goes down. Then, as Budget Available goes down, Training Days drop, too. This balancing loop functions like a thermostat, moderating Training Days. Also, like a thermostat, it won't let the first reinforcing loop spiral too high or too low. The balancing story in this loop is that Training Days are always capped by a budget. When the money is gone, no matter how much productivity has been increased, the training will be discontinued until the budget money is increased or refunded.

Here's another reinforcing loop. When Learning goes up, Existing Knowledge increases. When we know more, we can learn more, so this increases Learning.

Again, you may not agree with some of the mental models behind the links. For example, we do not believe that there is always a correlation between days of training and Learning. The Training Days could be delivered poorly, or pertain to content that is not timely. However, it is important when reading a model like this that you remember that it represents the reality of the people who created the model. When you create your own model, you will determine what the appropriate influences are.

Easy fixes don't work. Figure 8.7 shows why simply adding Training Days, New Technology, or Budget Available is not sufficient. Just increasing Training Days, for example, will grow the first loop a little, but that loop will ultimately be shut down by the loop that contains Budget Available. Typical fixes to this problem that have been tried unsuccessfully in the past become clearly flawed when you walk through this model. Multiple interventions must be made at different points along the loop; for example, CD-ROM training (more New Technology) might be done in concert with better appraisal rewards (more Opportunity to Apply New Skills).

How do you start? ST starts with a team that has a vested interest in a complex problem. The diversity of this team is critical to the quality of the results. Unfortunately, the diversity is also directly proportional to the amount of conflict in the analysis process, while this conflict is needed to move past the obvious and reveal mental models.

In practice, many participants prefer to work alone initially and then share with their team as their thoughts are clarified (see material on multiple intelligence, specifically Interpersonal vs. Intrapersonal, Lou Russell, *The Accelerated Learning Fieldbook*). Teams must be coached to honor the different processing styles and values as they work together so they know how to leverage their different processing styles.

Variables do not have to have a quantifiable or numeric measurement. They do, however, need to be nouns that will increase and decrease. For example, "Work to be done" is a good variable, since you can have more or less work to be done. "Time" is a poor variable, because time generally doesn't decrease. Adding more description by making it "Time remaining for the project" may fix the problem since it can increase and decrease.

Here are the steps to an ST session. Notice that there are two alternative approaches—Top Down and Bottom Up.

1. The Why Question

   The session starts by uncovering the question that the team wants to answer. The participants are asked to create a "Why" question. Using "What" and "How" should be avoided because they tend to create questions that suggest a specific problem and solution, like "What happened to the project management workshops?" Some examples are:

"Why can't I get through the day without caffeine?"

"Why don't our sales grow more steadily?"

"Why do I have to constantly cut price?"

2. Change the Question

Teams discover the power of the initial question time and time again. The question pinpoints the boundaries of the analysis. The question will evolve as the analysis evolves. It is very rare that a team ends up with the same question it started with. In fact, one of the benefits of ST is that it often provokes you to ask questions you hadn't thought to ask.

3. Top-Down Analysis

The top-down approach involves collectively brainstorming (with Post-Its) all the variables (nouns). The variables should be as neutral as possible (for example, avoid adjectives in the negative like "bad projects"). When the brainstorming starts to slow down, build models using reinforcing and balancing loops, hooking these Post-Its together on large white paper (more details follow). Using this method, teams may identify variables that are outside the scope, so revisiting the "Why?" question frequently helps to control this.

4. Bottom-Up Analysis

The bottom-up approach involves starting with a single variable, generally the noun related to the "Why" question. Successful projects could be the variable that you start with to answer the question "Why are our projects failing?" From here, the teams move forward and backward and tell the story, discovering new variables as they go. They would ask questions like, "If successful projects increase, what would happen?" or "What would happen to influence successful projects to increase?" Eventually the team would complete a whole loop.

From this point, the teams continue to add loops using either variables they have discovered using the top-down method, or by unveiling them through the bottom-up approach. Remember that each loop represents a story of what is really happening. When teams get stuck, the facilitators coach them to tell the story again, checking that the model represents this story correctly.

With practice, teams learn:

- The importance of starting with a shared vision by creating a good "Why?" question (example: Why is it so difficult to keep our skills up to date?)
- Recognizing reinforcing and balancing loops, and validating them against the behavior they observe
- Documenting delays that cause misdiagnosis and poor intervention
- Documenting at least one mental model for each influence
- Brainstorming intervention, even on the simplest models, and thinking through why traditional interventions in these specific situations have failed

ST is difficult, cognitive work. When a model is completed, it is tempting to just hang it up and move on. However, equal time and creative energy needs to be devoted to the interventions since they solve the original problem. We recommend that teams return to the model after a break to talk about intervention.

ST allows people to share their unique perspectives and work together. It can be used to facilitate the creation of a shared vision, common mental models, as well as innovative strategies to fix chronic business problems.

Exercise: Problem Solving

List three problems that you have been trying to fix since you moved into a leadership position. Think about the one that is most bothersome. Phrase that problem as a "Why" question. Then, draw a loop indicating the story of what would happen if there were no problem. Now build the loops around this center loop that are preventing success from occurring.

Building Intensional Networks

In the web-published white paper, "It's Not What You Know, It's Who You Know: Work in the Information Age" by Bonnie Nardi, Steve Whittaker, and Heinrich Schwarz, the authors introduce the concept of "Intensional." They use the term to describe people networks built with effort and deliberateness. They chose "intensional" to indicate the tension—stress, yet tensile strength—of these very personal, informal networks of people.

The emergence of these personal networks seems to have become the main form of social organization inside and out of the workplace to allow work. The rapid pace of organizational and market change makes internal organizational charts unstable, and makes business expertise tough to find and access. At the same time, the Internet provides access to a wider source of business knowledge.

What has replaced the organizational backdrop of work with predetermined roles is a personal assemblage of people who come together to collaborate and meet the needs of a current project. These are not just people who are customers, contractors, or suppliers. These are established relationships that may form the basis for future joint work or (minimally) that transform knowledge. The Internet has accelerated each individual's ability to manage her own intensional network.

Consider how you work today. Suppose you learn that your company has just hired a new executive who used to be at General Electric. You hear through emails from people in the company that Six Sigma is going to be implemented. You think there might be some opportunities for you in this rollout. What do you do?

First, you might search the Internet for something that will help you quickly understand more about Six Sigma. At one of these sites, you notice the name of someone you remember meeting at a conference. You email that person and ask what she is doing with Six Sigma. The contacts increase, and the knowledge is transferred.

The researchers found that it was the sender who determines the appropriate medium based on the needs of the recipient and the developmental history (habit) of interaction. For example, you decide, based on your need and your history, whether to email someone or grab the phone. It also appears to depend on what stage of the project you are in. One interesting phenomena seen in the research is that individuals consciously change their language depending on who they are working with and why. Think about how your language usage changes depending on who your email is going to. It's truly not what you know, but who you know.

Great heterogeneity through overlapping networks gives a sense of connection to workers—even under the conditions of flux that characterize today's economy. These relationships ebb and flow over time and have unique amounts of bonding strength. Emotional intensity, amount of time, intimacy, and ability for reciprocal services were all found to influence the strength of the relationship.

The challenge for individuals is managing the information overload and complexity of tracking the various strengths of different individuals on the network. This requires that you manage three tasks:

- Building a network; adding new nodes ahead of need
- Maintaining the network; keeping in touch
- Activating selected nodes when work needs to be done

As the authors noted: "Relationships are managed and fed over time, much as plants are."

Exercise: Leveraging Intentions

How do you currently leverage your intensional networks? Which of the following requires more attention than you have been giving it:

- Building a network; adding new nodes ahead of need
- Maintaining the network; keeping in touch
- Activating selected nodes when work needs to be done

How could your networks fill in the gaps in your leadership competencies? What do you have to offer to these networks in exchange?

Summary

Strategic Acumen is about seeing the business from the customer's point of view. It is the opposite of viewing projects from the silo of an IT organization. The techniques in this chapter will help you help your people see the perspective of the enterprise as a whole, not the limited perspective of individual stakeholders.

Lessons Learned

Strategic business acumen is composed of many dimensions, but as an IT leader you must have a good understanding of the business you are in. To continue to build this knowledge requires the ability to:

- Communicate with the customers
- Plan both strategically and tactically

- Problem-solve complex business issues
- Network with a global community to meet the business' needs

To build strategic business acumen requires multiple, parallel steps:

- To be an effective IT leader requires that you connect with the business, aligning the vision and work of your organization with the needs of the business and your team.
- Prioritization of work is critical to success; saying "no" to work is as critical as saying "yes." Filtering through a shared vision can accomplish this.
- Looking at multiple futures through scenario planning allows you to build a more flexible, more accurate strategic and contingency plan.
- An IT leader's ability to sell ideas and influence others is a critical competency.
- No business problem has an obvious, quick fix or it would have already been fixed. The discipline of ST allows a leader to think through the obvious, and intervene systemically, while coaching his staff to do the same.
- Intensional networks exist now, and they will grow in importance as business organizations fluctuate. Strong leaders learn how to build an effective network of their own, and respect and leverage the intensional network connections of their staff.

Action Plan/Journaling

In the following section, take a moment to reflect on your own strategic business acumen. Consider the following:

- Does your organization have a clear, shared vision? Does it actively use this vision to prioritize work? Is everyone in your organization clear what business they are part of, what the market influences are, and what the external customer demands?
- Does everyone on your staff agree on the set of products and services that you are chartered to deliver? Do they know how to "say no" to things outside of this scope without alienating the business customer?
- Identify people who are stakeholders in the success of your organization (staff, internal customers, vendors, etc.). How effectively do you influence and sell to them? What could you do differently with the stakeholders who you currently avoid or have conflict with?

- What competency, knowledge, and advice do you need to get from others to supplement your own? Who has it? How can you create an intensional network to fill these gaps? What will be required to nurture and invest in these relationships on an ongoing basis? What existing relationships need more attention from you right now?
- How can you help your staff build stronger intensional networks?
- What meeting processes make sense for your team? How can you get ownership and buy-in from team members to consistently follow the procedures?
- Is there a complex problem in your organization that you have tried to fix again and again, but it keeps coming back and seems to be getting worse? Is there a way to look at it more systemically using a technique like ST?

Take a few minutes in your journal, and describe yourself as you would like to be. What kind of strategic business acumen do you imagine yourself having in the future?

Finally, jot down some quick notes about some first steps you will take to grow into this competency.

Project Leadership

IT leadership requires work on yourself and others but, as in alchemy, the integration of these occurs when you apply the right techniques. Project management provides a systematic way to translate a business need into manageable, well-planned actions. Leaders need to apply strong project management techniques to their own work, since the nature of their work is project-oriented. Leaders also need to grow the project management abilities of those to whom they delegate through coaching. In addition, IT leaders must learn to leverage strong project management techniques to manage the expectations of their internal and external customers.

Opportunities for Growth

- Set, communicate, and monitor project milestones and objectives
- Communicate project status with all stakeholders; prioritize and allocate resources
- Manage multiple, potentially conflicting priorities across a project

- Create and define processes to translate business need into action
- Manage project risk
- Balance established project management and systems development standards with needs for exceptions
- Align decisions with needs of the business

Agenda

What Is a Project?

What Role Does the Leader Play?

Dare to Properly Manage Resources: Define, Plan, Manage, and Review
- Define: Creating a Project Charter
- Plan: Creating a Project Plan
- Manage: Monitoring and Controlling a Project
- Review: Learning from Post-Project Review

Project Management Trends

What Is a Project?

Five things characterize a project. A project has:
- A beginning
- One or more deliverables with criteria that determine whether the deliverables are acceptable
- Temporary resources, including resources that may not be fully available to the project team, and some that may be on a part-time basis
- Constraints, which are usually limits to time, budget, people, but may be in other dimensions as well
- An end

All these provide significant challenges to IT organizations. For example, the actual beginning of a project may be unclear. Tasks that begin as quick fixes often evolve into projects (sometimes on their own). IT is notorious for projects that never end, and the difference between development, production, and maintenance is often just a matter of semantics. How many times have you seen large IT projects go on indefinitely, perhaps with a new team or a new acronym, but essentially the same business need? These types of challenges demand strong leadership from the project manager who owns the planning, organizing, and control of the project, and from the executives who prioritize and fund project work.

Managing temporary resources is another issue that requires strong, pragmatic leadership. IT projects involve multiple roles and skill sets, some used temporarily from inside organizations and some rented from outside consulting firms. In many cases, the project manager does not have hire/fire control over these resources, and often cannot completely control their day-to-day tasks. The organizations to which they report directly can yank them back at any time. Following a post-project review, one organization we worked with realized that whenever a project was in trouble, they reassigned one of their star project members to that project to save it. The problem was, these stars were constantly being moved to new projects, and were never able to stay long enough to be anything but rookies. This revolving door of resources requires leadership with strong planning, organizing, and control, including contingency plans.

In *Getting Things Done: The Art of Stress-Free Productivity* (New York: Viking Press, 2001), David Allen differentiates between tasks and projects by suggesting that if something can be completed in two hours, it is a task; otherwise, it is a project. Two hours may be arbitrary, and each person should figure out what number makes sense for her. The important, underlying concept is that a task can be completed in one sitting. That means that many of the things that are currently sitting on your task list are actually projects, not tasks, and should be managed differently. Allen makes the claim that many of the things on our task list stay there because they are too big to be actionable, so we don't know where to start. He coaches people to begin by brainstorming the next step or two of a project, and putting these on your task list—with a separate list of projects.

What Role Does the Leader Play?

Projects seem to work best when there is a single project manager. However, this is not always feasible, and many companies use multiple project managers. This does add the risk of different visions and strategies, so roles must be designed very clearly to keep the project managers aligned. On many IT Enterprise projects, co-project managers may be from IT and the client area. Collaboration of these two is obviously critical to project success, but it is difficult, since they report to different authorities.

Many project management researchers, including Rob Thomsett, a renowned project management consultant, differentiate between a "technical" project manager and a "real" project manager. A technical project manager is in charge of technical decisions such as the choice of programming languages, architecture, and approval of software design. Real project managers are in charge of budgets, schedules, hiring/firing, and escalation. Individuals who are good at technical project management don't tend to have the same strengths at real project management, and vice versa. Often, subdividing the role of the real project manager into categories like technical project manager, training project manager, customer area project manager, and others can help a business manage the inherent complexity of large ERP projects by mapping the right competencies to the right role. I prefer to use the term "project leader" for these subcategories. The constant communication between these project managers is critical. It works best when there is a hierarchy, with a single real project manager at the top.

Consider the following additional roles:

The Project Sponsor(s)	The executives who are funding this project and own the prioritization and business need
The Project Manager	The person responsible for planning, organizing, and controlling the project
The Project Leader	The person responsible for planning, organizing, and controlling subprojects, and reporting to the project manager

Other roles may include:

The Developer(s)	The people responsible for translating the business need into a technical solution. They also create the resource and time estimates
The Business Experts	The people responsible for defining the need of the business. These people own the requirements and prioritize what is in and out of scope
Stakeholders	The people who will be impacted by this project's completion

As a leader, you may play the role of project manager on many projects. If you are playing the role of a project manager on a very large, mission-critical IT project, you will find it difficult to also play the role of a supervisor/leader. Both of these roles demand a lot of attention. When this is reality, and there is nowhere to delegate either of the roles, plan to time-box chunks of attention on your calendar to ensure that both get proper attention.

Dare to Properly Manage Resources: Define, Plan, Manage, and Review

Figure 9.1 shows a model for remembering the phases of managing a project: Define, Plan, Manage, and Review. In this chapter, our emphasis is on defining the project. The role of leader dictates that there be a strong, clear vision for each project, and this is what comes out of the Project Charter, the deliverable of Define. Many great project management books with additional techniques that are less related to leadership and more related to management are available (see the Bibliography). More detail on all these techniques can be found in Lou Russell's book *Project Management for Trainers* (ASTD, 2001), Alexandria, VA.

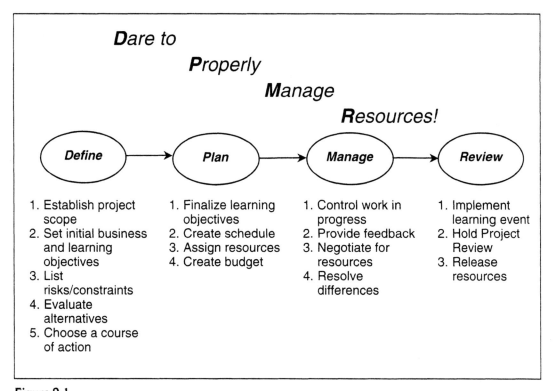

Figure 9.1
Four steps to managing great projects.

Note that the first letter of the mnemonic "Dare to Properly Manage Resources" helps you remember the first letters of the four project management phases. In the following sections, you will learn pragmatic techniques to Define, Plan, Manage, and Review a project.

Define: Creating a Project Charter

IT leaders can increase the success of a project by making sure there are Project Charters. Often, this strategizing phase is skipped, so the team can jump right into the excitement of the new project. Often, that's because the work initially hasn't been determined to be a real project. The Project Charter answers the questions:

- Why is the company doing this project? Why is it important to the business?
- What is the scope of the project? Where are the boundaries?
- What are the constraints and priorities of the project?
- What are the risks associated with this project?
- Who are the stakeholders? Who is the key internal customer contact?
- What are the alternatives for success? What is the cost/benefit analysis?

In the following sections, you will learn about pragmatic ways to answer these questions and build a Project Charter, including:

- Documenting the Why: The Business Objectives
- Documenting the Project Objectives
- Documenting Scope
- Documenting Risk
- Scenario Planning
- Documenting Constraints
- Creating a Stakeholder Communications Plan
- Evaluate Alternatives

Documenting the Why: The Business Objectives   Business objectives may seem obvious at the start, but they rarely are. As soon as possible, make sure all stakeholders are clear about why the business is doing this project and define the potential gains. The business objectives are both the purpose for initiating the project as well as the measurement to judge the business contribution of the project at its end. Often, IT projects proceed without any real business objectives, only to turn into systems that are never used or projects that are canceled long before they are completed. In other words, unless there is a business problem, there shouldn't be a solution.

Business objectives can be easily remembered through the mnemonic IRACIS, which represents the first letters in the phrases that capture the essence of business. All must be clear how the project will:

- Increase Revenue (IR)
- Avoid Cost (AC)
- Improve Service (IS)

In some situations, project work is required to react to government regulatory changes. For example, systems need to be updated to reflect tax law changes. This will not increase revenue, avoid cost, or improve service, although it does generally avoid the costs of fines or media embarrassment. Likewise, many projects strive to create a competitive advantage, such as salespeople who get customer relationship management (CRM) tools to increase their sales. The investment is hoping for long-term revenue growth, although in the short term, this type of speculative investment usually decreases revenue, increases cost, and degrades service.

Example: A Project Management Case to Think About

Here is a fictional leadership case example that will help demonstrate the types of project deliverables that are expected of a successful project manager. You'll see references to this fictional case throughout the entire chapter.

Pretend you have noticed that your team is composed of very talented technical individuals who perform their own tasks very well, but do not work well as a team. In fact, they often end up operating as solos when on projects that need multiple resources. Increasing and enabling collaborative behavior within an existing team is a project, and requires a clear Project Charter.

To uncover the business objectives keep asking, "Why?" Why are your staff members so productive when they are alone? Why do they resist asking each other for help, or holding each other accountable for missed deadlines? Why would the company benefit from increased team collaboration? Why would the individuals benefit? Why would the customer benefit?

Asking these questions could bring about immediate action, eliminating the need for a project. For example, if the customers and company believe there is a benefit to the team being more collaborative, but the team does not, the team is likely the wrong team. An immediate action might be to move the people around and construct a team that is more functional.

Here are the business objectives that you might build to review with the stakeholders:

- By adjusting individual communication to the needs of another team member, the staff can make more timely, higher quality project decisions. *Avoid Cost (of late projects)*
- By establishing team rules of engagement and holding others accountable for following these rules, the staff can work more effectively and efficiently together toward project goals. *Avoid Cost (of late projects)*
- By working more collaboratively, the teams will be able to deliver new products to the market more quickly, gaining market share. *Increase Revenue, Improve Service*
- By working more collaboratively, we can reduce turnover (assuming the turnover was caused by stress, which is not always the case). *Avoid Cost (of hiring and retraining)*

Given these objectives, it's possible to measure turnover after the project is completed, using it to judge the project's success. Measuring collaboration is not as straightforward, and could be done with staff surveys and meetings. Revisiting the business objectives also keeps the project focused, providing criteria for auditing whether project tasks are moving toward or away from the business goals. In a sense, it gives you a way to remain focused on the forest, even when ensconced deeply within the trees.

Documenting the Project Objectives   Creating project objectives can be difficult because they are often created before the requirements are understood. At this point, a one-day discussion with key stakeholders is usually sufficient to build a list of objectives that will be used to measure the completeness of the project. The business objectives specify the return on investment to the business, while the project objectives define the project's deliverables, which will be created to achieve the return. Here is a simplified approach to creating objectives:

A = Audience: Who will be involved in the activity? Who is this objective for?

B = Behavior: What will be done? How will it be measured?

In the fictional case study offered earlier, after discussion with the stakeholders, we might determine the project objectives to be:

- After completing individual and team communication assessments, the business staff member will be able to adjust his/her communication behavior to the needs of another team member.

- The team will create a consensus "Rules for Engagement" agreement for immediate use by 10/1.
- The team will be assessed during performance reviews on its adoption of both new communication patterns and the "Rules for Engagement" next year.

The business objectives clarify why this investment makes sense to the business. The project objectives specify the measurable tasks that must be completed to make sure this investment pays off. Figure 9.2 illustrates this relationship.

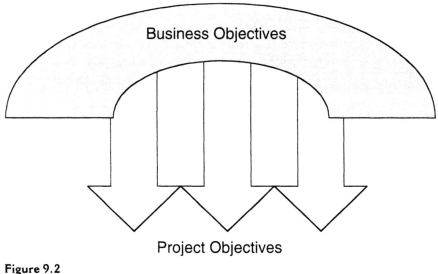

Figure 9.2
Relating the objectives.

Documenting Scope   Scope creep is a common threat to projects. No matter what a project manager does, the business needs *will change* over the duration of the project, and in IT, the technical needs will often change, too. The longer the project, the more likely the needs will change drastically. We cannot freeze scope any more than we can eliminate change. The best tactic for an effective project manager is to *manage* the scope so that all stakeholders understand the change; you can't *control* scope.

At the start of the project, the project manager, customer, and project team members should jointly document the scope. The more stakeholders contribute to creating this document, the more successful the project is likely to be. Also, the customers and project team will know when the scope changes, because they were both involved in the original baseline. A visual model is the best way to document scope, since most people prefer to learn things visually (see Chapter 7, "Customer Orientation"). Many project teams make the mistake of creating scope documents as long texts, and many customers sign off just to avoid the torture of reading the document. In those cases, scope problems won't be uncovered until the project is well under way.

Figure 9.3 is an example of a visual scope model for the fictional case study derived from Ed Yourdon's "bubble charts" used for structured systems analysis. Notice that the boxes show the interfaces to the project—where the input to the project comes from, who receives benefit (output) from the project, and who monitors the project. All the stakeholders are drawn as boxes, and outgoing arrows indicate their needs. This example is very basic, and your models would show the names of the groups or people with whom you are working. You can also identify which project objectives impact which stakeholders by indicating them on the arrows. This gives you a working visual model of the project's scope.

As the project progresses and the business needs change, the project objectives and scope diagram need to be revisited and updated. The business

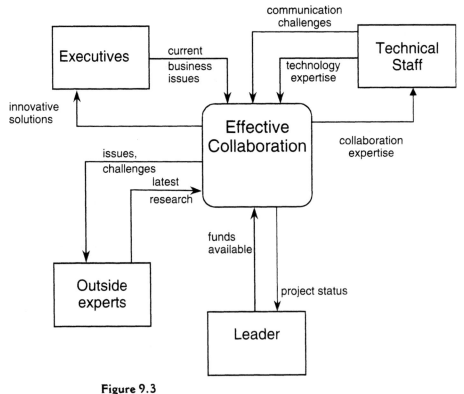

Figure 9.3
A visual scope model.

objectives are not likely to change, but the project objectives will do so as the scope changes. All the deliverables of Define are used in the Manage phase to organize and control the project.

Documenting Risk   Risk is the likelihood that your project will fail. It could fail to meet the needs of your staff, be late, or over budget. The higher the risk, the more likely that one or all of these will happen. So, the higher the risk, the more time the project manager must spend on project management tasks such as status meetings, troubleshooting the schedule or budget, evaluating quality, and other activities necessary to avoid trouble. In other words, the more risk, the more time you'll have to devote to project management.

Although the concept of risk management is familiar, IT project managers tend to do a poor job of it for a number of reasons:

- Businesses tend to "shoot the messenger" of bad news, so project managers talking about bad news even before it occurs are often treated poorly.
- IT practitioners are amazingly optimistic at the start of projects. They are gifted problem-solvers, and love a new problem. Tainting the glow of a new project with negative thoughts is distasteful to them.
- Some believe that if you anticipate a risk and it happens, you will be blamed for the problems created, but if you don't anticipate a risk, you can't be accountable for the impact.

All of these behaviors contribute to project failure that is far worse than the short-term impact feared above. Risk is inevitable, but analyzing and managing risk upfront allows a project manager to strategically:

- Anticipate situations, glitches, and problems to build contingency plans
- Gauge the amount of project management time needed to the amount of risk (more risk, more project management time)
- Manage the expectations of the stakeholders and the project team

A "Quick and Dirty Risk Assessment" technique (see Figure 9.4) can be used with the team and stakeholders to share their expectations of risk relative to others you may have worked with in the past. This technique works best if you do it with your entire project team. Ask each member to privately write down his or her answers (rating 1 through 10) to the following questions:

1. How big is this project compared to others you have been a part of? 1 indicates it's the smallest; 10 indicates it's the largest.
2. How well do you understand the requirements for this project compared to others you have been a part of? 1 indicates that the needs are

completely clear; 10 indicates the needs are undefined. In considering this number, think of:

- How many business areas will be involved? The more business areas, the more disagreement.
- How cooperative are the stakeholders? Will they be able to devote the time, people, and resources? Will they get to the meetings? How hard was it to get this meeting scheduled?
- How supportive is the project sponsor? How much is she willing to risk her reputation to defend the project when it's in trouble?

3. How experienced are you with the technology you will use for this project? 1 indicates the team is very experienced with the technology; 10 indicates the team has no knowledge of the technology.

	small									huge
Size	1	2	3	4	5	6	7	8	9	10
	defined									unclear
Structure/requirements	1	2	3	4	5	6	7	8	9	10
	known									unknown
Technology	1	2	3	4	5	6	7	8	9	10

Average = [   ]

Figure 9.4
The Quick and Dirty Risk Assessment technique.

Now ask all to average their answers and share them. Like the other deliverables you have created up to this point, this is an important step toward managing expectations—yours and others.

Example: Risk Assessment

Think back to the fictional project. Here is how a "Quick and Dirty Risk Assessment" might work out:

SIZE = 4   Assume your five staff members are the only ones involved.

REQUIREMENTS = 8   Although collaboration is obviously needed, you are really not completely sure what that means. Defining what behavior is appropriate for your team and how you will provide incentives for it will be a challenge.

TECHNOLOGY = 1   The only technology needed will be basic.

Average: 4.3

This is a low-risk project that shouldn't require a lot of project management time, especially since the stakeholders are all within your team. However, the requirements number is fairly high, so this is a place that will require more monitoring. If any of the assumptions change, the risk would change as well. This is another deliverable that should be revisited every time the project team gets back together to discuss status.

Here's an example of how things could change on our fictional project as it progresses. Suppose your boss decides that you will include your primary internal customers in this initiative to improve your collaboration with the internal business areas. Technology remains unchanged, but the size of the project would begin to climb to, say, 6, and the requirements would get very complicated, say 10. This project is now more likely to run into some surprises, and the new average of 5.6 reflects that. The project manager must plan to pay very careful attention to the communication patterns and requirements since both could seriously impact the project's success.

Scenario Planning   Another option for risk management is the use of scenario planning, which is more detailed. The concept is similar to the scenario planning technique we used to create a strategic plan in Chapter 8, "Strategic Business Acumen," but its application in project management is not as time-consuming. This technique allows you to document the probability of a risk as well as the consequences to the business. By doing this, the project manager has the data to prioritize her contingency planning investment. We now show how to apply this powerful learning organization technique, which was popularized by Peter Senge in *The Fifth Discipline*.

Gather your project team members and ask them to list glitches that occurred in other projects they have worked on, especially things they wish they had known at the beginning of the project. Then, ask them to brainstorm other potential surprises during this project that relate to people, processes, organizational issues, or technology. Use this brainstormed list to create data as shown in Table 9.1. The group will then rate each scenario's impact to the project—high, medium, or low. Low-impact scenarios can be ignored.

Table 9.1
Risk Scenario Planning

Risk Factors	Likelihood	Impact	Action
Business priorities delay the project activities	M	M	Add time for this likely scenario
Project Manager gets transferred	L	H	Plan meetings for backup to PM
People resources not available	M	H	Prioritize activities to cut if insufficient resources

H = High
M = Medium
L = Low

High-impact (and if time allows, medium) scenarios should be addressed in a contingency plan. The team has the option of either creating a preventative response to the scenario or a reactive response. Sometimes creating both makes sense. For example, for the scenario in which the project manager leaves:

Preventative: Cross-train a backup project manager from the start

Reactive: Freeze the project while the project manager is brought up to speed

This technique provides the following benefits:

- It promotes common, realistic expectations.
- It drives more accurate (and less idealistic) estimating.
- It removes "blinders," helping the project team members anticipate disaster and encouraging them to look for symptoms of glitches so they react more quickly.

This is a good point for the project manager and sponsor to discuss problem escalation procedures. There are always problems that are not anticipated, including external problems (like the software vendor going bankrupt pated, including external problems (like the software vendor going bankrupt in the middle of the project). There should be a mechanism that allows the project manager to escalate the issue up to a higher level where she can get the help and support the issue requires.

Documenting Constraints   All projects are constrained by time, money, and/or quality. The constraints drive the manner in which the project is managed. A project to automate brain surgery should be managed entirely differently than a project to create new standards for filling out timesheets. As part of the project definition, your team can use the technique below to capture the prioritized constraints. Once again, this visual document (Table 9.2) can be used throughout the project to identify when any of the constraints change.

Imagine Table 9.2 shows the consensus of your staff and stakeholders regarding the fictional collaboration project. Quality is the #1 priority, because this is a strategic project and doing it quickly or inexpensively without regard to quality would not make sense. Time is the #2 priority for the same reason that Cost is #3: the longer the behavior goes unchanged, the more money the business loses due to missed project goals.

	# 1	# 2	# 3
Time		X	
Cost			X
Quality	X		

Table 9.2
Prioritizing Constraints

Given these constraints, this project may well cost more or take a little more time than originally planned. Alternately, quality can be maintained by narrowing the scope of the project so as not to increase time or cost. For example, focusing the collaboration improvement on just the senior managers might make sense, allowing the project to be done in phases. When faced with a lack of time or money, a smaller piece can often be delivered without compromising quality.

To create this constraint matrix, ask each person to select his or her first, second, and last priority privately and then share the results as a team. The entire group must agree on these before the project can continue. In situations where the stakeholders were in direct conflict over the priorities, those conflicts must be resolved before proceeding—even if it requires escalating to higher levels of management to do it. No project can be successful when serving two different priorities.

These constraints must be revisited like the other deliverables, because they will almost always change. Whatever the #3 priority was at the start, it will eventually be challenged. For example, if money started out as #3, eventually someone will start putting pressure on the project manager to lower costs. Since most business constraints are relatively arbitrary, they will fluctuate frequently. The project manager can use this deliverable to revisit the priorities whenever the stakeholder's behavior indicates that the constraints are no longer the same.

Creating a Stakeholder Communications Plan   The success of a project often depends as much on the stakeholders and their perceptions as it does on the project manager and the real status of the project. Project managers who neglect to communicate proactively with the people surrounding and influencing the project make a fatal mistake. A stakeholder communications plan lays the groundwork for consensus and buy-in on an ongoing basis. Think of it as project public relations.

The scope model in Figure 9.3 is a good starting place for a communication plan. Each square represents areas with which the project team will need to communicate. With a little additional brainstorming, other people who will be less directly impacted by the project, but are still critical to its success, can be added to the list.

Table 9.3 shows a sample communication plan for the fictional project. Columns 2 and 3 help you gear the communication to the specific business and learning goals of each particular stakeholder. This upfront plan forces you to consider the specific information that each stakeholder needs and when. If in doubt, always err on the side of too much information.

Table 9.3
Communication Plan Layout

Stakeholder	Business Objective	Goal	Communication	Frequency
Team members	Improve service	Collaboration	Strategy	After analysis
			Schedule	After analysis
			Feedback	Mid design
			Performance Review	After design
Executives	IRACIS	Grow business	Strategy (high)	After analysis
			Baseline	Monthly
			Budget	Monthly
			Results	Monthly
Outside experts	Increase revenue through visibility	Collaboration research	Strategy	After analysis
			Schedule	After analysis

Evaluate Alternatives   There are always alternatives to every project, including "don't do it." It's difficult to cancel or end most projects, so think very carefully about initiating one when you have the choice.

There are usually alternate ways in which business problems can be solved. Minimally, there are solutions that are mechanized or not. Each possible configuration should be evaluated in terms of its cost/benefit ratio: what are the initial and ongoing costs balanced against the initial and ongoing paybacks? There are many ways to calculate cost/benefit including Return on Investment (ROI), Internal Rate of Return (IRR), and Payback Period. For project management use, it is not as important which calculation you use but more that you apply the same calculation to each alternative the same way.

Exercise: Define Deliverables

Using a project you are about to begin, or one you are currently working on, create the following Define deliverables:

- Business Objectives
- Project Objectives
- Scope Model
- Quick and Dirty Risk Assessment
- Risk Scenarios
- Stakeholder Communications Plan

Plan: Creating a Project Plan

In the Project Plan, your tasks include:

- Creating the Schedule
- Creating the Work Breakdown Structure
- Critical Path Method: Activities and Dependencies
- Estimating
- Assigning Resources
- Project-Related Work
- Environmental Factors
- Gantt Charts
- Project Management Software
- Creating the Budget

A project never goes exactly as planned. Most projects will require a major shift in strategy at some point. Think of the plan as the strategy—when you notice the Project Charter is changing, your strategy will change as well. You will have a *new* Project Plan, but you will still *have* a Project Plan. We call this "flexible structure." Refusing to abandon a flawed project plan destroys projects.

As you read in the previous section, the Project Charter is never done. The same is also true for the Project Plan. As you begin to do more research into the project requirements, you will discover more about both the business and the project objectives. It isn't surprising to learn of new objectives after the project has been started. Often, the complicated or troublesome issues are not revealed to the developer or project manager until the project is well underway. People don't like to start with bad news, so expect surprises.

Creating the Work Breakdown Structure   A Work Breakdown Structure (WBS) is a hierarchy chart that helps you brainstorm activities for a project. Figure 9.5 shows a WBS for the case study project. The WBS is created from your organization's development standards and your experiences. This is a working document that is not retained as part of the Project Plan once it is turned into a schedule.

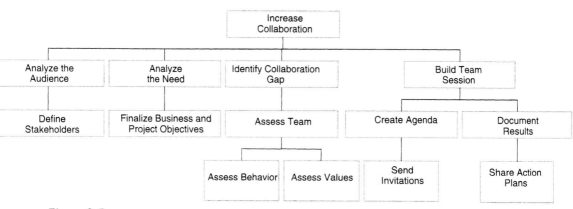

Figure 9.5
The Work Breakdown Structure.

When building a WBS, brainstorm to an activity level detailed enough for you to estimate how long it will take to complete each activity. These low-level activities are called tasks. Using David Allen's definition, a task is something you can complete in one sitting. Depending on the complexity of the project, your lowest level may end up representing a subproject, whose subproject plan describes activity to the lower task level. If you are responsible for all the activities on the WBS, the lowest level should be at task level.

You may find that you are not comfortable thinking in a top-down fashion such as this. Some people prefer brainstorming at a detailed level, with piles of Post-Its, and then grouping them from the bottom up into a WBS. Others prefer to begin in the middle, and work up and down. Whichever method fits your personal style is the right one for you to use. If you are part of a team, remember to honor the needs of others to process in different ways.

Sharing these charts with other people may help you discover gaps in your thought process. Even if you have to do the project alone, consider borrowing the brains of your friends to help you in this strategic planning activity. Here's a checklist to help you succeed:

- Have you considered project management activities like status meetings, reviews, and the construction of project communication plans?
- Have you considered all the activities that will have to be done by people outside your direct influence, such as printing, design, programming, or video work?
- Have you considered all the research that you will need to do?
- Have you considered all the groups with which you must interface, including support services, operations, testing, security, disaster recovery, etc.?

The WBS is a stepping stone toward the schedule. If you find it easier to brainstorm in other ways, replace this step with other techniques. For other brainstorming alternatives, I recommend reading Michael Michalko's *Thinkertoys* (Berkeley, California: Ten Speed Press, 1991).

Creating the Schedule   The schedule is composed of four parts:

- The tasks that need to be completed
- The sequence of the tasks
- The people that will do each task
- The time each task will take

The sequence of the tasks is best shown with a visual diagram (see Figure 9.6) illustrating which tasks are the most critical, which depend on other tasks, and which should be done first (and second, and third . . .).

Figure 9.6 shows the beginning of a critical path chart based on the generic WBS in Figure 9.5. Notice that this diagram shows that some tasks must be completed before others can begin. The tasks are identified with square boxes, and the lines between the tasks show dependencies. By definition, if a task follows another connected with a dependency, the first task must be completely finished before the next can begin. In practice, dependent tasks are often started before the predecessor is completely done. This diagram shows that some tasks can be done in parallel, some can start at any time, while others must wait for predecessor tasks. This type of predecessor dependency is often called task or activity dependency. As people are assigned to tasks, new dependencies may emerge. One person cannot work on two different tasks at the same time, so a choice must be made to place one ahead of the other. This is called people dependency.

A critical path diagram.

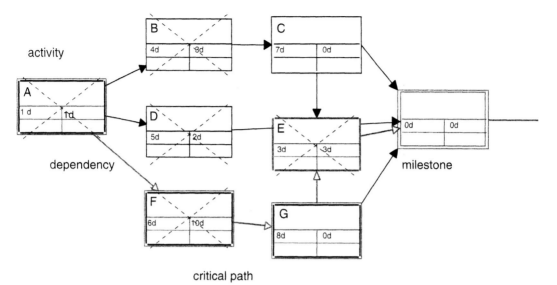

Figure 9.6
Critical path diagram.

Milestones are different than tasks because they do not take any time. They provide places to stop and check progress. Tasks usually precede milestones for status meetings, or some other review activity, and some people use these tasks for milestones. Milestones may also be used as approval points at which contracted work is paid for or interim deliverables are completed.

The next step is to estimate how long each task will take. This will depend on the complexity of the task, the expertise of the people working on it, the number of people and organizations involved, and the culture of the company where the work is to be performed. In the next section, you will learn a process for estimating that takes all of these into account.

Estimating   There are two different types of estimates: duration and elapsed time. Duration is how long an activity would take if a person of average experience worked on it non-stop. For example, an average IT staff member at your company might need four hours to install a new version of Windows. Upgrading 50 desktops would then take 200 hours duration.

However, we cannot expect a developer to work on something for 200 hours without stopping, even armed with very good coffee. This is where the second kind of estimating comes in: elapsed time. Elapsed time is the amount of calendar or clock time that will pass before the activity is completed. For example, the duration of 200 hours of upgrade work might actually take 10 weeks of elapsed time. Elapsed time is calculated using three add-ons: expertise, project relation, and environmental.

Assigning Resources   Risk is reduced when more experienced people execute the project. Expertise can significantly lengthen or shorten the duration of an activity. For example, a person who has never done upgrades will take much longer to complete the upgrade than a person who has been doing them for many years. There are two different kinds of expertise: expertise in the activity and expertise in the content. The example we just cited is upgrading expertise, which involves expertise in the activity.

Many IT projects benefit from business expertise, which is knowledge of the business area. Similarly, if you have a choice between one installer who has significant knowledge of the business area in which the upgrades are taking place, and one who does not, you'll probably choose the developer with knowledge. She will need less elapsed time to complete the project and won't have to perform as much research or needs analysis about the order in which she should upgrade the machines.

Programmers at AT&T during the late 1970s were taught how to apply estimating factors to project plans based on Bell Labs research that is no longer published. The expertise of a project team member was regarded as the single most influential factor upon elapsed time. Before you can judge the elapsed time of an activity, you must find out (or decide) who will work on it, because that can change the duration of a project by .5 to 4.0 percent.

To adjust for activity expertise, the project manager multiplies the duration by .5 to 1.5 (.5 for a great deal of expertise and 1.5 for none). For knowledge expertise, the project manager multiplies duration—which has already been inflated by the activity expertise factor—by a factor between .75 to 4.0 (high expertise to low).

Let's assume our developer has average experience in upgrading this type of computer, but no expertise in the business area. The calculation would be:

Duration = 200 hours

Activity Expertise = 1.0

Subtotal (200 × 1) = 200 hours

Content Expertise = 2.5

Adjusted Duration (2.5 × 2) = 500 hours

The figure is daunting, but it speaks loudly to the fact that almost all up-grades exceed time and budget. As seen below, the existing relationships in a business area—as well as a clear understanding of the business priorities—can dramatically influence the success of this kind of project (as can the absence of both).

No experience adjusted duration: (200 × 1.5 × 4) = 1200 hours

Highly experienced adjusted duration: (200 × .5 × .75) = 75 hours

Project-Related Work The second add-on to the original duration is project-related. This is the amount of time you add to the duration for the communication necessary to ensure a successful project. This figure is most influenced by the number of people involved in the project, but also by the risk of the project as described earlier. As the number of players and organizations ratchets up, communication takes exponentially more time. A factor of .10 (less risk) to .20 (more risk) is now added to the adjusted duration. Continuing our example, assuming moderate risk:

Adjusted duration after expertise add-on: 500 hours

Adjustment for project-related communication: + .15

New adjusted duration (500 + 75) = 575 hours

Adding Environmental Factors The final adjustment is for environmental tasks, which are non-project tasks (.25 to .35). This accounts for the time a business requires employees to do tasks other than project work, such as checking and responding to their voice or electronic mail. It also builds in a cushion for illness, vacations, and events like company meetings. The best way for a project manager to estimate how much should be added to account for this factor is to track the percentage of the average workday that is devoted to non-project work. For example, if you work an eight-hour day and can usually spend six hours on project work, you have 25% overhead for environmental work. This add-on will be the same for each activity, so many project managers add an activity before each milestone—holding 25% of the adjusted duration for that chain of tasks for environmental work, rather than inflate each activity. It is critical to remember that this factor is not fluff and is not a safety net for project problems. It is the actual time that is going to be used for non-project-related tasks. Returning to our example, the final adjustment is:

Adjust duration so far (after expertise and project related): 575 hours

Environment adjustment: + .25

Elapsed time (575 + 143.75) = 718.75 hours

Essentially, this estimating method converts duration to elapsed time. Duration does not tell how long it will actually take to finish a task. This is a common mistake. If you think your project is going to take the total of all the activity *duration*, say, 40 hours, you and your stakeholders will be very upset when you find that projects actually take the *elapsed* time of all tasks, which might be as much as 200 percent more. This is how many projects get into trouble right at the start.

The Critical Path   At this point, it's time to add the people dependencies and the elapsed time estimates to the critical path diagram. When there is more than one parallel path, the longer path is called the *critical path*. The shorter path has *slack time*, which is the difference between the longest path and this path. In other words, the shorter path allows a little extra time. This extra time is for the whole path, not each activity (a common misconception). This final critical path diagram, shown in Figure 9.7, makes it easier to see the

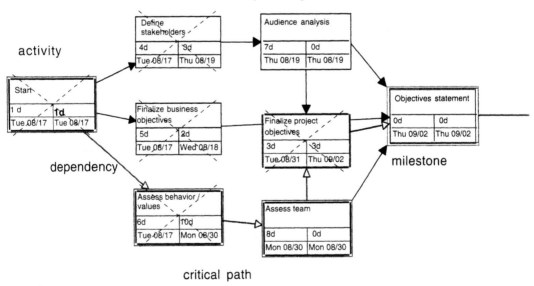

The final critical path diagram.

Figure 9.7
The final critical path diagram.

dependencies involved in the tasks. This diagram is excellent for monitoring the work on the critical path, which impacts the completion of the overall project when behind schedule.

PERT charts are special types of critical path diagrams laid out with a timeline across the bottom. This adds a management dimension that is missing from ordinary critical path diagrams. Many people prefer to use a separate diagram called a Gantt chart to view tasks by calendar date.

Gantt Charts   A project manager also needs to be able to manage a timeline, and needs to know what tasks should be happening at any given point in time. This calendar view can be represented with a chart called a Gantt chart, or bar chart. Gantt charts can represent different views of the project activity against a calendar. Figure 9.8 shows an example of a Gantt chart.

Partial Gantt Chart

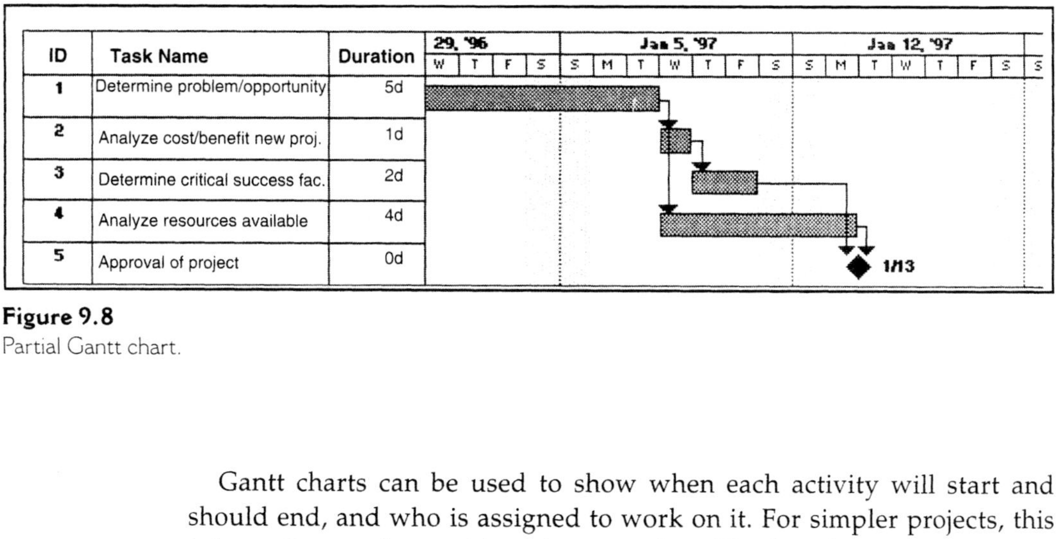

Figure 9.8
Partial Gantt chart.

Gantt charts can be used to show when each activity will start and should end, and who is assigned to work on it. For simpler projects, this information can be combined into one chart like that shown in Figure 9.9. With more complex projects, Gantt charts may be created for each milestone, or for each person, showing only her tasks. However, this type of chart may make it more difficult to discern the critical tasks and their dependencies. As the project struggles and the project manager needs to reassign people, the original critical path diagram can be used to stay focused on dependencies, while the Gantt chart can be used to monitor elapsed time and people loading.

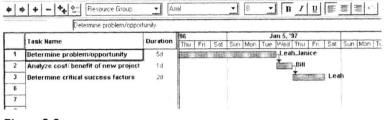

Figure 9.9
Partial resource Gantt chart.

Project Management Software   If your project is fairly complex, you may find it cost-effective to use project management software to create a plan and maintain it. Some software products like Microsoft Project™ keep all your information in one place, but allow you to view it in different ways. You can look at your project as a critical path diagram, as a Gantt chart, from an individual's perspective, from a date perspective, or in almost any combination you can imagine. Here are some considerations about using software, and how to manage it if you do:

- PM software can be very time-consuming. Sometimes you can waste a lot of time trying to do something that the software cannot handle easily. Time-box your computer time so you don't end up doing project management software work instead of project work.
- Sometimes, if your project is small-risk, a simple drawing is sufficient for managing the project. A good drawing package, without all the calculations and logic of project management software, may be enough to make it attractive—but not so complex that it draws your attention away from the project.
- Consider asking someone with knowledge of the tool to enter your hand-drawn project plans into the computer. This way you can stay focused on project management, and he or she can help you with administration.
- A good guideline for project management software is to let the software calculate dates from your task estimates as much as possible. In other words, avoid entering dates, unless they are fixed. This gives the software more flexibility to re-flow the dates when actual activity time is more or less than planned.

Creating the Budget   The more complex the project, the more critical it is to manage the budget carefully. The costing worksheet in Figure 9.10 is an example of a worksheet used to document the budget at the start of the project and then manage the budget as actual project work is completed.

EXPENSE ITEM	PROJECT COST	ACTUAL COST
Labor		
• People		
• Contractors		
• Vendors		
Environment		
• Work space		
• Supplies		
• Computer equipment		
• Software		
• Services		
Process		
• Books		
• Methodology		
• Training		
Organization		
• Meeting expense		
• Conference calls		
• Travel		
• Room rental		
• Refreshments		

Figure 9.10
Managing costs with a worksheet.

If you are the only one on the project, you may not find it necessary to be this rigorous in your budget management. However, one difference between an IT manager and an IT leader is that the leader is aware and accountable for managing costs, because they matter to the business.

Exercise: Timing Your Project

Create a plan for a project that you are about to begin. Brainstorm the activities, then use the estimating loading factors to determine the actual elapsed time. Build a critical path network of the tasks, and calculate the end date of the project.

Manage: Monitoring and Controlling a Project

Unfortunately, the minute the project begins your plan is out of date. Throughout this chapter, you have learned about the importance of "flexible structure." Your Project Plan will change often, if not immediately. Many of the deliverables your customers thought they wanted during the planning steps will have changed by the time the tasks begin. This may include new tasks, removed tasks, and changed resources—but the most common change will be that the time estimates are now too short. Scope, money, and quality may change as well. In this section, you will learn how to manage inevitable, but normal, project change.

It is impossible to anticipate all the events that will occur in a project before you get into the nitty-gritty. It is also impossible to freeze the customers' needs since business and technology change is constant. Keep yourself from getting too attached to the Project Plan. This is not to say that you will make every change requested of you. Your focus needs to remain squarely on the project stakeholders who have requested that you meet the project objectives in order to meet the business objectives. This is a critical concept: it is not *your* project, it is *their* project. You are the manager of their request. They make the decision as to when to change the plan to reflect a new need, and you implement the changes. Project managers trying to fight the needs of the business as it changes will expend a great deal of energy on futility. Managing well requires that the project manager implement her communications plan and share information about the trade-offs. In this section you'll learn to:

- Establish Monitoring Criteria
- Manage Project Change
- Troubleshoot

There are two steps to dealing with project change: identifying the change and managing the change in an effective way. Establishing monitoring criteria is the way you ensure that changes are visible. A costing worksheet such as the one shown in Figure 9.10 will help track variance.

Establish Monitoring Criteria   In this section, you will learn how to build the monitoring criteria from the documents in the Project Definition, including:

- Risk assessment
- Constraints
- Scenarios

In addition, you will draw monitoring criteria from the Project Plan, including:

- The Schedule
- The Costing Worksheet

Each of these components will be monitored so that you can implement "flexible structure."

Risk   You'll recall from earlier in this chapter that the risk assessment for the collaboration case study project was a 4.3. The fact that the requirements are not clearly understood created project risk, and making a list of anticipated risk factors was part of the risk scenario document (Table 9.1). During this time, the project manager must remain vigilant in looking for signs that these risk factors are actually coming to fruition. Some of the signs that might indicate trouble are:

- A staff with different "favorite approaches" to development
- A "we must build it here" attitude prohibiting research and/or external help
- A "we must get it outside" attitude prohibiting flexibility and/or creativity
- Reluctance from anyone to attend meetings
- Reduction in customer involvement

One of the highest risk factors for the fictional case was that the key business sponsor leaves. This is always a serious event, because without sponsorship, the project will founder. As a project manager, you can keep your ear to the ground by:

- Meeting regularly with others who might know of sponsor changes
- Listening for rumors of reorganizations and asking questions directly

Constraints   Another part of the Project Definition involved prioritiz-ing the project's constraints (Table 9.2). As you'll remember, only one con-straint—time, cost, or quality—can be the top priority of a project at a time, although these priorities can and do change.

Here's an example of how this might happen. In the fictional case study, the constraints during the Define phase were prioritized as #1 quality, #2 time, and #3 cost. The Project Plan would reflect the importance of having a high-quality product, so there would be many checkpoints, reviews, and walk-throughs. Sending multiple customers and multiple developers to these meetings would take time and build up a significant labor cost.

Suppose on the first day of the project none of the customer staff members show up to the first meeting. As you call to see what's going on, they each tell you that they are too busy with business issues to participate in this meeting. However, they would like to be involved in the final—but not the prelimi-nary—walk-through of the plan so that they can offer suggestions. Obvi-ously, it will be impossible to deliver a high-quality product in a timely fash-ion without staff involvement.

What do you do? You might ask for a quick one-hour status meeting. You tell them that you have stopped the project until they are available for the meetings. You revisit the constraints and explain that if quality is truly #1 (which is also supported by business objectives that were created jointly in the Define phase), then the project will need their participation all the way through. Anyone who does not participate in the beginning will not be per-mitted to critique later because of the second constraint, which is time. If new voices show up at the end of development, then the project will have an ex-tended timeline. Since cost is the lowest constraint, you suggest the follow-ing alternatives:

- Stop the project until involvement is possible
- Designate one dedicated staff member to help develop a prototype plan
- Hire some temporary help to free up the staff members so they can par-ticipate (spend money to "buy" quality)
- Change the scope of the project so that quality is maintained for a smaller piece, reducing some time and cost of involvement
- Change the constraints and the Project Plan

If these options do not work, then the customer's behavior tells you that the constraints are not prioritized correctly. If business staff members are un-willing or unable to spend time or money, as their behavior indicates, then quality is not #1 and money is not #3. That makes it critical to revisit the con-straints diagram and come to an agreement consistent with current behav-iors, because the project cannot be successful in its current state.

Schedule   Time is monitored through the critical path diagram and Gantt charts. In most project management software packages, you can view both planned and actual times for each activity. This is critical if you plan to use the software to help you monitor the project.

Check your project management software to see how it handles actual and planned activity times. As a project manager, you want to look forward using the planned tasks, but monitor trends and glitches through the actuals. The critical path (or longest path of time), which the project manager must monitor carefully (see Figure 9.6), can change due to those actuals. When the duration of a task that is not on the critical path increases, it can push that path to become the critical path, giving you a new critical path as seen in the second example (see Figure 9.7).

If you have a fixed due date for a milestone or for the end of the project (which is not unusual), adding actual completion times that extend the project beyond the initial due date will place every activity on the critical path. When using software, this becomes obvious because the critical path tasks are often color-coded. It feels staggering to watch your whole plan "go red" after entering actual completion times.

This is where the guideline noted earlier (about letting the software calculate dates from your activity estimates) becomes critical. This gives the software more flexibility to re-flow the dates when actual activity time is more or less than planned. Some software packages can do unpredictable things with tasks that require more time than the fixed dates allow, including loading resources up to 24 hours of work in a day, or allowing resources to work on 10 tasks at the same time. Always view these charts with a good dose of common sense, watching for these kinds of unrealistic adjustments.

Budget   During the Manage phase, the project manager must track the actual costs of the project and compare them to the budget items. There is capacity for managing dollars at activity levels in most project management software packages, but some prefer to track using a spreadsheet. Either way, keep an eye on the costs, watching for the start of insidious trends. The quicker you spot these trends, the quicker you can take corrective action.

Manage Change   The phrase "Manage Change" differs significantly from "Control Change." Managing change requires that you create a change management plan before project work begins, because such plans are seen as defensive if they are developed out of panic. This deliverable is part of a development approach and is traditionally not thought of as a project management deliverable, although it is critical to the progress of a project. Sadly, developers often bypass this document to avoid conflict with the customer at the start of the project. A change management plan should document the following:

- What will happen when the scope appears to change?
- How will the customer and the development team prioritize changes?
- How and when will problem escalation occur?

Imagine change management based on a boat metaphor. A Level I change request means that the boat is taking on water, but could easily survive with a little bailing. A Level II change request means that the boat is taking on enough water that it has started to sink, but could probably hang in there for a little bit of time. The Level III change requests are "Titanics," which require immediate attention. If the project manager communicates the trade-offs well, the customer ultimately makes the final choice.

More likely, a change will initially be stated as something that was in the original requirements. For this reason, the scope diagram created in the Define phase is critical for determining whether something is truly a change or not. The scope document can never be clear enough to resolve all debates, but it will be a useful tool in the negotiation process.

Troubleshooting (What To Do If You're Behind and It's Your Behind)

Here are some tips for managing project problems. Remember, you *will* have project problems, and something *will* slip. Time is almost always trouble because it is the easiest to measure. Many projects are given arbitrary due dates simply to have a date. Any project date with a "1" in it, like 09/01, is usually arbitrary, especially if these dates fall on a weekend. The first thing to do when you need more time is to challenge the due date. If you find that things are taking much longer than you had expected, here are some other options:

- BEST: Cut the scope of the project and roll out the objectives in phases. Do a great job on a smaller piece, deliver it quickly, and then leverage that success to roll out the rest. Many of the up-front bottlenecks, such as agreeing on terminology, the look of the screens, the flow, and the overall form, will be resolved by the first piece, easing the way for the later modules.

  Risk—if the project is not something you can subdivide while maintaining the required business performance, quality suffers.

- MIGHT WORK: Get some money to add resources to the project. Outsource tasks such as programming or video production that are chewing up lots of time. Hire an expert in a skill area that your team lacks.

Risk—adding people to a project always adds communication time and can put you further behind. Remember, for every one person you add to a project team, you lose some percentage of everyone else's time to bring the new person up to speed.

- PROBABLY WON'T WORK: Ask for more time. If time is the #1 priority, this won't work. If it does, it wasn't really the #1 priority. It's always a good idea to test the constraints. If it does work, this is the easiest solution.

  Risk—work expands to fill time.

- BAD IDEA: Pretend everything is okay. This forces everyone to deliver poor quality, creating piles of rework and distrust.

Cost   Surprisingly, money is a pretty difficult commodity for project managers to measure. If you've brought in a lot of outside people; purchased expensive software, hardware, or equipment; or spent money on "hard" dollar items that are easy to notice, you will encounter pressure to reduce cost. Internal people costs are somewhat measurable, although the numbers are often artificial. You may get pressure to cut staff to reduce costs. Project development hours themselves are also difficult to measure accurately. Here are some options for cutting costs:

- BEST: As previously mentioned, cut the scope of the project, and roll out the learning objectives in phases. Do a great job on a smaller piece, deliver it quickly, and then leverage that success to quickly work on the rest. If people are really cost-conscious, because the project is more strategic than tactical, adding phases will be well received.

  Risk—if the business need is not something you can subdivide and still get the performance, quality will suffer.

- MIGHT WORK: Ask for more time so that the resources currently aligned to the project can continue to work on it.

  Risk—adding labor time actually adds cost (of hours for the work). Sometimes this is not an issue, depending on how closely you account for hours.

- PROBABLY WON'T WORK: Ask for more money. If money is the #1 priority, this won't work. If it does, it wasn't really the #1 priority and you'll get some money to add resources to the project. Hire an expert in a skill area that your team lacks.

  Risk—adding people resources to a project always adds communication time and can often get you further behind.

- BAD IDEA: Pretend everything is okay. This forces everyone to deliver poor quality, creating piles of costly rework.

Quality   Project managers are often emotionally stunned when quality becomes an issue. The customer wants the best and may have many ideas about how to improve things—your area of expertise. The most critical aspect is to keep your ego out of the way, which is a very difficult thing to do. As a developer, you take great pride in your work and want to be appreciated for it. Being critiqued by someone outside the field can be humbling. However, it is critical to remember at all times that this is not your deliverable—that it belongs to, and is being funded by, the customers. They are the ones who will judge whether it is good or not. They are the ones who understand the business context in which it will be implemented. Here are some other thoughts on how to handle quality critique:

- BEST: If the change is within the scope, make the change quickly. If the changes start to cycle (changing something back after it was changed to something new), begin to log the changes so you can explain the cost of this constant tuning to the customer. If the project has quality as the #1 constraint, you should be tuning at all costs and time; otherwise, inform the customer as to the effects of the changes in terms of time and cost. Draw a line at what you can change for fixed-bid contracts. Cut the scope of the project and roll the objectives out in phases.

   Risk—negotiating changes is a critical success factor for project trust. It is critical that you are honest about how you feel with yourself and with your customer.

- MIGHT WORK: Ask for more time so that resources currently aligned to the project can continue to tune the project.

   Risk—adding labor time can sometimes hurt quality because of the increased communication.

- PROBABLY WON'T WORK: Ask for more money. Money is commonly not useful for buying quality, because it adds new people and technology, which adds complexity to a project. It might work if you obtain money to hire an expert in a skill in which your team is lacking.

   Risk—adding people to a project always adds communication time and can often put you farther behind.

- BAD IDEA: Pretend everything is okay. This forces everyone to get angry at one another. A project cannot be successful if the customers and the developers are at odds. Avoid this at any cost because it creates a negative reinforcing loop from which it is very difficult to break out.

Review: Learning from Post-Project Review

When the project is completed, it is tempting to move on. A review allows learning to occur after projects are over. As project teams move quickly from finished projects to new projects, they fail to take time to reflect upon what happened and the ramifications on future project work. The Post-Project Review, discussed in this section, identifies lessons learned and helps you change the behavior you bring to future project work. This activity grows an organization's project management expertise.

Unfortunately, very little post-project reflection occurs. Research from the Project Management Institute (PMI) points out that most projects fail to meet quality, cost, and/or time goals—and these statistics have not changed by much since the original measurements were made more than 20 years ago. Even with advancing technology, new methods, and lots of new research, project teams still make the same mistakes.

That's not to say that your project will be exactly the same as someone else's. There are certain events that occur in many projects, such as scope creep and communication problems. Issues like these will be revealed in a Post-Project Review. In this section, you'll learn about:

- A Sample Post-Project Review Template
- A Sample Process for Post-Project Review

A Sample Post-Project Review Template   The Post-Project Review gathers information about a project's manageable items:

- Time and deadlines
- Costs and budget
- Specifications and learning objectives
- Staffing
- Technology, tools, and techniques
- Monitoring performance
- Corrective action
- External vendors and stakeholders

If you remember the initial Project Charter, the three high-level components of risk were size, requirements, and technology. The four project priorities documented as constraints were time, cost, quality, and scope. Basically, these review questions cover these areas. In addition, it helps to revisit any scenario planning performed as part of the Project Charter, and to reflect on the accuracy of the scenario events brainstormed and the action plans proposed.

A Sample Process for Post-Project Review   As we mentioned in the beginning of this chapter, even if you are the only one executing a Post-Project Review, there is tremendous value in answering the questions (see

Figure 9.11). Personal reflection creates personal improvement, so your time is well invested. However, there is real organizational leverage when the whole project team answers these questions together. Here's a suggested process for performing this while investing minimal time:

Step 1: Individually reflect on the project using the Post-Project Review questions (time needed: < 1 hour).

Step 2: Summarize all the responses in one document, without using names, for review by all (time needed: summarization = 2 hrs., review < 1 hour).

Step 3: Spend a half-day with the entire team covering the following agenda:

- Create a list of the Top 10 lessons learned, based on the survey responses and any new thoughts.
- Create a statement for future projects: Helpful Hints.
- Plan a strategy for sharing this information with future project teams (include the Project Charter information so the context of the project is clearly understood).

1. How close to the scheduled completion date was the project actually completed?
2. What did we learn about scheduling that will help us on our next project?
3. How close to budget was the final project cost?
4. What did we learn about budgeting that will help us on our next project?
5. Upon completion, did the project output meet customer specifications without additional work?
6. If additional work was required, please describe.
7. What did we learn about writing learning objectives that will help us on our next project?
8. What did we learn about staffing that will help us on our next project?
9. What did we learn about monitoring performance that will help us on our next project?
10. What did we learn about constraints that will help us on our next project?
11. What techniques were developed that will be useful on our next project?
12. What recommendations do we have for future research prior to a project?
13. What lessons did we learn from our dealings with outside contractors?
14. If we had the opportunity to do the project over, what would we do differently?
15. What would we do the same?

Figure 9.11
Post-Project Review questions.

If possible, use a neutral facilitator to manage the face-to-face meeting. The project manager will be tempted to perform this meeting, but she will be too close to the issues to do a fair job. Since it may be difficult to get funding for a facilitator (especially when the project is already over budget), you may be able to borrow a facilitator from another project with the promise of reciprocity.

Systems Thinking (see Chapter 8) is a technique that can be used for more systemic project review. Consider investing in the use of ST when mission-critical projects are completed.

Exercise: Questioning Your Project

Using the Post-Project Review questions from this section, reflect on a project that you have completed. What lessons are you surprised to find that you could have used on a current project?

Project Management Trends

If the risk of unstable requirements is high, you have customer commitment, and the project is mission-critical, consider taking a more agile approach to your project, such as what's spelled out in "The Agile Manifesto," *www.agilealliance.org*. This new approach to development is being adopted in many different areas, from IT system development (Kent Beck's "XP"—Extreme Programming) to course development ("Agile Development," Lou Russell, *Training Magazine* electronic (email) newsletter, 11/01). This iterative method ensures that customer-prioritized business value is delivered quickly and often. Here's an overview of how you might apply this approach to projects:

- Meet with the customers to brainstorm all the features they would like.
- The IT developers create time estimates for each of the features.
- Work is divided into short iterations (one day to six weeks). Customers choose the amount of features they would like for the first iteration.
- The first iteration is completed. The velocity is equal to how much of the features were actually approved as complete by the customer. In the next round, the customer can only select this many.
- The rounds continue until the customer says "done."

The roles involved in this type of approach must be very clear: the developers own the estimates and the customers own the requirements, including their prioritization. The developer can suggest requirements but can't implement them without the customer's approval. The customer can challenge an estimate, but he can't change it without the developer's agreement.

Summary

You have read about how to Define, Plan, Manage, and Review a project—critical competencies for any IT leader. If you do nothing else, invest in the activities of Define and Review. These two will give you the most return for your time, and are the two that make Manage such an ongoing challenge. The techniques in this chapter will help you teach your staff how to improve their initial definition and post project review capacities.

Lessons Learned

When creating the Project Charter, here are some tips:

- Asking the right questions of the right people can create an environment for success.
- Managing the scope, risk, and constraints of a project depend on a mutually agreed-upon baseline which is created during Define. If you skip this Define phase, your project will run over on time, quality, scope, or cost goals, if not all four. A little time upfront can save a tremendous amount of time and stress during the project.

Here are some lessons learned about creating and managing a Project Plan in the Plan and Manage phases:

- Projects always take longer than you expect, due to business politics, other people, or surprise glitches such as weather, illness, and even promotions. The work done in the risk assessment earlier in this chapter should help you deal realistically with changes and surprises.
- It is very tempting (no matter how experienced you are) to skip the planning. In fact, the more experienced you are, the more tempted you will be to skip it. *Don't.* Even if you never look at the plan again, creating it will improve your project success because it will influence the approach you take.

- If you do not believe the plan is possible, you're right. Be honest with yourself and to anyone who is trying to coerce you into a schedule that you do not think is possible.
- Everyone's expectations—yours, the customers', and the other team members'—are strongly influenced by a common visual picture and language. The Project Plan creates a central place of understanding, and should be a living, breathing, evolving document as the project progresses.

All projects will struggle, and learning from these struggles helps to ensure that they won't occur on the next project. The teams that look back and learn from their mistakes will be much more successful in the future than teams that hide from these lessons. The Review phase allows a team and an organization to:

- Build knowledge about project critical success factors for their business culture
- Create a team consensus that leaves the participants on an open and forward-thinking note, rather than hiding from a less than successful project result; this builds bridges (instead of burning them) for future project teamwork
- Create a building block for implementing knowledge management in a pragmatic manner, so knowledge can be created, exchanged, and transformed for measurable business return

Projects are always unique, always exciting at the beginning, and always terrifying once they start. Keeping the documents created in the Define phase close at hand, and constantly keeping the lines of communication open between the team and the customers is the only way to drive project success. Post the following nuggets of truth on your wall:

- It's usually time.
- Manage scope to manage quality.
- It is the customer's project, not yours.
- Change is necessary, good, and inevitable.
- You will learn something new in every project, every day.

To be a leader means to direct others. To direct others effectively requires the ability to:

- Define a vision with measurable outcomes.
- Plan a project by organizing appropriate resources.
- Manage the surprises that always occur, and control them.
- Review work completed for critical nuggets of truth for the future.

Action Plan/Journaling

In the following section, take a moment to reflect on your own project management abilities. Consider the following:

- Are you successful at prioritizing the multiple tasks and projects on your own to-do list? How could you improve that?
- Are you able to coach your staff on more effective ways that they can manage their own projects?
- Are you clear about the objectives, scope, risks, and constraints of projects before trouble arises?
- Do you have a repeatable process for assigning the right resources to the right project tasks?
- Do you forgive yourself when projects don't go exactly the way you've planned?
- Do you have a strategy for managing customer expectations during project work that you or your team is involved in?
- Do you take the time to learn from past project work?

Take a few minutes in your journal and describe yourself as you would like to be. What kind of project management abilities do you imagine yourself having in the future?

Finally, jot down some quick notes about some first steps you will take to grow into this successful project manager.

Creating and
Actualizing Vision

Every endeavor, grand or small of scale, begins with vision. What are we hoping to create? What are we striving for? What is our desired outcome? These are the visionary questions that drive all individual, team, and organizational energy. Think of any effort or achievement from history and you can identify the vision that propelled it forward. In the 1880s, Susan B. Anthony imagined women in voting booths. At the dawn of the 20th Century, Henry Ford had a vision of an automobile in front of every home. In the 1960s, Dr. Martin Luther King, Jr. expressed his dream of equality. In the 1980s, Steve Jobs and Bill Gates built their fortunes and helped to launch a revolution by foreseeing the power and possibilities of desktop computing. In the 1990s, thousands of companies were born upon a vision of business at Internet speed.

Vision is the ultimate sulphuric leadership competency. Sulphur is the alchemy principle that aligns with expansion, spreading, connecting, and combining. Vision is all of that. A well-crafted and boldly implemented vision has the expansive power to spread throughout an organization, connecting and aligning people and processes and combining with human energy to create remarkable results.

Vision has long been acknowledged as an essential quality of leadership. Of the alchemy of competencies required by leaders in any field, none gets more attention than the ability to create compelling visions. Yet vision is still something not entirely understood; and even when understood, rarely mastered. In this chapter, you'll learn about the dynamics of vision—how we understand vision as a concept, how we create it, and how we apply it to inspire and achieve in a fast-paced, challenging world.

Opportunities for Growth

- Gain new insights and different perspectives on vision as a process
- Learn and explore the power of compelling vision
- Apply vision as a management tool in an unpredictable world
- Create a business unit vision via a co-creation process
- Align business unit visions with the larger organization
- Enroll stakeholders in the business unit vision
- Convert vision into action
- Enact the leadership role of vision keeper

Agenda

Creating Common Terminology

Thoughts on Vision

The Power of Vision

Vision in an Unpredictable World

Vision Creation

Vision Alignment

Vision Enrollment

Vision Actualization

Leader as Keeper of the Vision

Creating Common Terminology

Terms like vision, purpose, mission, goal, and strategy are often used in confusing ways, sometimes even interchangeably. You'll read where an author uses "strategy" to refer to the direction an organization is moving and then later hear a speaker apply the term "vision" in the same way. You're left to question: Strategy or vision, which is it? It's not so important what you call your organizational process of planning for and framing your future; what is important is that you understand the need to conduct such a process. Terms like mission and purpose describe concepts, and you are free to apply what terms you like so long as you understand and implement the concepts they describe. Acknowledge the confusion these conceptual terms may cause and clarify your terminology prior to beginning to define your organizational purpose or create the future vision for your business unit.

For the sake of our exploration here, we'll apply these terms as follows:

Values—the core behavioral guidelines organizations live by. Values articulate the moral character of an organization and determine the code of ethics for its operations. A statement of values affirms where the organization places its priorities and what it can be counted upon to stand for. (See the discussion of personal values in Chapter 2, "Leader Self-Alignment.")

Purpose—the reason for being. A purpose (sometimes also called a mission) is a broad statement explaining why an organization is brought into being and sustained in existence. The purpose behind most business ventures is profitability, though such ventures often also include some sense of purpose connected to service, innovation, or some other constructive end within the organizational field. A statement of purpose is often sweeping enough that it may never be fully realized. (See the discussion of individual purpose in Chapter 2.)

Vision—the path traveled in pursuit of the purpose. A vision (sometimes also called a strategy) is the "story" we create about the future we seek within the bounds of our purpose. It is where we are going and how we propose to get there. Vision ranges in terms of time frame—it is the way in which we carry out our purpose over the next period of time. A carefully crafted vision provides an organization with a sense of direction, and gives the individual members an identification of their place in a greater whole. Vision may be impacted by significant change and may need to be clarified and realigned over time. As the shifting landscape closes off some opportunities and opens new possibilities, vision must remain somewhat dynamic. (See the discussions of vision in Chapters 3, "Resiliency," and 8, "Strategic Business Acumen.")

Action Steps—the specifically defined actions designed to move us down the path of our vision. Action steps (sometimes also called goals) represent the day-by-day and week-by-week benchmarks by which we measure our movement toward fulfillment of our vision. Action steps govern the focus of our attention and the deployment of our energy.

There is a flow in the relationship between these concepts. Values shape purpose; purpose is given life through dynamic vision; and vision is enacted via a series of measurable, day-to-day action steps. Here's an example of how these pieces fit together:

- Organizational values direct how we do business. We might hold a value around exceptional service to our customers or innovative technical solutions to organizational business needs.
- Purpose is influenced by our values. In Chapter 8, we offered a sample Help Desk statement of purpose: Enable, support, and learn from clients about the technology infrastructure. This statement speaks of a value around customer service and defines the role of the Help Desk in providing client-focused solutions within the technology infrastructure. This is the reason for the Help Desk's existence.
- Vision is created within the scope of our purpose. It articulates how we seek to enact that purpose over time. A vision connected to the Help Desk purpose statement above might involve a plan for partnering with Help Desk clients more fully so as to better anticipate their support needs. This is how the Help Desk will live its purpose—through service-based partnership with clients.
- Action steps define the specific tasks we will implement in carrying out our vision. Action steps accompanying the vision of partnering with clients might include Help Desk staff spending two hours each week on-site with clients or offering user-training programs to more fully enable clients in their use of the technology supported.

This chapter may focus specifically on the creation and implementation of vision, but an understanding of these related concepts is important as well. Values and purpose provide the foundation upon which vision is constructed. Action steps are the means by which vision comes to life. Vision is the critical leadership competency enabled and enacted by and through these related elements.

Thoughts on Vision

Vision is a vividly imagined sense of a desired future. It is the destination we aim for; the outcome we endeavor to realize. We've alluded to the notion that vision is also a path we travel in carrying out our purpose—not just a destiny but also the journey in pursuit of that destiny. Vision is not only an answer in response to "What do we want?" or "Where are we going?," but also to "How do we get there?" Vision is the destination and the path all in one. While it may seem that knowledge of the destination must precede the choice of paths, this may not always be the case. Certain destinations only become clear once the journey down a specific path has begun—thus, the need to keep vision dynamic.

We might choose to think of vision as a story. There is great power in a story as a medium for communicating a message. A story captures the imagination, creates powerful images, and conjures strong connections. Vision is the story we tell about our future. As we tell and retell the story, it becomes familiar to us. We come to know how the story unfolds, how it ends; we become attached to that ending. Vision as a story implies a need for authorship—we write our own story, we direct the flow of it, and we enact it. As performers enacting the story, we know our roles and our place in the context of the whole; clear roles allow us to better perform them. Stories become a part of us; they shape our behavior, direct our interactions, and guide our choices. Vision portrayed as a story behaves much the same.

In *Leadership and the New Science* (San Francisco, California: Berrett-Koehler Pub., 2001), Margaret Wheatley describes vision through the context of field theory. Simply put, field theory is the premise that space is filled with invisible energy fields. We are familiar with and apply some of these fields in everyday life—radio, radar, and electromagnetic fields, for example. We don't see the fields, but we know they exist because we have witnessed their effects. Wheatley suggests that we gain a new perspective on vision by thinking of it as a wave of energy rather than the more linear model of a force pulling us from our present state toward our desired future. As an energy field, vision could spread out and permeate an organization, influencing everyone coming into contact with it. The field would grow stronger as larger segments of the organization become connected to it, adding their energy, their ideas, and their momentum. In conversation, you've probably used the phrase "on the same wavelength" to describe an instance in which you and others have a common understanding and alignment. Vision as a field creates a scenario in which you, the team, the customer, and the entire organization are on the same energy wavelength.

The Power of Vision

Imagine yourself in a training session. The facilitator asks you and the other participants to rise from your seats and walk around the room. You stand and you walk. You're confident in your ability to walk, to avoid the chairs, tables, and other obstacles that lie in the path before you. You can decide where in the room you wish to go and you get there easily. Now imagine the facilitator asks you to close your eyes and continue walking. Suddenly you're not so confident. You hesitate. You worry about what you may collide with. You don't have a sense of direction any longer. You wander aimlessly, moving cautiously in an attempt to avoid crashing into something.

This is an exercise we use when we do training on the importance of having a guiding vision for our endeavors. Operating without vision, without a sense of direction, is like walking around with your eyes closed. Without vision, movement is hesitant and cautious; the best we can hope for is to stumble blindly across an opportunity to make forward progress. With vision, we move more confidently. We know where we are going. We can see the path before us and anticipate the challenges that lie along it. We aspire not only to arrive at our hopeful destination in good time, but also to reap the benefits of a well-planned journey.

Aside from providing something of a road map for our journey, vision brings other powerful benefits to us as individuals, teams, business units, and organizations, as outlined here.

Vision provides focus. In a world full of opportunity and distraction, a clear vision enables us as individual performers, teams, departments, and organizations to remain focused on our commitments to ourselves, our customers, and other organizational business units. It defines our place in the flow of things. Constant connection with vision keeps us on course, allowing navigational correction when we drift. You may recall from Chapter 3 that maintaining a focus on our desired future destination is a key characteristic of resiliency, a means of navigating our world of white water change.

A few years back, we were doing some work with a product development team from the health care division of a large company. The group was struggling with its team process. After some initial assessment, we recognized that the team lacked a clear focus for its work. Team members knew, of course, why they were meeting weekly and conceptually understood the ultimate desired result from their efforts, but they seemed to have a hard time staying connected with their day-to-day focus on this work. Because they couldn't "touch" what it was all leading up to, it wasn't entirely real. In processing this missing element, we came up with the idea of creating a physical model of the product packaging they were developing—something real, something they could see and touch. Based on their best sense of what the final product would be, the team members created a mock-up of the packaging for their new product. Now they could see what they were working toward and pass it around and speak of it as though it was already complete. This vision in physical form sat in the center of the table for every team meeting that followed and lent an effective focus to their work.

Vision provides inspiration. This is the factor that makes vision such an inseparable component of the leadership equation. Leadership is about harnessing human potential and human energy toward a desired end. It is about inspiring performance—and vision is the medium through which inspiration flows.

In the era of World War II, General Eisenhower is said to have illustrated a point about inspirational leadership using a piece of string. With the string stretched out on a table, he pushed it from one end toward the other. Watching it bunch up, he commented that human energy cannot be driven forward with a push. Stretching the string out again and now pulling from one end forward, the string moved in whatever direction he chose to lead it. Human energy flows more freely when directed by a pull. An inspirational vision provides such a pull, drawing people forward and channeling their energy in the desired direction.

A compelling glimpse of the future that is articulated through clear vision allows us to tap into an unseen source of power. If the vision presents a future that aligns for us, we are drawn to it, inspired by the story it tells, and driven forward to fulfill our character's role in the unfolding tale.

Vision provides hope. Throughout this book we've discussed the challenging nature of the world in which we operate. As the demands for speed, results, and constant change grow ever stronger, it is easy to become frustrated and disillusioned. We surmount challenge after challenge, with trials that seem to have no end. When the burden becomes too much to bear, solace can be found in the hopeful end offered by vision.

Exercise: Seeing Clearly

Reflect back on a time when you were firmly connected to a clear vision—maybe a business-related project or perhaps a personal achievement you sought to realize. Spend a moment reliving that experience now in your mind. Bring forth the memories of being clear about your destination and what you need to do to get there. In a few words, capture what the vision brought for you, how it made you feel, and what having a clear sense of it added to your pursuit of your hopeful outcome. What words or concepts come to mind?

Now let's play with the opposite scenario. Reflect back on a time when you were without vision—again, perhaps on a business project or at a time in your life when you were not holding any particular sense of direction. Spend a moment reliving that time. What was it like being without vision?

Vision in an Unpredictable World

Before we immerse ourselves more deeply in our exploration of vision, we need to address a significant question about creating and holding vision in a rapidly changing world. As we look around at the ever-shifting landscape, it would be easy to discount vision as too rigid for such a dynamic business environment. We could even prove this point (albeit for the short term), as many companies did during the Internet boom of the late 1990s. In such expansive times, it may seem that holding to a vision is limiting. Don't be fooled. Even in years of tremendous opportunity, where growth and profit appear around every bend, vision is a critical element in organizational success. It contributes to maximizing growth, and to channeling energy and focus in times of widespread opportunity. More important, it provides a solid foundation upon which to stand when the bottom inevitably drops out.

In a *Fast Company* interview (from the article "Michael Porter's Big Ideas," by Keith H. Hammonds, March 2001), Harvard Business School's Michael Porter points to Dell, Intel, and Wal-Mart as companies with proven track records that also live by vision (or strategy, as he prefers). In high times and low, such companies work their plans, live their visions, and excel in their markets. Adhering to their guiding visions has created legendary success.

Porter believes that strategy is about making choices; his viewpoint: Strategy forces you to set limits on what you're trying to accomplish. He comments that strategy must have continuity; it cannot be constantly reinvented. He defines strategy as being about the basic value you're trying to deliver to customers, and about specifically identifying which customers you're trying to serve. A clear strategy is essential for communicating to staff and customers what you are all about and where you are going as an organization.

The principles of organizational strategy or vision remain steadfast, even in times of rapid change. In fact, the boundaries and guidelines framed by vision help us to navigate such change successfully. Granted, the dynamics of change make creating vision a more complex process—and carrying out that vision must itself be dynamic. The essence of vision remains, regardless of the pace of change. Vision declares who we are, where we're going, and how we are going to get there—invaluable insight to hold in any world, but especially in one of dramatic and rapid change.

Vision Creation

In a traditional leadership model, the leader himself (remember, we said "traditional") was the visionary. He alone held the clear sense of the organization's future and set its course. His goal: to create and communicate a vision so compelling that the rest of the organization was inspired to act in support of it. This tradition of the leader creating the vision more or less in isolation and then revealing it from on high can still work in these less-than-traditional times. Every process has its place, depending on context, and we may find ourselves in cases calling for such traditional visionary leadership. Sometimes, it comforts people. In this era of participatory leadership, however, shared processes usually meet with less resistance and more enrollment.

A shared vision creation process implies the inclusion of the best ideas and most heartfelt sense of purpose from throughout the organization. It is a process with built-in enrollment and a real sense of attachment and ownership. In *The Fifth Discipline Fieldbook* (Doubleday, 1994), Peter Senge and colleagues describe shared vision as a process for building shared meaning—a collective sense of what is important and why. This is a shift from the traditional "create, tell, and sell" methodology in which members of an organizational community are left to derive inspiration from what they've been told carries importance or why they *should* care about the work they are doing. The shared approach allows the participating community to create and build the meaning behind the work, empowering their efforts in fulfillment of that shared vision.

Leadership development researcher Ronald Heifetz of Harvard claims that, while leaders can and should provide direction, this should take the form of framing clarifying questions as opposed to providing definitive answers. Heifetz's visionary leader is one who operates from the premise that leadership is about facilitating the organization in facing its challenges and maximizing its opportunities. In other words, facilitating the creation of shared vision.

Inviting input into the vision creation process can be difficult for some leaders. It requires them to accept that they don't know all of the answers. It requires trust of and from those who they invite to participate. It demands that they enter the process open to its outcome, without any direct influence upon what that outcome should be. The process can be long and daunting. It is a risk that some leaders are not willing to take. For those brave enough to engage it, though, the shared vision process adds value from the strength of diverse perspectives, to the enhanced sense of organizational community, to the richness and depth of the final output.

So far, we've portrayed the vision creation process as either/or: Either you as the leader create the vision as a solo act or you invite full input from the organizational community. In actuality, the process is carried out in degrees along a continuum with the above examples representing the extremes. In *The Fifth Discipline Fieldbook,* the points of this continuum are described as telling, selling, testing, consulting, and co-creating. As co-creation of vision is the most challenging for a leader, we've chosen to discuss it at greater length here.

One of the techniques we've used in the past to help teams and business units co-create a vision of their desired future is a six-step vision merger process. This process begins with individual visions, brings those together into small-group collaborative visions, merges these into a collective vision, gains input and feedback from additional stakeholders, refines and finalizes the vision, and concludes with the packaging and communication of the vision in its final (but still dynamic) form. The detailed steps are as follows:

1) *Individual Visions:* This first step allows individuals participating in the visioning process to express what they see for the future of the business and their affiliation with it. This is their opportunity to articulate what they feel is important from their own individual perspective. Participants in this process may include any person or representative of a group that has a stake in the outcome of the process—the team or business unit leader, the team members or business unit staff, higher-level management, customers, or representatives from other interconnected business units. Any of these stakeholders not able to participate in this part of the process can be invited to offer input and feedback on the rough vision during the fourth step of the process.

We advocate that this initial step of the visioning process be without bounds, and we strive to clarify our ideal outcome and not limit ourselves by applying too much reality (that time will come). We do suggest that some visioning focus be applied to create some basic boundaries for this work—what we call the visioning playground. The playground is established by specifically clarifying what it is you have gathered to create—a three-year vision for the expansion of Help Desk services or a strategy for building a strong service provider relationship with a new user group account, for example. The purpose and values of the organization further define the playground. A vision of the future must be aligned with how the organization defines its reason for being and its operational ethics.

Once we've established the boundaries of the visioning playground, the creative process can begin. As visioning is a creative process, we like to begin by accessing the creative right brain via a drawing exercise. The right brain is more open to possibilities and less constrained by the limits of what is or has been. Equipping individuals with large sheets of paper and markers, we challenge them to render in pictorial form the future as they would have it within the bounds of the visioning playground. We usually guide an imaging process—a little mental trip into the future—as a way of getting people started and then ask them to record on paper what they "saw" in their mind as they imagined their future.

We allow participants plenty of time to express their individual visions. We often seek to enhance the creative atmosphere in the room by adding some background music and nurturing a lighthearted spirit.

2) *Collaborative Visions:* Step 2 of our process has the participants come together in small groups (no more than eight or so per group) to share their individual visions. Interpreting their drawings as they go, each participant reveals an idealized version of the team or business unit's future. As this sharing process unfolds, the group identifies commonalties in their individual visions, and tracks the vision concepts that the group aligns with or finds particularly interesting. Participants expressing an idea not embraced by the group can advocate their idea if it is important to them. All participants should be heard, whether or not the group aligns with what they propose.

3) *Collective Vision:* Now we bring the collaborative vision ideas together into a collective view of our common future. One by one, each small group presents its common or interesting vision concepts. The larger group may ask for further clarification and interpretation if required. Reality may now begin to influence the ideal. The group should be encouraged to exercise creativity here, exploring questions such as: How can we have the essence of this ideal within the bounds of our current reality? This sharing, discussion, and creative process often requires a strong facilitator to guide the focus and flow.

As each group presents, key vision components are captured on sheets of paper, one per sheet. This capture method allows vision components to be moved around and grouped with others as part of the process. Building a vision using this method is similar to assembling a puzzle. These vision components represent the puzzle pieces and they need to be laid out, rearranged, and fit together in order to complete the vision puzzle.

When each small group has had its opportunity to present, the large group should review all of the vision components currently "on the table." This is also the time for individuals still holding onto a vision idea to which they feel connected, but their small group failed to embrace, to give that idea another airing. If accepted by the larger group, this idea becomes another piece of the puzzle. If not accepted, individuals are asked to release the idea without prejudice. With the pieces in place, the goal is now to begin fitting them together. Some basic themes or tracks should emerge. Arranging and outlining these into a workable form, something that can be communicated outside of the group, is the final action for this step of the visioning process.

4) *Stakeholder Feedback and Input:* Depending upon the nature and purpose of the vision you're creating, this step may be skipped. If there are no other stakeholders beyond those who participated in the steps above, there may be no need to solicit additional input. Often, though, there are other individuals or groups who could offer input of value to the visioning process. In addition to gaining additional valuable insights, this step extends the ownership of the process and its final outcome to a wider stakeholder group.

There are many ways to carry out a feedback process of this sort. You could run a focus group, host an all-inclusive stakeholder "sneak peek" at the vision in its unrefined form, or do some kind of email survey. The essence of this step is to solicit broader perspectives with regard to the vision components and build a sense of stakeholder ownership. Select whatever feedback method will most effectively provide these results.

5) *Refine and Finalize the Vision:* With all of the vision components having been collected, laid out, discussed, and rearranged, the vision must now be given its final form. A smaller team from the initial group of participants may best carry out this process. The goal of this step is to synthesize all of the perspectives gathered from the previous steps of the process and articulate the final vision product. This effort may require a stronger dose of reality than had been previously applied in this work. This is also the final opportunity to test the vision against the organizational values to ensure alignment. Questions to address in this step include:

- What is the ultimate outcome for which we are striving through the articulation of this vision? What is the broadest statement of our vision?
- What are the specific components of this vision that we bring together in support of this outcome?
- What is our time frame for realizing each of these vision components?
- What are the specific accountabilities for each vision component? Who oversees or carries out each piece?
- What benchmarks will we set as a means of measuring our progress along the way?
- What communication process will we implement to keep all stakeholders aligned and informed of the vision as it unfolds?

As the vision is being finalized, some input from the broader group may be necessary. This may take the form of a back-and-forth communications process as vision components are made more clear, specific, and solid. Though a small group is finalizing the vision, it is important not to lose sight of the shared process.

6) *Package and Communicate the Vision:* If the vision, now in its final form, is going to become an energy field sweeping through the organization, it must be packaged in a way that supports this. What form best enables this in your organization is for you to determine. Rather than the standard written format for articulating vision—a broad statement of the outcome followed by a more specific outline appearing as a poster or handout—we enjoy the idea of a story as a package for vision. Earlier in this chapter, we mentioned how a story has the power to capture the imagination. Tell the story of your vision, describe the chapters of the story, introduce the characters and their roles, bring the vision to life in the imaginations of those hearing and interacting with the story. If we can't sell you on the story concept, try some other creative form of communicating the vision. You could employ a visual form, such as a series of graphics or a game board that follows the journey toward completion of the vision. The hard work of formulating the vision has been carried out, but the vision is not yet alive. Now it requires essentially an advertising job—breathe life into the vision you've created via clever packaging and a sound communication strategy.

You can see that these steps require a significant commitment of time and energy. It certainly may seem easier (or at least faster) if you as the leader simply decree the vision—and sometimes this is necessary. In most circumstances, however, this kind of shared vision process supports a richer overall outcome, a stronger final vision, one with built-in enrollment by the stakeholders. The ongoing benefits of the relational bonds forged between those coming together through this process—managers, staff, customers, and other stakeholders—more than pay back the investment of time and energy required to do it well. (For another example of a visioning process, see Chapter 8.)

Vision Alignment

Vision is the path we create and travel in pursuit of fulfilling our purpose for existence. Each entity within an organization—divisions, departments, business units, teams, and the individuals who comprise the organizational community—has a reason for being and, whether consciously declared or not, also has a vision it enacts in fulfillment of that reason. Each of these visions must align with the broader vision hierarchy within the organization.

Like a set of Russian nesting figurines, each vision must "fit" inside the next. This is vision alignment.

It is a function of leadership to ensure that those who carry out the work we oversee understand the value they bring to the whole as a result of this work—that they understand their purpose within the broader organization. In IT, such purpose usually takes the form of building, supporting, and continuously enhancing the technology infrastructure of the business. Each entity within the organization should recognize the piece of the organizational puzzle it fulfills and realize that the puzzle cannot be complete without it. With this understanding in place, it follows that the vision puzzle created by a project team, for example, must align and fit within the broader vision puzzle created by the business unit under which the project falls. Each piece must fit within and add to the next.

Alignment of vision involves not only vision-to-vision alignment but also vision-to-values alignment. All organizational visions must align with the organization's values. Achieving vision alignment is largely a matter of awareness. It requires clarity of vision at multiple levels and an intimate connection to the context of the organizational values. Alignment can be tested through a series of questions:

- If vision is energy moving in a chosen direction, how does the energy of our business unit vision flow with and add momentum to the energy movement of the broader organizational vision? Where do these energy currents run counter to one another?

- If our vision is a piece of a broader organizational puzzle, how precisely does our piece mesh with our designated space in that puzzle? Where do "rough edges" in our vision challenge our fit?

- How can our vision be viewed as a vision component of the broader organizational vision? What does our vision contribute to the fulfillment of this broader vision? Where does our vision limit or detract from this fulfillment?

- To what degree does our vision honor the organizational values to which we're committed? In what ways does the vision support and advance these values?

Exercise: Exploring Alignment

Select an affiliation you have within the organization: a project team you serve on, the business unit you lead, the division under which your IT-related function falls. With this as a basis for your thinking on this exercise, complete the following steps:

- In only one or two sentences, write out a statement of vision for the organizational affiliation that you choose to focus on.
- Under this vision statement, list several components of this vision—pieces of the puzzle.
- In one or two sentences, write out a statement of vision for the next level up in the hierarchical structure of your organization from the affiliation you worked with above.
- Using one of the alignment questions above, reflect on the "fit" of these visions. To what degree and in what ways does the smaller context vision support the broader context?

Vision Enrollment

The vision generation methodology you choose to implement will largely determine the degree of enrollment required once the vision has taken shape. In a co-creative visioning process, the enrollment is somewhat integrated. If the members of the organizational community charged with carrying out the vision had a role in its determination, enrollment is largely built-in. To the degree that the vision generation methodology falls closer to the "create, tell, and sell" end of the vision creation continuum, enrollment becomes more of a requirement.

Communicating vision should be viewed not just as an announcement or informing process, but also as one for capturing the attention and securing the commitment of those to whom the vision is being communicated. Enrollment is the direct result of how the vision is packaged for and communicated to the audience—so it demands the basic rules of effective communication, the first of which is *know your audience*. (See Chapter 5, "Communication Skills.")

When seeking vision enrollment, we must first be clear as to whom we're seeking to enroll in the vision. Who is our audience? Are there several different audiences we're seeking to enroll? With the audiences identified, we need to determine what each wants to hear, and which elements of this vision will capture their imaginations. Some might call this motivation, but we prefer to call it inspiration. Inspiration refers to the fire within each of us and to a process for fueling these internal fires. Knowing your audience means knowing what will inspire them and packaging your message accordingly. The following questions may help you clarify this:

- If this vision is a story, how clearly will this audience identify themselves as vital characters in it? How can their character roles be clarified further and brought to life more fully?

- What lies at the core of what this audience most wants to hear? How can this vision provide for that desire?
- In which aspects of this vision will this audience find inspiration? How can this inspirational quality be maximized?

Keep in mind that enrollment is an ongoing process. While commitment and inspiration may be secured through the initial communication process, they must be reasserted and reinforced constantly as the vision unfolds. The road of carrying out vision can be long and arduous, and the initial enthusiasm we build for the journey will wane over time. You must nurture the connection your stakeholders have to the vision to remind them of the value of the work they do and to continue fueling their internal fires for that work.

Vision Actualization

Vision has power. It inspires, it connects, it energizes, it shapes us and the organizations of which we are part. Yet this power is wasted if the vision is not brought into reality through action.

The creative work has been done, the vision has been articulated, and the key players are primed for action. Now what? How do we turn a long-term vision into a step-by-step action process that is carried out a bit at a time every day?

The lure of vision lies in the product—the outcome of vision fulfillment that we desire to see and experience in the world. The energy lies here, rather than in the actual process of bringing this about. The road to actualizing vision can be long and difficult. There are unforeseen challenges along the way. Unexpected change creeps in and alters the path. We lose sight of where we're headed, and lose the energy required to bring it about.

Actualizing vision requires a carefully laid yet flexible, step-by-step plan that never takes its eyes off of the desired result. In turning vision into action, we must first find a way, in fact, several ways, to keep the ultimate destination and the reasons we chose that destination in front of us.

Putting a step-by-step action process in place for carrying out vision requires that we can see within the breadth of the vision to its key components, and within those key components to their basic elements. The key components of the vision should already be clear and fairly specific as a result of the vision generation process. Working with each component individually, but not losing sight of their interconnectedness, we can work backward from the future to the present, identifying key steps along the way. We might imagine the journey from present to desired future as the act of crossing a river, our desired destination being on the far bank. What are the stepping stones we need to put into place in order to allow us to cross without getting wet?

As we examine this process, we'll likely discover that some stepping stones are already in place, or at least partially so. We'll also discover that there are large gaps where no steps exist and perhaps even just the opposite, a barrier of some sort awaits. We can think of both the existing stepping stones and the barriers as driving and restraining forces—things already in place that drive us forward or hold us back (see Figure 10.1). These may be physical things or forces of some kind—attitudes, knowledge, technology. We must become aware of the drivers and restrainers and explore their leverage upon our plan.

Action Initiative: Upgrading payroll system software

Driving Forces

- Most users agree that the upgrade is necessary—positive attitudes
- Half of the staff has already been trained on the new system
- The new software requires minimal hardware upgrade
- The upgrade is cost effective—minimal investment

Restraining Forces

- Mixed messages from management—prefer to wait on upgrade
- Upgrading will affect one pay cycle—checks may be missed
- System shutdown may create unexpected problems

Figure 10.1
Examples of driving and restraining forces.

Exercise: Force Field Analysis

Consider an action initiative currently underway in your business area. Write a short statement encapsulating that initiative. For this action initiative, list three driving forces (things already in place that support or propel the initiative forward) and three restraining forces (things that block or inhibit forward progress).

With clear awareness and solid understanding of the drivers and restrainers, we can now begin to explore how we work with these forces. How can we leverage or maximize the driving forces? How can we eliminate or minimize the impact of the restraining forces? As we respond to these questions, specific action steps begin to take shape.

There is no magic to actualizing vision—it requires effort and commitment. As with any difficult undertaking, maintaining an appropriate attitude, gaining an intimate understanding of the landscape, breaking broad goals into specific, measurable actions, and identifying and celebrating milestones along the way are all essential pieces of the vision actualization equation.

Leader as Keeper of the Vision

The notions of the co-creative vision generation methodology and the packaging, communication, and enrollment processes imply that the vision belongs to all members of the organizational community and that all share the responsibility for carrying it out. This is the essence and the power of vision. While the ownership of and energy behind the vision may be organization-wide, there must be one individual designated with the responsibility for maintaining and enforcing the highest sense of the vision. There must be one person who has intimate knowledge of the strategy as articulated in the vision and who shepherds it forward—a chief strategist or keeper of the vision.

In *Fast Company*, Michael Porter talks about vision or strategy as helping our organizations maintain boundaries around their efforts. He describes this as a process of choice-making. Making appropriate choices, ones that uphold the boundaries as set forth in the vision, requires insight into the intention of the vision and discipline for protecting that intention. This becomes the role of the leader once the vision has been created and unleashed.

As a leader, you are the keeper of the vision for your business unit. You must maintain the energy behind the vision, guide the way when the path turns murky, make the hard choices in support of the vision as you encounter crossroads, and alter the vision when the times demand.

Summary

Powerful vision is the foundation underlying every successful endeavor. Vision provides focus in times of change, inspiration when performance needs to be mobilized, and hope when challenge darkens the horizon. Vision needs to remain somewhat dynamic, to flex and flow with the shifting landscape while still providing a guiding point of light. As leaders, we are the keepers of our organizations' visions. Just as alchemists applied sulphur to drive their chemical processes, leaders apply vision to drive organizational achievement.

Lessons Learned

- Vision is the path we travel in pursuit of our purpose over a specific period of time. It is both a vividly imagined end and the journey toward that end.
- There are many ways to consider vision. It can be viewed as a compelling future drawing us forth, a story we tell about our future and our journey toward it, and an energy field influencing our organization in the shaping of its future.
- Vision has power. It maintains focus, inspires performance, and provides hope.
- Vision is at once both a set of boundaries and a dynamic pathway. While it is easy to discount the value of a set vision in an unpredictable world, flexible vision provides an important tool for navigating that world.
- There is a continuum of vision-generation approaches, ranging from the directive to the collective. Each degree along the continuum has value, given different circumstances. A collective or co-creative vision-generation process provides the richest diversity of perspectives and an integrated enrollment of stakeholders.
- Business unit visions must align with the visions and values of the broader organization.
- Vision enrollment requires knowledge of the audience and the ability to recognize and tap into what inspires them.
- Actualizing vision is a process of breaking vision components down to their elemental pieces, exploring the forces acting upon these elements, and leveraging these forces through specific actions.
- The leader's ultimate role in vision is to maintain the integrity of the vision as adopted, guide the choice-making process to reflect the essence of the vision, and utilize the inspirational quality of the vision to maintain energy and progress toward its achievement.

Action Plan/Journaling

In the following section, take a moment to reflect on your own leadership abilities in the creation and actualization of vision. Consider the following:

- How powerful are the visions currently held within your organization?
- To what degree do they inspire and guide your daily actions?
- From our exploration in this chapter, what elements of effective vision are present in your organization? What elements are missing?
- Within your own sphere of influence as a leader, what will you do to more fully tap into the power and potential of vision in your organization?

Take a few minutes in your journal and describe yourself as you would like to be. What kind of visionary leader do you imagine yourself being in the future?

Finally, jot down some quick notes about some first steps you will take to grow into this competency.

The Journey to Change

Alchemy is change. It is a process of transformation, taking what is and creating what can be. The alchemical process blends multiple inputs—material elements, heat, time, pressure—to induce transformation and a hoped-for output, something of value. Leadership alchemy is much the same. There are various inputs: self-insight, a solid skill base, technical competence, organizational culture, and constantly shifting external forces. Blended together, these create an environment for transformation that not only induces change, but demands it. While this is true of every industry, it is especially so in IT. As those performing the role of leadership upon this stage, we must become intimate with the process of change as it transforms us individually, exerts pressure upon our people, and impacts our organizations.

Opportunities for Growth

- Clarify the distinction between change and transition
- Map out the human journey of transition

- Assess the challenges of the transitional journey
- Manage your own personal leadership transformation
- Discover the essential components for successful organizational change
- Develop strategy for leading individuals with different change styles
- Build the skills necessary for leading change

Agenda

The Challenge of Change

Transition: The Human Process of Change

Understanding Organizational Change

Leading Change

The Challenge of Change

Change is hard. There can be no argument. That doesn't mean that we always run from change or even resist it all the time, but making the journey from what is to what can be/needs to be always presents challenges. The challenge of change stems from its uncertainty—the questions for which there seem to be no immediate answers. What will it be like on the other side of this change? How will this change impact me? Will I find a comfortable place in the changed world? We can't know the answers to these questions until we complete our journey through the change and see firsthand how the new way works and whether or not we're comfortable there. The difficulty lies in the recognition that change is a journey into the unknown.

To fully understand the challenges of this journey, we must make a careful distinction between two terms that are often confused: *change* and *transition*. People (including us) often say that change is difficult, but that's not actually true. Change is change—it is not good, bad, difficult, or easy. Transition, the human process of adapting to change, is where the difficulty comes in.

Change is an external event, a shifting of circumstances in the world created by a natural occurrence or human-made choice. Change is outside of us, around us, and does impact us. How change impacts us depends upon the transitional process and the insights, beliefs, and attitude we bring to it as individuals affected by the change event. Those events always launch transitional processes within those influenced or impacted by the change.

Transition is a process of adaptation, of the human process of getting used to the change. This human process and the multitude of variables influencing such human processes often brings challenge to change.

Exercise: Distinguishing Change and Transition

Think of two or three professional or personal changes you have experienced in your life. Select changes that were dramatic, with some impact. List each change using a general descriptor. Reflect on each change and make a distinction between the event or decision that launched the change and the transitional process that surrounded it. Jot a few notes based on your memory of each of these components. We've provided an example to get you started.

Example:

Change: SAP Implementation

Event: Study of future business needs and ROI led to decision to switch systems

Transition: Marked by fear of downtime during implementation, period of staff retraining, gradual acceptance, and then widespread success with system

Transition: The Human Process of Change

Insight into the process of individual change benefits leaders for two main reasons:

1. In seeking to grow and develop our full leadership potential, we will experience (actually create) individual change in a very real, personal way. (See Chapter 12, "A Plan for Action.")
2. The insight we hold into the individual change process provides the foundation for effectively leading change within our organizations.

As we seek to transform ourselves, support our people in their growth and performance in a changing world, and help our organizations adapt to the shifting business landscape, we will need to forge a deep understanding of and compassion for the difficult journey that is transition, the human side of change.

Well-known transitional process authority William Bridges describes transition as unfolding over three distinct stages: Endings, Neutral Zone, and

New Beginnings. According to Bridges, one of the rules of transition is that before something new can begin, something old must first end. Abiding by this rule—and we really have no choice but to abide by it—often presents a struggle. Even in situations where we are truly discontent with our present state and where the new beginning we seek to create promises to be alluring, we often find ourselves strangely reluctant to let go of the old way. The knowledge or the expectation of what comes after the ending—the Neutral Zone—brings about this struggle. We don't like endings because they inevitably launch us into a limbo state, a place in between the "way" we know and are leaving behind and the "way" we are coming to know but have not yet arrived at. This explains much of the change-averse behavior we sometimes see within ourselves and those around us. Remember the panicked uproar when your organization upgraded to Windows 95? Welcome to the difficulties we have with letting go!

The Neutral Zone (or "the wilderness" as Bridges sometimes refers to it) is the place in between the old way and the new. At this stage of transition, we have managed to tear ourselves loose from what we were used to and comfortable in and are now lost in the wilderness of transitional process. We are now "in between worlds." This is a psychological sense of being lost. Depending upon the degree and perceived impact of the change in our world, we may find ourselves asking defining questions here such as:

- Who am I? (Who are we?)
- Where am I (are we) going?
- Why am I (are we) on this road?
- How do I (we) fit in the new way now that the old way is gone?

This is an awkward and uncomfortable time. It is a place of wandering in the fog, with no assurance that we are moving in the desired direction. The Neutral Zone is a place of low productivity both individually and organizationally. It is hard to make forward strides and produce value while feeling lost. The tendency here is to focus energy on finding our way and rediscovering or redefining ourselves.

The Neutral Zone seems like a fine place to avoid if at all possible, but the reality is that we need this time being lost in the wilderness. As mentioned above, this is not a place of external production, but one of important internal work. This "in between" state pushes us to ask important but rarely considered questions, to explore, to learn, to create vision, to rekindle energy, and ultimately to emerge somewhat transformed and ready to step forward into the new world created by the change. The Neutral Zone is a time of reflection and introspection, of learning about our world and of defining our place within it. Without enduring this stage of the process, we would discover that while the world around us has changed, we have not and therefore may not fit. Every change launches a transitional journey for those impacted by the change. There is no escape nor should we seek one. The process of transition begins when we accept that the world has changed and therefore so must we. Is the journey painful? Sure. Is it necessary? Absolutely!

The New Beginning represents our emergence from the wilderness. This is the stage of the journey where we "find our feet" again and begin moving forward. It is still a time of learning, fueled by hopeful optimism and a sense of direction. There may still be some grieving for the old way, especially in times of challenge, but this mostly takes the form of memories rather than a longing to return. New Beginnings can be exciting times, filled with energy, discovery, innovation, and a sense of creating the future. This stage represents the arrival and should be recognized and celebrated.

So what does all of this insight into individual transition mean for us personally as leaders? If you have used this book as intended—as a tool for assessing leadership competencies in the challenging and rapidly changing world of IT—then you should be well on your way to designing an action plan for enhancing skills and growing as a leader (see Chapter 12). In doing so, we are seeking to create a change, one that will have impact upon us and those around us. This change will come with a transitional journey—and despite the fact that we have chosen this change, it will bring its challenges. We will be tempted to cling to the leader we know, rather than struggle with transforming into the leader we wish to be. As we commit to letting go of old habits and comfortable approaches to our role in leadership, we will find that new habits take time to root themselves and become a natural component of our leadership style. There may be a period of "playing the role" before the role becomes a part of who we are. (See the discussion of character versus persona in Chapter 2, "Leader Self-Alignments.") Navigating this process requires a willingness to be lost for a time. Acceptance of our fate is the first step to beginning the journey. Transition is about growth and learning and that is where our transformative process needs to focus. Keeping this in mind brings us the courage and commitment we need for finding our way to the new beginning we seek.

Understanding Organizational Change

Having painted a basic picture of the individual journey we take through change, we now have the foundational understanding for connecting with what it means to implement organizational change. Organizations are communities of people, and organizational change is all about supporting our people through the transitional process that's connected to the organizational change being implemented. Sounds easy? The challenge is that each member of our organizational community will respond differently in the face of that change. The very fact that they probably had little input into the decision to change—that it was perhaps thrust upon them—only increases the challenge of gaining acceptance and moving people into transition.

IT organizations inherently need to constantly change, regularly and rapidly adapting to the shifting business landscape. Factors driving the need for organizational change include:

- The speed of change in the world within which the organization exists
- The visibility and predictability of the future
- The complexity of the marketplace—customers, competitors, suppliers
- The technological infrastructure the organization is built upon
- The stability of resources—human, material, financial

As organizations struggle to adapt and recreate themselves in response to these forces, it is easy to forget about the people element involved in creating change. William Bridges declares that organizations are often very good at creating change—but not so good at managing transition. As we've already noted, we can't achieve change without transition. The organization cannot successfully institute change without bringing its people along. Management can make all the decrees that it pleases, but the people throughout the organization ultimately bring about the change. And they do so only when they are ready, having moved through transition at their own pace.

In *Resistance to Organizational Change*, Michael Ayers discusses his findings on individual resistance factors that occur within organizations seeking to create change. At any point in time during the change process, each of your team members may be resisting along one of these factors. Resistance corresponds with individual needs within the transitional journey and it is rare that all team members would resist for the same reason. Ayers has documented these five factors:

1. The Belief that Change Can Occur—People resist when they do not believe that the change proposed is possible.
2. A Challenging Vision—People resist change that does not have a challenging vision, one that they can get passionate about. If the vision is missing or illogical, there will be resistance.
3. A Clear Pathway—People resist change when they don't see how it's going to change their life directly.
4. Congruent Values—People resist change when they perceive the change as inconsistent with their personal values.

5. Autonomy—People resist change when they do not see the place they play in it. If the change can be accomplished without them and they add nothing, they will resist.

Exercise: Organizational Change Post-Mortem

Consider a widespread organizational change you have experienced in your career. Dissect this change effort and note your observations with the clarity of hindsight. Respond to the following questions and add more of your own reflections:

1. What was the organization trying to accomplish? What was the change?
2. How was the change introduced to the organizational community? How effective was this method of introduction and enrollment? What might have been done to improve its effectiveness?
3. How did the transitional journey flow? What sort of responses did you personally experience and witness in others to the need to adapt?
4. How did the organization strive to support people in making this transitional journey? How could the leadership have done a better job at providing such support?

How do we as leaders support and facilitate the transitional journey? We need to consider several key elements:

• Vision—People need a clear sense of where they are going, even if the broader vision remains cloudy and is clarified only a step at a time. Vision helps to manage the uncertainty and adds confidence for navigating the vast unknown. (See Chapter 10, "Creating and Actualizing Vision.")
• Skills—People need a skill base compatible with the challenge of moving through change (see Chapter 3, "Resiliency") as well as skill development in the areas necessary for success upon arrival at the new beginning.
• Incentives—People need to understand why the change is necessary and what is in it for them. What reward (extrinsic and intrinsic) will they receive for making the transitional journey?
• Resources—People need resources—physical, human, informational, psychological/emotional—to support their journey.
• Action Plan—People need a clear sense of day-by-day action with measurable milestones worthy of celebrating upon accomplishment.

Each of these factors working in concert supports the organization and its community of people in creating lasting change. Table 11.1 explores how the absence of any of these factors impacts the process and the outcome of change.

Table 11.1
Critical Elements for Effective Change

Elements Supporting Change					Outcome
Vision	Skills	Incentives	Resources	Action	Change
	Skills	Incentives	Resources	Action	Confusion
Vision		Incentives	Resources	Action	Anxiety
Vision	Skills		Resources	Action	Gradual change
Vision	Skills	Incentives		Action	Frustration
Vision	Skills	Incentives	Resources		False starts

Rarely is organizational change revolutionary. Change is evolution, and evolutionary processes, because they rely on adaptation, take time to fully integrate. People must assimilate new circumstances, regain their footing, and develop new comfort structures with regard to new processes and procedures. It takes time to become fully productive again. While the choice to change may be determined at the speed of management decision-making, the unfolding of the change takes place at people speed. Change only takes place as quickly as people move through transition. Successful organizational change is bound by the success the organizational leadership has in facilitating its people through the transition associated with the change.

Leading Change

There is an exercise we sometimes use in training that involves people in pairs, with the first partner blindfolded at one side of the room and the second partner with full vision at the other side of the room. Between them, the floor is scattered with paper plates creating an obstacle course of sorts. The sighted partner must offer verbal directions to the blindfolded partner so she can navigate across the room without stepping on any of the plates. The challenge is heightened by the fact that there may be as many as 15 pairs of people shouting directions and blindly navigating the obstacle course at the same time.

We usually run two rounds of this exercise. In round one, the partners are separated across the room, blindfolds are tied, the guidelines are explained, and the exercise begins. It's usually pretty chaotic. The blindfolded person often can't hear the directions from her sighted partner amid the din of everyone shouting. The sighted person often watches helplessly, vainly offering unheard guidance. The blindfolded people begin initially trying to pick their way through the obstacles on their own, often finally giving up and just walking through without concern for where they step. In our experience, we have witnessed blindfolded participants actually sit down in the middle of the obstacles in a fit of frustration.

Before beginning round two of the exercise, we allow the partners a few minutes of planning time. Together they strategize how they will handle the noise and confusion of the exercise, often working out some sort of communication strategy for a more direct and effective flow of guidance, feedback, and information. Pairs often also create a specific common understanding of how movement will take place—for example, how big a step should be or how they'll describe the need to turn a certain number of degrees in one direction or another. Pairs often get fairly creative in their approach to the task at hand—given the guideline that they can't step on any of the plates, one blindfolded person actually grabbed a broom and simply swept the plates aside!

We can make an analogy between this exercise and the notion of leading others through change. The blindfolded excursion through the obstacle course represents the journey into unknown terrain that contains unseen challenges. The blindfolded people are hesitant to make that first step into the obstacle course; once in the middle, they move slowly and tentatively. The sighted partner represents leaders trying to guide their people through the process of change. The exercise points out the importance of clear and effective communication, of strategy, of vision, of ongoing "navigational" feedback, of creativity and innovative problem-solving. The first round of the exercise, in which no strategy is present and no structures have been established, points out the futility of simply shouting "Go!" and letting people fend for themselves in times of change.

As we described in the previous section on Understanding Organizational Change, an important part of change leadership is recognizing where the individual members of the organization stand with regard to their view of the change. In some ways, we lead change one person at a time and must begin doing so from that individual's perception and attitude about the change. Table 11.2 introduces four viewpoints on change and cites some emotional, behavioral, attitudinal, and contribution-oriented factors for each. The chart also shares a sense of how we as leaders need to support people in each category and direct their energy in positive ways.

Table 11.2
Approaches to Change

Descriptor: Grievers
Feelings: Victimized, Helpless, Pessimistic
Behavior: Anger, Fear, Blame, Reluctance
Attitude: Change will pass and the old way will return
Contribution: Negative
Immediate Need: Opportunity to grieve and support toward acceptance of
  change

Descriptor: Adapters
Feelings: Not happy with but accepting of change
Behavior: Go with the flow of change
Attitude: Change effort is just another hoop to jump through
Contribution: Neutral
Immediate Need: Enrollment into the vision of change and clarity of their
  potential contribution and reward

Descriptor: Explorers
Feelings: Hopeful, Curious, Supportive
Behavior: Takes some risks, willing to try something new
Attitude: Change presents some new opportunities
Contribution: Positive
Immediate Need: Focus positive energy toward maximum contribution

Descriptor: Visionaries
Feelings: Excited, Optimistic, Engaged
Behavior: Creating and driving change
Attitude: The future is ripe with possibility
Contribution: Positive, contagious
Immediate Need: Evangelize the change effort and support and enroll
others

Exercise: How Do Your People Approach Change?

Identify individuals under your leadership who in your opinion represent
each of the change approaches cited in Table 11.2. Make some notes as to
how you have observed the specific change approach "playing out" be-

haviorally in each case. For each person, plot a brief strategy—a few action points—for taking an individualized approach to leading this person through change.

The following are some general support structures that leaders need to build to facilitate people's journey through change:

1. *Create Ownership.* When people understand the force driving the change and have some say in how the change will unfold, the impact of the "victim mentality" is minimized and change is accepted more readily (see Chapter 10).

2. *Communicate! Communicate! Communicate!* We're saying it three times because leaders often think they have adequately communicated the vision and the change strategy—when in reality, they need to send the message over and over and through different channels to help people stay connected with it (see Chapter 5, "Communication Skills").

3. *Manage the Ending.* The process for letting go of the old way is very similar to the classic grieving process people go through when they lose a loved one—shock, anger, and denial are all emotions they may experience. Create opportunities for the expression of this grief and recognize that grieving is a step along the road to acceptance.

4. *Respect Diversity.* Recognize and allow for the reality that everyone is different and will therefore move through the transition in a different fashion, at a different pace, and with different needs. This requires some balance, as there may be people already at the doorstep to the new beginning while others are only just letting go of the old way. Be clear but realistic as to your performance expectations and provide the appropriate support to each person as an individual (see Chapter 4, "Interpersonal and Team Skills").

5. *Be a Coach.* Accept that in times of change, leaders need to become coaches, providing the sort of support that comes with any new skill development process. Clarify the vision for each performer, help them see their connection to it, and provide navigational feedback on their journey toward actualizing it (see Chapter 6, "Coaching").

6. *Foster a Learning Environment.* Change often forces people to try things they've never done before and a learning curve must be expected. Create an appropriate atmosphere for learning: Make it safe for people to try and fail, facilitate a positive learning attitude, and model learning behaviors.

Summary

In IT, where the necessity for and pace of change are high, we must master the competency of leading others through change. Modeling change management within ourselves, demonstrating resiliency and seeking to coach and develop it within our people (see Chapter 3, "Resiliency"), honoring the human process of change, and building sound support structures for organizational change are essential components to our change leadership role.

Lessons Learned

- The transitional process associated with all change often brings challenge to change.
- Change is based in external events and decisions.
- Transition is the internal process of adapting to the change.
- Endings, Neutral Zone, and New Beginnings mark the three distinct stages of the transitional process.
- As we seek to transform ourselves in our role as leaders, we will experience and must manage the challenge of this personal transitional journey.
- Successful organizational change is based on successfully supporting the organizational community (people) through the transitional journey.
- Supporting people through organizational change requires: Clear vision, Skill Building, Incentives, Resources, and Defined Action Steps.
- There are four basic individual styles or approaches to change: Grievers, Adapters, Explorers, and Visionaries. Each requires a different style of leadership support in times of change.
- Some basic structures for supporting change include: Create Ownership, Communicate (×3), Manage the Ending, Respect Diversity, Be a Coach, and Foster Learning.

Action Plan/Journaling

In the following section, take a moment to reflect on your own individual and leadership abilities around change and transition management. Consider the following:

1. How do you as an individual typically view change?

2. How do you create a supportive transition environment within your sphere of leadership? What steps could you take to enhance your support of the transitional process?

3. How effective are you in the various key roles of a change leader—communicator, coach, visionary?

Take a few minutes in your journal and describe yourself as you would like to be. What kind of change management and change leadership do you imagine yourself practicing in the future?

Finally, jot down some quick notes about some first steps you will take to grow into this competency.

A Plan for Action

At this point in your reading, you have explored the competencies that you believe are relevant to your personal leadership needs. You now face a critical decision. You have a choice of two future paths—forward, to becoming a new kind of leader with transition ahead, or back to your old frustrating work self, probably not as effective as it could be. Only you can make the decision whether to put this book back on a shelf, or to work at applying the relevant thoughts and techniques to your own situation. Alchemy and leadership are explorations that never end. The next step in the journey is your choice—and your choice alone.

Opportunities for Growth

- Identify your leadership strengths and development needs through personal and 360-degree assessment
- Assess where you are and where you want to be in your leadership role

- Apply the insights gained through assessment to create a personal Action Plan
- Schedule feedback and coaching sessions with your leader on a periodic basis as you work through your personal Action Plan

Agenda

Review the Personal Assessment

Initiate a 360-Degree Process

Identify Opportunities and Needs

Build a Personal Action Plan

Beware of the Neutral Zone

The Journey Begins

Review the Personal Assessment

In Chapter 1, "The Value of Technical Leadership," you were asked to do a personal assessment of your current leadership skills using the IT leadership competencies in this book. Return to this assessment and reflect on what you wrote. Make a copy of Figure 12.1 to re-evaluate your own competencies.

Initiate a 360-Degree Process

Also make copies of Figure 12.1 for others to provide feedback on your IT leadership competencies. Take the important step and risk asking your team, your customers, and your supervisors to give you this feedback. The transition necessary to create lasting change demands such courage. Step forward to become the leader you know you should be. By asking these people for their feedback, you will begin to build trust and collaboration and gain new allies as you begin your journey.

Evaluate your current strengths by selecting High, Medium, or Low for each:

Inner Work—Self-Awareness:

- Clarify and acknowledge that leadership comes from within the leader
- Understand the difference between leadership character and leadership persona, and evaluate this distinction with regard to your own approach to leadership
- Identify your personal values, purpose, and vision and explore their interplay and alignment with your actions as a leader
- Design a strategy for receiving honest feedback regarding your leadership style from those within your leadership sphere
- Build your own personal brand as a leader

Inner Work—Resiliency:

- Assess your personal strengths and areas from development around the attributes of individual resiliency
- Adopt and maintain an empowered attitude in the face of adversity
- Create and hold a vision as a guide through uncertain times
- Build a flexible thinking approach to challenges
- Utilize a process for effective decision-making and establishment of priority actions
- Recognize and seize the opportunities hidden within challenging situations
- Balance the modes of "doing" in the present, planning for the future, and processing learning from the past

Interpersonal and Relationship Skills:

- Understand the essential nature of strong relationships for effective leadership
- Identify the key elements of healthy relationships
- Develop strategies for building trust as the foundation of strong relationships
- Apply effective communication strategies as an expression of interpersonal caring
- Build skills for more effective conflict management
- Recognize and leverage the value of individual diversity

Figure 12.1
Self-assessment profile.

Communication Skills:

- Be clear as to the intentions of your communications
- Recognize the two messages comprising every communication
- Select the appropriate communications channel for sending messages
- Manage interference for clear communication
- Strengthen your presentation performance
- Practice multiple levels of listening

Coaching:

- Motivating employees to high performance
- Coaching for development and improved performance
- Manage with appreciation/respect for diversity of individual values and needs
- Delegate tasks as needed and with awareness of employee development opportunities
- Select appropriate staff to fulfill specific project needs and responsibilities

Customer Orientation:

- Understand and apply customer needs and expectations
- Gather customer requirements and input
- Partner with customer in gathering requirements, maintaining communication flow, and managing work
- Set and monitor performance standards

Strategic Business Acumen:

- Demonstrate ability to ethically build support for a perspective you feel strongly about
- Holistic view—think in terms of the entire system and the effects and consequences of actions and decisions
- Operate with an awareness of marketplace competition and general landscape of related business arenas
- General business acumen—functions of strategic planning, finance, marketing, manufacturing, R&D, etc.

Project Leadership:

- Build cohesive teams with shared purpose and high performance
- Set, communicate, and monitor milestones and objectives

Figure 12.1 (Continued)

- Gain and maintain buy in from sponsors and customers
- Prioritize and allocate resources
- Manage multiple, potentially conflicting priorities across various/diverse disciplines
- Create and define systems and processes to translate vision into action
- Maintain an effective, interactive, and productive team culture
- Manage budget and project progress
- Gather and analyze appropriate data and input and manage "noise" of info overload
- Manage risk versus reward and ROI equations
- Balance established standards with need for exceptions in decision-making
- Align decisions with needs of business and organizational/team values
- Make timely decisions in alignment with customer and business pace

Creating and Actualizing Vision:

- Gain new insights and different perspectives on vision as a process
- Learn and explore the power of compelling vision
- Apply vision as a management tool in an unpredictable world
- Create a business unit vision via a co-creation process
- Align business unit visions with the larger organization
- Enroll stakeholders in the business unit vision
- Convert vision into action
- Enact the leadership role of vision keeper

The Journey to Change:

- Clarify the distinction between change and transition
- Map the human journey of transition
- Assess the challenges of the transitional journey
- Manage your own personal leadership transformation
- Discover the essential components for successful organizational change
- Develop strategy for leading individuals with different change styles
- Build the skills necessary for leading change

Figure 12.1 (Continued)

Identify Opportunities and Needs

Compare the results of the 360-degree process with your own self-assessment. What have you learned about yourself? What are your priorities for development? What would you like to accomplish? Reviewing this material, pick your top three strengths.

Figure 12.2 is a worksheet that will help you leverage your own leadership strengths. As you have read, learning to leverage your innate strengths is the best way to jump-start your leadership abilities. Through the questions in this worksheet, you will build a plan for doing just that. Take the final intentions and add them to your daily intention list (see Chapter 6, "Coaching.")

Strength 1	Strength 2	Strength 3
Description:	Description:	Description:
Known Successes:	Known Successes:	Known Successes:
Leveraging Opportunities:	Leveraging Opportunities:	Leveraging Opportunities:
With staff:	With staff:	With staff:
With customers:	With customers:	With customers:
With bosses:	With bosses:	With bosses:
With vendors:	With vendors:	With vendors:
With process:	With process:	With process:
List of Actions:	List of Actions:	List of Actions:
Top Three Goals / Actions	Top Three Goals / Actions	Top Three Goals / Actions

Figure 12.2
Leadership strengths worksheet.

Measurement for Top Three Actions of Progress:	Measurement for Top Three Actions of Progress:	Measurement for Top Three Actions of Progress:
Intentions: 1. 2. 3.	Intentions: 1. 2. 3.	Intentions: 1. 2. 3.
Keepers of the Gate:	Keepers of the Gate:	Keepers of the Gate:
Allies:	Allies:	Allies:
Trials:	Trials:	Trials:

Figure 12.2 (Continued)

Now, go back to your assessments and pick the three areas that are currently weak and need to be improved. Figure 12.3, an opportunity worksheet, will help you shore up the competencies that you find most challenging. Some of the strategies might be:

- Consciously practice techniques to grow that competency (for example, new meeting facilitation techniques, communication tips, change management models, etc.)

- Build intensional relationships with people who have these strengths that are a challenge for you, and trade your expertise in your strengths with them. For example, invite a co-worker to facilitate a difficult meeting for you and offer to edit a difficult document for him.

Something that represents a large challenge for you will probably never become a strength. However, you can build both relationships and techniques to grow that competence to a level that is more than adequate for supporting your leadership role. Again, use these worksheets to build a plan and then copy your intentions to your daily list.

Build a Personal Action Plan

Reviewing the worksheets you have just created in Figures 12.2 and 12.3, use Figure 12.4 to build a project/task list. This will give you a one-stop place to examine your goals, your measures of progress, dates, and completion. This mini-project management tracking worksheet will help you focus on the activities that you have prioritized as important, while providing a way of "checking off" activities to show progress. It may make sense for you to integrate this into your personal office system, such as Outlook or Lotus Notes. This process will provide the infrastructure you need to support your ongoing leadership growth. Here are a few additional tips:

- Return to Chapter 9, "Project Leadership," to review how to schedule.
- Look at each item you want to enter on the table—is it actually a task or a project consisting of multiple tasks?

Put only task-level activities on this table. This will provide measurable accomplishment and encourage you along the way. Find someone to whom you can report your progress. Consider sharing this progress with your own leader, or consider hiring an executive coach.

Use this space to set and monitor your plan:

Goal	Measurement	Date

INTENTIONS:

Figure 12.4
Tracking your goals.

Beware of the Neutral Zone

Choosing the more demanding (but rewarding) path of leadership growth brings with it all of the challenges of transition we explored in the previous chapter. A leader must be willing to let go of the comfortable familiarity of certain behavioral ways and move into the unknown of the neutral zone. Navigating this transitional space is difficult for everyone. As we have been coached through past transitions, we've noticed that the immediate result is a feeling of fear and chaos—but this is part of getting to the reward. Revisit the tips in Chapter 11, "The Journey to Change," to connect with supportive tools and insights.

In *Hero with a Thousand Faces* (Princeton University Press, 1949), Joseph Campbell describes what he calls the Hero's Journey. Our model (shown in Figure 12.5), adapted from Campbell's work and based on the premise that we are all heroes, is a roadmap for transformation in which an ordinary person embarks on a heroic adventure. Driven by choice (internal) or circumstance (external), the hero crosses a threshold of change and is challenged by a series of trials. On the surface, the journey is one in search of reward—riches, power, or perhaps recognition. To get the rewards, however, requires the hero's discovery of self and the realization of individual potential and capacity—which is our hope for you. The hero is transformed by the journey, and through the insight and abilities sharpened along the way, is able to transform her world. You have planned your journey across the threshold of change in Figures 12.2 and 12.3.

When you chose this book, you decided to embark on a transforming adventure, a Hero's Journey. Choice or circumstance has brought you to the threshold of change. How you weather the challenges ahead is up to you. There is no need to rush this process; after all, journeys of this scale should be taken one step at a time. There is learning to be gained along the way.

People who are accustomed to seeing you act a certain way ("Keepers of the Gate" in Campbell's model) may feel threatened by your new behaviors. For example, your team may be uncomfortable when you do not join its "customer bashing" at lunch. They may try to get you back to the way you were. Resist them without anger or pious sermons. Model, rather than talk about, the behaviors you'd like to grow and reinforce.

Pay attention and be patient with yourself. Return to the worksheets you created in Figures 12.2 and 12.3, and prepare yourself emotionally for the trials that may occur as you begin to change your own behavior. Though it may seem that you are alone in your travels, you will encounter allies. Tap into their insight, strength, and support when you need it. Return to the worksheets and think about who your allies will be. In parallel, consider that you are an ally for your people as they make their own transitions.

The Hero's Journey

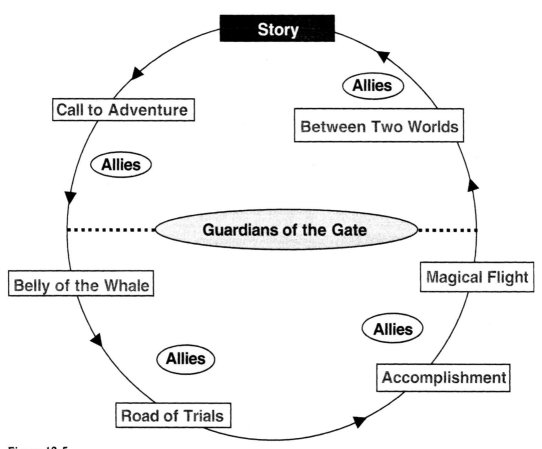

Figure 12.5
A model for transformation.

The ultimate reward from this adventure is the discovery of your own answer to the question: "What do I need to become to fulfill my place ?" As you move through the next 30 days, remind yourself (with a trigger in your calendar) to pause for two minutes and think about what you have learned about the answer to this question. Congratulate yourself for your victories. Leadership is a hero's role. This is your opportunity to develop your potential and realize your capacity as a heroic leader.

If you are having trouble working through this planning process, you'll find an example in Figure 12.6.

Strength 1

Description:
Clarity of personal values, purpose, and vision

Known Successes:
Clarity of purpose, strong sense of values

Leveraging Opportunities:

With staff: *Review the purpose of our team at the start of each weekly status meeting. Ask a different he or she each week to share a way he or she modeled this purpose the week preceeding.*

With customers: *Communicate the purpose of the group to each key customer. Create a weekly mini email newsletter with the notes from the status meeting, sharing the weekly story above.*

With bosses: *Talk to supervisor about purpose, and how it fits into the overall purpose of the organization.*

With vendors:

With process:

List of Actions:

Use the "three verbs / one noun" exercise to come up with a team statement of purpose.
Have weekly status meetings with purpose (see above).
Share purpose with the customer.

Top Three Goals / Actions:
Schedule the "three verbs / one noun" meeting by 3/1.
Hold the "three verbs / one noun" meeting.
Assign the customer email newsletter summary to staff member by 4/1.

Measurement for Top Three Actions of Progress:
Statement of purpose (consensus)
Email newsletter out by Friday every week

Figure 12.6
Sample planning (all worksheets).

Intentions:
1. *The purpose of my team is clear and shared.*
2. *My team's customers are clear about our purpose and support it.*
3. *My boss is clear about our team purpose and supports it.*

Keepers of the Gate:
Customers with negative history who don't believe we have a purpose.
Boss who keeps expanding our purpose (scope of responsibility).
Staff who continue to perform work for the customers which is outside the purpose of our team.

Allies:
Key customers who want to know how we can help.
Staff who want to know how they will be measured.
External coach—supporting transformation.

Trials:
Anticipate work will still be done outside the scope of the purpose. Will need to provide direct feedback. Anticipate a customer testing of our boundaries—conversations of the boundaries will be a success.

Opportunity 1

Description:
Manages transition with employees—guiding and supporting the change process

Known Successes:
Survived last chaotic process with regular "venting" meetings

Leveraging Opportunities:

With staff: *Need to create a unique strategy for each of the team members. Put some thought together about what they individually need to go through to change.*

With customers:

With bosses:

With vendors:

Figure 12.6 (Continued)

With process: *Would like to create some sort of consensus process to give my staff a safe way to express to me resistance, and to help them understand their own resistance better so they can communicate it more effectively to me.*

List of Actions:
Build an individual change profile for each of my team members (use assessment?).
Ask each team member to email change status (1 thru 5 [high]) before weekly meeting.

Top Three Goals / Actions
Create an individual change profile for each team member and review it with each of them by 4/1.
Ask for secret ballot (Post-It) voting on change feelings at the start of each status meeting (effective next meeting).
Share my change profile with team members to model the behavior I expect from them.

Measurement for Top Three Actions of Progress:
Individual profiles completed (phase 1) and reviewed (phase 2).
Change process (secret ballot) implemented by next meeting.

Intentions:
1. I appreciate the differences in each of my staff.
2. I successfully monitor and coach the change tolerance and adaptation of each staff member through a unique profile.

Keepers of the Gate:
Staff will be uncomfortable sharing their fears with me.
Some staff fear assessments.

Allies:
One staff member is more in tune with her emotional intelligence. Do her profile first!

Trials:
Expect staff to avoid turning in assessment, scheduling review session, and avoiding status meetings.

Figure 12.6 (Continued)

The Journey Begins

You opened this book because you recognized a need in yourself to grow your ability to lead in IT. Perhaps you are painfully aware of the lack of good IT leadership and want to raise the bar in your organization. Perhaps you want to honor your leadership commitment and make sure you are doing as much as you can for the company that pays you. Perhaps you want to better serve the staff or project team that you have been entrusted with. We hope you realize the enormous power you have to influence the world through your work with the people with whom you come in contact every day.

But it would be unfair to say that the road ahead is straight and clean. The business world is currently in chaos—technology is changing faster than ever before—and the IT organizations stand in the center of it all. People like you will choose whether IT will make the world a better or worse place.

There will be days when you will feel you are not up to the challenge. On these days, look back at your assessments and recognize the unique strengths you bring to this role. Look at other leaders, if necessary. Notice that they all have weaknesses behind their sometimes more-obvious strengths.

There will be days that you wish you could find a leadership pill to take—something easy. But deep in your heart, you know that there is no finish line to this race and no easy way to propel you forward. If there were, there wouldn't be such a problem in IT.

You are truly a hero. Enjoy your transformation to IT leadership gold.

Bibliography

Books and Articles

Allen, D. *Getting Things Done: The Art of Stress-Free Productivity.* New York: Viking Press, 2001; ISBN: 0-670-89924-0.

Barnes, B. Kim. *Exercising Influence.* Berkeley, California: Barnes & Conti Associates, Inc., 2000; ISBN: 0-970-07100-0.

Beck, K. *Extreme Programming.* New Jersey: Addison Wesley, 1999; ISBN: 0-201-61641-6.

Bridges, W. *Managing Transitions: Making the Most of Change,* Cambridge, MA: Perseus Press, 1991; ISBN: 0-201-55073-3.

Campbell, J. *The Hero with a Thousand Faces.* Princeton, NJ: Princeton University Press, 1972; ISBN: 0-691-01784-0.

Cashman, K. *Leadership from the Inside Out.* Provo, UT: Executive Excellence Publishing, 2000; ISBN: 1-890-00931-8.

Covey, S. *The Seven Habits of Highly Effective People.* New York: Simon and Schuster, 1990; ISBN: 0-671-70863-5.

Dahle,C. "Natural Leader." *Fast Company,* December 2000, #41.

Davenport, T., and Prusak, L. *Working Knowledge.* Boston, MA: Harvard Business School Press, 1997; ISBN: 1-578-51301-4.

Galwey, W. *The Inner Game of Work,* New York: Random House, 1999; ISBN: 0-375-50007-3.

Garfield, C. *Peak Performers.* New York: Harper Collins, 1991; ISBN: 0-380-70304-1.

Goleman, D. *Emotional Intelligence: Why It Can Matter More Than IQ.* New York: Bantam Books; ISBN: 0-553-37506-7.

Goleman, D. *Primal Leadership: Realizing the Power of Emotional Intelligence:* Boston, MA: Harvard Business School Press, 2002; ISBN: 1-578-5148-6X.

Goss, T. *The Last Word on Power.* New York: Currency/Doubleday, 1995; ISBN: 0-385-47492-X.

Greenleaf, R. *Servant Leadership: A Journey Into the Nature of Legitimate Power and Greatness.* Mahwah, NJ: Paulist Press, 1977; ISBN: 0-809-12527-7.

Hammonds, K. "Michael Porters Big Ideas." *Fast Company,* March 2001, #44.

Hartmann, F. *The Life of Paracelsus and the Substance of His Teachings.* London: Wizard's, 1997.

Highsmith, J. *Agile Software Development Ecosystems : Problems, Practices, and Principles.* New Jersey: Addison Wesley, 2002 ; ISBN: 0-201-76043-6.

Jones, L. *The Path.* New York: Hyperion Press, 1998; ISBN 0-471-96639-8.

Kotter, J. *What Leaders Really Do.* Watertown, MA: Harvard Business School Press, 1999; ISBN: 0-875-84897-4.

Michalko, M. *ThinkerToys.* Berkeley, CA: Ten Speed Press, 1991; ISBN: 0-898-15408-1.

Nonaka, I., Takeuchi, H., and Takeuchi, H. *The Knowledge-Creating Company: How Japanese Companies Create the Dynamics of Innovation.* Oxford University Press, 1995; ISBN: 0-195-09269-4.

Peters,T. "The Brand Called You." *Fast Company,* August 1997, #10.

Russell, L. *The Accelerated Learning Fieldbook.* San Francisco, CA: Jossey-Bass, 1999; ISBN: 0-787-94639-7.

Sacks, P. *Generation SX Goes to College: An Eye-Opening Account of Teaching in Postmodern America.* Chicago, IL: Open Court Publishing Company, 1996; ISBN: 0-812-69314-0.

Seligman, M. *Learned Optimism.* New York: Simon and Schuster, 1998; ISBN: 0-671-01911-2.

Senge, P. *The Fifth Discipline.* New York: Currency/Doubleday, 1990; ISBN: 0-385-26095-4.

Senge, P., and others. *The Fifth Discipline Fieldbook: Stratagies and Tools for Building a Learning Organization.* New York: Currency/Doubleday, 1994; ISBN: 0-385-47256-0.

Sittenfeld, C. "I've Seen the Future." *Fast Company,* October 1998, #18.

Thomsett, R. *People and Project Management.* Upper Saddle River, NJ: Yourdon Press/Prentice Hall, 1980; ISBN: 0-136-55747-3.

Thomsett, R. *Third Wave Project Management: A Handbook for Managing the Complex Information Systems for the 1990s.* Upper Saddle River, NJ: Yourdon Press/Prentice Hall, 1992; ISBN: 0-139-15299-7.

Vaill, P. *Learning as a Way of Being: Strategies for Survival in a World of Permanent White Water.* San Francisco, CA: Jossey-Bass, 1996; ISBN: 0-787-90246-2.

Vaill, P. *Managing as a Performing Art: New Ideas for a World of Chaotic*

Change. San Francisco, CA: Jossey-Bass, 1989; ISBN: 1-555-42140-7.

Wheatley, M. *Leadership and the New Science*. San Francisco, CA: Berrett-Koehler Publishing, 2001; ISBN: 1-576-75119-8.

Yourdon, E. *Death March: The Complete Software Developer's Guide to Surviving 'Mission Impossible' Projects*. Upper Saddle River, NJ: Yourdon Press/Prentice Hall, 1999; ISBN: 0-130-14659-5.

Yourdon, E. *Managing High-Intensity Internet Projects*. Upper Saddle River, NJ: Prentice Hall, 2002; ISBN: 0-130-62110-2.

Yourdon, E. *Modern Structured Analysis*. Upper Saddle River, NJ: Yourdon Press/Prentice Hall, 2000; ISBN: 0-135-98624-9.

Yourdon, E. *Time Bomb 2000: What the Year 2000 Computer Crisis Means to You!*, Upper Saddle River, NJ: Prentice Hall, 1999; ISBN: 0-130-20519-2.

Yourdon, E. *The Y2K Financial Survival Guide*, Upper Saddle River, NJ: Prentice Hall, 1999; ISBN: 0-130-25663-3.

Articles and Web Sites

Nardi, B., Schwarz, H., Whittaker, S. "It's Not What You Know, It's Who You Know: Work in the Information Age" [http://www.firstmonday.dk/issues/issue5_5/nardi/]. 2000

Russell, L. "Agile Development" [http://www.trainingsupersite.com/tss_link/trainset.htm]. 2001

Index